CREATIVE PROBLEM SOLVING FOR MANAGERS

This text provides an essential introduction to the ideas and skills of creative problem solving. It demonstrates how and why people are blocked in their thinking, how this impairs the creative problem solving process and how creative problem solving techniques can help overcome these difficulties. Theories of creative thinking are critically examined and utilised to justify the variety of techniques which can be employed to discover insights into difficult management problems.

Contents include:

- Paradigm shift and the need for creative thinking in management
- Blocks to creativity and how to overcome them
- Defining and redefining problems
- Extensive explanations and illustrations of the methods and techniques of the creative problem solving process – Lateral Thinking, Morphological Analysis and Synectics
- Evaluating ideas – qualitative and quantitative approaches
- Implementing ideas and effecting the management of idea acceptance

Using case studies and case histories, together with extensive diagrams, examples and thought-provoking questions, *Creative Problem Solving for Managers* provides the most up-to-date and extensive approach to this important topic.

Tony Proctor was formerly a Senior Lecturer in Marketing and Head of the Department of Management at Keele University. His previous publications include *Marketing Management* (ITBP, 1996) and *The Essence of Management Creativity* (Prentice-Hall, 1995). He is also a regular contributor to several management journals, including *Management Decision* and *Creativity and Innovation Management*.

CREATIVE PROBLEM SOLVING FOR MANAGERS

Tony Proctor

Routledge
Taylor & Francis Group

LONDON AND NEW YORK

First published 1999 by Routledge
11 New Fetter Lane, London EC4P 4EE

Simultaneously published in the USA and Canada
by Routledge
29 West 35th Street, New York, NY 10001

Reprinted 2002 (twice), 2003

Routledge is an imprint of the Taylor & Francis Group

© 1999 Tony Proctor

Typeset in Plantin and Rockwell by Keystroke,
Jacaranda Lodge, Wolverhampton
Printed and bound in Great Britain by
TJ International Ltd, Padstow, Cornwall

British Library Cataloguing in Publication Data
A catalogue record for this book is available from the British Library

Library of Congress Cataloguing in Publication Data
Proctor, Tony.
    Creative problem solving for managers / Tony Proctor.
        p.   cm.
    Includes bibliographical references and index.
    1. Problem solving. 2. Management. I. Title.
    HD30.29.P763 1999
    658.4'03—dc21   98–39630
                                                        CIP

ISBN 0–415–19678–7 (hbk)
ISBN 0–415–19679–5 (pbk)

Contents

Figures

Preface

I began the first chapter of a book I wrote some years ago called *The Essence of Management Creativity* by saying it was about creativity and problem solving in management. This book too follows a similar theme but I have expanded my ideas somewhat since I wrote the other book.

I am often asked whether the various approaches I outline in this book really work. The answer to this I feel is really only known by those who use the methods. Moreover, it is always difficult to know if you would have been able to find an answer to a problem which you did not know existed without the aid of the techniques I outline here. Or, indeed, for that matter, whether you might solve the problem more to your satisfaction by using other methods.

The material contained in this book should appeal to a wide audience. I originally thought the subject matter was something which would perhaps most interest experienced and mature adults. I discovered that not only was it something which appealed to experienced managers but it also held the attention of students of management of all ages and backgrounds. One of my most enlightening experiences has been getting final year management studies undergraduates interested in the subject.

In 1998 I taught the subject to a class of over seventy undergraduate students studying Management as a joint honours subject. The class also included European ERASMUS students, US exchange students and comprised students from many different ethnic backgrounds. I have reservations about teaching the subject to such a large and diverse class but it was interesting to note that when perusing feedback and other indicators of how successful the course had been I found that the student assessment of my presentations was only marginally worse than the average of my presentations on the subject over the previous ten years with much smaller classes.

The subject matter of this book will appeal to people who have a variety of different interests in management. Whether your primary interest is in accounting, personnel management, marketing, production, research and development and so on, does not really matter since the subject matter contained in this book is relevant to all these interests. However, you must approach the subject with an open mind and all the methods, no matter how ridiculous they may seem, should be treated seriously – but not too seriously that they cannot be enjoyed. The greatest barrier to appreciating the subject matter of this book is scepticism.

In terms of its contents the book first sets the scene for management creativity. First it explains what creativity and creative problem solving is thought to be. It then considers why creativity management is considered to be important. The various blocks to creative problem solving are explained, as are the actions that are required to get around these difficulties. A chapter outlines some of the most recent ideas on theories relating to creativity and creative problem solving. This chapter is important since it provides a background and explanation for many of the steps in the creative problem solving process which are considered in subsequent chapters. Each step in the creative problem solving process is explored in some depth and illustrations are given of some of the principal mechanisms used to help structure and stimulate thinking. The final chapter in the book is given over to considering how interaction with computers can help to stimulate creative problem solving.

Throughout the book there are ample illustrations of the key points. There are specific case studies attached to each chapter and an additional set of twenty case studies in Appendix 2. The latter invite the reader to make use of all the knowledge he or she has gained about the creative problem solving process through reading the book.

Tony Proctor
July 1998

chapter one

CREATIVITY AND ITS IMPORTANCE IN BUSINESS

INTRODUCTION

In this chapter we will review some definitions of creativity and highlight the importance of creative problem solving in enabling business executives to cope with novel or new problems. First we give some consideration to defining creativity and then to distinguishing between creativity and innovation. Various notions exist on how ideas arise in our minds. These are introduced in this chapter and developed further in Chapter 3. Creativity in business is important and managers need to possess the ability to gain creative insights. We look at the importance of creativity to business and managers, picking out those instances where it is most needed and relating it in particular to the notion of paradigm shift. In the later sections of the chapter we look at characteristics of creative thinking and creative thinkers, highlighting the qualities of a creative person and pointing to how creative skills can be achieved through training.

SOME DEFINITIONS OF CREATIVITY

Creativity involves an ability to come up with new and different viewpoints on a subject. It involves breaking down and restructuring our knowledge about the subject in order to gain new insights into its nature. However, any definition of creativity is complicated because the concept has many dimensions.

What is creative thinking?

Creativity is a concept which we often come across in our everyday conversation. We hear of creative people, admire creative objects of art or read creative books. Yet despite our almost innate understanding of what it means to be creative there is much confusion about the nature of creativity.

Wertheimer ([1945] 1959) suggested that creative thinking involved breaking down and restructuring our knowledge about something in order to gain new insights into its nature. Understanding our own cognitive model of reality may therefore be an important determinant of our ability to think creatively. Kelly (1955) and Rogers (1954) both supported this argument by maintaining that we can be creative by gaining an understanding of how we think about a subject. Creativity is something which occurs when we are able to organise our thoughts in such a way that readily leads to a different and even better understanding of the subject or situation which we are considering.

Maslow (1954) thought of creativity as having two levels. He envisaged primary creativity as the source of new discovery, real novelty, or ideas which depart from what exists at a given point in time. He saw secondary creativity as a characteristic possessed by many scientists in their collective search for discovery achieved by working alongside other people, extending the work of previous researchers and exercising prudence and caution in their claims about new insights or ideas. He envisaged creativity as an aspect of human nature that was to be found universally in all human beings. In children he felt it to be an easily observable phenomenon but suggested that it seemed to become lost in adults, surfacing mainly in dreams with the relaxation of repressions and defences. It was a view that was echoed subsequently by Stein (1974) who argued that without such an assumption the techniques for stimulating creativity would have no application.

Torrance (1965) defined creativity as:

> The process of becoming sensitive to problems, deficiencies, gaps in knowledge, missing elements, disharmonies, and so on; identifying the difficulty; searching for solutions, making guesses or formulating hypotheses about the deficiencies; testing and retesting them; and finally communicating the results.

This contrasts with that of Newell *et al.* (1962). They adopted a criterion based approach, which suggests that any problem solving may be creative. Indeed, Haefele (1962) argues that everyone of us must be creative to some degree because we have to find new solutions to newly presented problems.

Rickards (1985: 5) defines creativity as: 'the personal discovery process, partially unconscious, which leads to new and relevant insights'. Rickards (1988: 225) also advocates a view of creativity as a universal human process resulting in the escape from assumptions, and discovery of new and meaningful perspectives or as an 'escape from mental stuckness'. In broad terms he believes creativity is to do with personal, internal restructuring.

Creativity is very much concerned with how we imagine things in our minds. Although language is a medium of expressing our creative feelings our creativity is often gained through images and sensations which are difficult to express in words. As Koestler (1964), said: 'True creativity often starts where language ends.'

Weinman (1991) considered that creativity is the ability to go beyond the mundane and obvious and reject the traps of repetition and pre-set categories. Similarly, Gilliam (1993) defined creativity as a process of discovering what has not been considered – the act of making new connections.

More simply, creativity can be thought of 'as the production of novel and useful ideas in any domain' (Amabile *et al.*, 1996: 1155).

Yet one more approach, along with many others is offered on the Internet: 'Being creative is seeing the same thing as everyone else but thinking of something different.' http:www.ozemail.com.au/~caveman/basics/definitions.htm

These various definitions seem to agree that creativity involves an in-depth thought of a subject and an ability to come up with new and different viewpoints. However, any definition of creativity is complicated because the concept is multi-faceted.

INVENTION AND CREATIVITY

> **Invention is an act of creativity that results in a device, process, or technique novel enough to produce a significant change in the application of technology.**

Invention is an act of creativity that results in a device, process, or technique novel enough to produce a significant change in the application of technology. The application is fundamental to invention. The element of novelty has various forms; it may be a new device or process, or even material, but it may also consist of a combination of existing knowledge in a manner not previously considered. For example, James Watt added a separate condensing chamber – a new device – to Thomas Newcomen's atmospheric engine and created the steam engine.

INVENTIONS, INNOVATIONS OR JUST CREATIVE RESEARCH?

Gene research

In 1988 Rudolf Jaenisch and co-workers succeeded in implanting in mice, the gene for a hereditary disease of humans. It was thought that it would open the way to the study of such diseases and to improved treatment.

Superconductors

In 1911 Heike Onnes discovered that electrical resistance in mercury disappears when the mercury is cooled to absolute zero. This phenomenon is known as super-conductivity. It was found subsequently that other metals and alloys also become superconducting at very low temperatures. Today superconductors are used in large and powerful magnets, mainly in particle accelerators and the magnetic-resonance imaging machines used in medicine. Other potential applications still exist.

Infinity of non-smooth four-dimensional spaces

In 1987 Clifford Taubes discovered that the infinity of non-smooth four-dimensional spaces is uncountable (an infinity is countable if each element in it can be matched to one of the counting numbers).

Quarks

When physicists first began to think deeply about quarks they were puzzled because isolated quarks had not been observed. One idea was that quarks might be the ends of strings. Assuming that a particle was a string and that quarks were just the ends of the string, then it was plausible why one never found a quark without the other. A string is essentially a one-dimensional object in a space of four dimensions (counting time as a dimension). Physicists turned to topology, the mathematics of knots and surfaces, to find out what the implications might be of using strings instead of particles in their calculations. To their surprise they discovered that strings simplified the calculations.

Question

How would you classify each of the above four illustrations in terms of inventions, innovations or just creative research?

The two general theories of invention are the *deterministic* and the *individualistic*. The deterministic theory holds that when economic, technical, and cultural conditions are ripe, an invention will be made by one inventor or another; who does it is just historical accident. This theory has some support in the numerous instances of simultaneous and independent invention. It also helps to explain the competing claims that emerged over the invention of the steamboat, the electric telegraph, the incandescent lamp, and the aeroplane. The theory is also plausible because timing is unquestionably important in invention. Also, inventors are likely to focus on projects that are reasonably attainable and for which there is a recognisable need or demand.

THE WHEEL AND THE MEASUREMENT OF TIME

Perhaps the most important invention in the history of the human race was the wheel, for which there have been many applications. These include the ability to measure the passage of time itself accurately.

IDEAS AND HOW THEY ARISE

Generating ideas is not just a chance process. Ideas appear to arise by chance only when people are actually looking for them. It does not happen to people who are not curious or inquiring or who are not engaged in a hard search for opportunities, possibilities, answers or inventions.

One might, indeed, think of ideas as 'the sentences of thought'. Ideas are mental phenomena which somehow drift into the mind, wander through and often vanish into obscurity, never to be recalled again. Making notes on ideas, as they arise, is extremely important. Graham Wallas (1926) tells the story of a man 'who had so brilliant an idea that he went into his garden to thank God for it, and found on rising from his knees that he had forgotten it, and never recalled it'.

In terms of problem solving we might prefer to think of 'insights' rather than ideas. The gaining of insights into a problem can lead to a restructuring of that problem and the development of further insights into the solution of the problem. There may not be a perfect solution to a problem which requires creative thought but only different solutions, more acceptable solutions and, often, only further insights into a problem.

Many ideas seem to occur by chance. Fleming discovered the effects of penicillin quite by accident – it was blown in from an open window and killed bacteria in a saucer which contained a strain which he was investigating. While searching for a way to hear the sounds of the heart, Laennec found his answer when he noticed two boys playing in an unusual way with a see-saw. The one was hitting one end of the wooden see-saw with a stone while the other listened with his ear pressed close to the other end of the see-saw. The idea of the stethoscope leaped to Laennec's mind. Westinghouse discovered the idea of the air-brake when he casually read in a journal that compressed air power was being used by Swiss engineers in tunnel building. Kekule gained his clue to the nature of the benzene ring from his dream of a snake swallowing its own tail. Rutherford used the solar system to understand the structure of the atom. He viewed the electrons as revolving around the nucleus in the same way that the planets revolve around the sun. Einstein's theories came from analogies about riding on light beams and travelling in elevators.

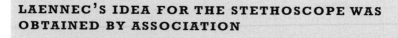

LAENNEC'S IDEA FOR THE STETHOSCOPE WAS OBTAINED BY ASSOCIATION

The idea was sparked off by seeing two boys playing with a see-saw in an unusual way (see text).

However, generating ideas is not just a chance process. Ideas appear to arise by chance only when people are actually looking for ideas. It does not happen to people who are not curious or inquiring or who are not engaged in a hard search for opportunities, possibilities, answers or inventions.

It is also widely recognised that immersion in one's subject matter can be an important factor in gaining creative insights. Newton, for example, arrived at the law of gravitation by being preoccupied with the problem all of the time. It is also known that Einstein tried for years to clarify the problem of the relation of mechanical movement to electromagnetic phenomena. Creative insights appear to be easiest to gain in fields where we have considerable prior knowledge and experience. Nevertheless, there is a paradox here, for we tend not think about what we think we know already. Existing ideas tend to make us myopic about new possibilities. The paradox reveals itself in that it appears that creative ideas do not come to us unless we spend much effort engaged in just the activity which makes their emergence most difficult.

Motivation also plays an important role in our ability to be creative. Again there is a paradox for creative work demands both a passionate interest on the part of the thinker and a certain degree of detachment from the work and ideas. Creative thinking, however, does not appear to occur where the individual's interest in the subject matter is relatively low. There seems to be a delicate balance whereby the creative thinker has to remain sufficiently detached from the work.

CREATIVITY AND INVENTIONS

Christian Doppler gave his name to a well known principle which he discovered in the nineteenth century (the Doppler effect). We can observe it any time a motorist sounds his or her horn while passing us by. As long as the source of the sound approaches us the pitch seems higher than when it moves away from us. Sound waves are just one form of *wave* subject to this effect.

Can you think of how twentieth century inventors might have made use of this principle to come up with commercially applicable inventions?

See Appendix 3 for solution.

THE IMPORTANCE GIVEN TO CREATIVITY IN BUSINESS

> Logical thinking progresses in a series of steps, each one dependent on the last. This new knowledge is merely an extension of what we know already, rather than being truly new. The need for creative problem solving has arisen as a result of the inadequacies of logical thinking. It is a method of using imagination along with techniques which use analogies, associations and other mechanisms to help produce insights into problems which might not otherwise be obtained through conventional, traditional methods of problem solving.

In management, problems arise as different or new situations present themselves and they often require novel solutions. Frequently, it is difficult to see solutions to problems by thinking in a conventional fashion. Logical thinking takes our existing knowledge and uses rules of inference to produce new knowledge. However, because logical thinking progresses in a series of steps, each one dependent on the last, this new knowledge is merely an extension of what we know already, rather than being truly new. It would seem, therefore, that logical thinking has only a limited role to play in helping managers to be creative. The need for creative problem solving has arisen as a result of the inadequacies of logical thinking. It is a method of using imagination along with techniques which use analogies, associations and other mechanisms to help produce insights into problems.

Over the past few decades creativity has become a highly fashionable topic in both the academic and business worlds. That is not to say that creativity did not exist before, but its importance to the continued success of an organisation had yet to be recognised. Many management problems require creative insights in order to find satisfactory solutions. Nowadays, the majority of organisations are fully aware of just how vital creativity is to their prosperity. Over time, considerable research has been undertaken which enables us to obtain a better understanding of creativity and become more innovative ourselves.

AN ECONOMIC CLEANING JOB: FINDING A LESS COSTLY WAY OF PERFORMING A TASK

Tank Refurbishers clean out and reline industrial storage tanks. In an increasingly competitive market, margins are becoming tighter and profitable business ventures more difficult to find. Nearly all the tanks the firm refurbishes are cylindrical ones and vary considerably in terms of the volume of liquids that they contain. The procedure is to remove the ends, clean and repaint the inside of the cylinder, clean and repaint the end sections and re-weld the pieces after completion of the repainting.

How might the firm seek to be more competitive in the pricing of its jobs?
See Appendix 3 for possible solutions.

Even thirty years ago it was reported that the 'accelerating pace of change is now widely accepted . . . Alvin Toffler found evidence that the pace of change was causing "Future shock" and social disorientation' (Rickards, 1985: 186), and this change is an ever present phenomenon to which businesses of all kinds are forced to respond if they want to stand the best chance of survival and prosperity. But how should they respond? An increasing number of problems have no precedents and there are fewer and tested ways of approaching them. This poses problems for organisations. Many suggest that creativity is indeed the answer and as Majaro (1991: 1) suggests 'It is universally assumed that enhanced creativity can provide a company with a competitive edge.' A survey sponsored by Porter/Novelli among 100 executive readers of *Fortune 500* in 1993 found that people thought creativity was essential to ensure success in business.

A plethora of literature emphasises the need for creativity in business. Indeed, Oldman and Cummings (1996: 609) note that 'numerous commentators have argued that enhancing the creative performance of employees is a necessary step if organisations are able to achieve competitive advantage'.

> **Organisations face a large number of problems of about equal importance, but only a few solutions. Thus the chance of finding a solution to a particular problem is small.**

Why is creativity in management important? The main problem in management according to James March (1988) is that: 'Organisations face a large number of problems of about equal importance, but only a few solutions. Thus the chance of finding a solution to a particular problem is small.'

In order to identify and so solve many of the problems that arise in business it is necessary to challenge the problem solving capabilities of those in charge. In many cases the creative process which is used to approach problems has to be restructured and redeveloped in order to produce new ideas and perspectives.

Change is an intrinsic necessity for a company that wishes to perform well in the long term. As Sir John Harvey Jones stated: 'Unless a company is progressing all the time, it is in fact moving backwards. It is quite impossible to maintain the *status quo*' (Rogers, 1996). Attempting to do things in the same way as they have always been done in the past can lead to difficulties in a business environment which is experiencing rapid cultural, economic or technological change. Change is an ever present phenomenon to which businesses of all kinds are forced to respond if they want to stand the best chance of survival and prosperity.

The rapid growth of competition in business and industry is often quoted as a reason for wanting to understand more about the creative process (see for example Van Gundy, 1987; Rickards, 1990). Many firms are continually experiencing pressure to enhance old systems and products. Growth and survival can be related directly to an organisation's ability to produce (or adopt) and implement new products or services, and processes (Van Gundy, 1987). One of the key aspects of any organisation's success or failure is its ability to stay ahead of the competition in a rapidly changing environment. The modern business, with its emphasis on competition, building larger markets, strategic planning, team working, etc., has created the need for new problem solving and decision making strategies.

An increasing number of problems have few or no precedents, hence there are fewer tried and tested ways of approaching them with the anticipation of reaching a successful outcome.

Another reason is that managers need to discover new and better ways to solve problems (Ackoff and Vegara, 1988). In particular, an increasing number of problems have few or no precedents, hence there are fewer tried and tested ways of approaching them with the anticipation of reaching a successful outcome. To stay in business a company has to respond creatively to the problems it faces. Problems may exist in both the external and internal environments. The former poses problems such as how to cope with slow economic growth, how to deal with new entrants to an industry, how to grow sales at the pace of competition in high growth markets, how to deal with new technological developments and how to cope with shorter product life cycles. The latter poses problems to do with poor internal communications, financial problems, alienated or poorly motivated staff and inadequate planning.

Creativity is considered to be a vital asset for any person who is involved in a leadership situation.

Changes within a company, either forced by internal or external factors, create an unhappy climate for the company and its workers. Management needs to respond positively to such situations. Creativity is considered to be a vital asset for any person who is involved in a leadership situation (see for example Bennis and Nanus, 1985 and empirical evidence provided by Ekvall, 1988). Creative leaders actively hunt for new problems and are especially successful in handling new challenges which demand solutions outside the routine of orthodox strategies. They often possess significant vision and are able to inspire others by their creative talents.

It is argued that creativity is an important human resource (Barron, 1988) which exists in all organisations. Organisations have to try to make use of this resource by devising settings which permit creative talents to thrive.

How creative thinking may be used in management

ILLUSTRATIONS OF HOW CREATIVITY CAN BE USED IN MANAGEMENT

To make more effective use of a manager's time.
To improve a product's appeal to customers.
To improve motivation amongst staff.
To appeal to customers' wants and needs.
To cut costs through more efficient/effective production methods.
To identify new and profitable product-market opportunities.

Creative thinking benefits all areas and activities of management. It is required to dream up better ways of marketing goods, to devise new production methods, to find new ways to motivate people, and so on. Creativity turns up in every business situation where there is a chance that things can be done in a more business-like, more profitable or in a more satisfying way.

The following is typical of the kind of problems which require creative thinking:

- How to make more effective use of a manager's time.
- How improve a product's appeal to customers.
- How to improve motivation amongst staff.
- How to appeal to customers' wants and needs.
- How to cut costs through more efficient/effective production methods.
- How to identify new and profitable product-market opportunities.
- How to get skilled and experience staff to stay with the company without paying them excessively high salaries.

Problems which require creative thinking are 'open-ended' problems; that is, problems for which there is not just one solution. Executives have to make decisions which require creative problem solving in planning, organising, leading, and controlling their organisations:

Planning
Determining the mission of the organisation.
Determining the organisational objectives.
Identifying strengths, weaknesses, opportunities and threats.
Adjusting the organisation behaviour and strategies to competitors' strategies.
Deciding how to implement competitive strategies.

Organising
Deciding what jobs need to be done within an organisational unit.
Deciding how various jobs within an organisational unit can be grouped together, etc.
Deciding how much authority should be delegated to various organisational positions.
Determining how best to train people for their jobs.

Leading
Finding ways of increasing productivity in the workplace.

Controlling
Deciding what systems of control are needed.
Setting standards.
Identifying why standards/objectives have not been achieved.

CONDITIONS WHEN CREATIVE THINKING IS REQUIRED MOST

> **The need for creative thinking often becomes paramount when *paradigm shift* occurs or is likely to occur soon.**

It is argued that in an organisational sense creative thinking is required most when there is a lack of consensus regarding goals and also a lack of understanding about cause–effect relationships (Thompson, 1967). Disagreement often occurs when problems arise which have not been previously encountered and when outcomes and goals are uncertain. The need for creative thinking often becomes paramount when *paradigm shift* occurs or is likely to occur soon.

CREATIVITY IN ACTION

Who could have envisaged fifty years ago the retail development complexity of travel agents or the shopping complexes at airports such as London Heathrow, London Gatwick, Manchester International, Amsterdam, Kuala Lumpur, Munich, Madrid and Barcelona – just to mention a few. Indeed some of the major airport complexes have developed almost into mini-shopping centres in their own right. The planners of such development complexes continue to exercise their creative problem solving skills in order to find more ways of satisfying their customer *en route* to various destinations.

The airlines themselves have become more creative in their thinking and in the way in which they approach problems. Not everyone, however, is always happy with the outcome of such creativity, as was evidenced in the manner of some distinguished members of the public's reaction to the novel tail fin logo adopted by British Airways in 1998. In recent years airlines have come to pay more attention to the logo on their aircraft, seeing it as an important way of portraying their brand image.

Traditionally, Air Canada planes were white with bright red lettering and a big red maple leaf on the tail. However, research showed the strong image was a real problem with Canadian users because of its association with government bureaucracy. Apparently, Canadians adore Canada, but are much less favourably disposed to its government. Canadians tend to attribute a host of hearth-and-home values to themselves and their country: compassion, friendliness, a progressive outlook and a law-abiding nature. It was decided to emphasise these latter associations while de-emphasising the government part. The maple leaf was also kept but it was rendered in a more natural earthy red on a new evergreen tail – the reasoning being that the stark red-on-white contrast was too much associated with the government image. The overall effect makes the new planes look a lot less like flying Mounties.

British Airways too has had its dose of creative thinking. It was revitalised by Sir Colin Marshall in the 1980s with a particular directive to focus on the customer. An effective internal marketing programme was based on the notion that employees would not treat customers better until they themselves were treated better. He established profit sharing and a two-day seminar at which attendance was compulsory for all employees. The seminar focused on all relationships employees might have with other employees, bosses, customers or even family members. It was felt that the programme contributed significantly to raising staff morale and better customer relations. Among the creative ideas to emerge was the installation of TV cameras in passenger disembarking areas enabling them to register complaints immediately on landing. These are then dealt with in a timely manner and the customer is informed of what action is taken. Changing the image of British Airways was also something to which attention was given. New uniforms for staff, new exterior paint on planes, new interiors for planes, new passenger lounges and an expensive advertising campaign were employed to promote the new image of British Airways. The airline business is immensely competitive and all companies have to strive to find ways of identifying means of establishing a competitive advantage for themselves. This is often sought by trying to improve the quality of service offered in relationship to the price charged or through the nature of the *augmented service* offered.

Service quality includes such things as:

1 Tangibles – do the physical facilities, equipment and appearance of personnel associated with the service promote confidence in the quality of the service?
2 Reliability – is there evidence of an ability to perform the promised service properly the first time?
3 Responsiveness – is there a willingness to help customers and provide prompt service?

4 Competence – do the personnel possess knowledge and skill and have they an ability to convey trust and confidence?

5 Credibility/trustworthiness – is the organisation trustworthy and does it always deliver what it promises to deliver?

6 Empathy – does the provider of the service provide its customers with individualised attention?

7 Courtesy – do customers perceive the service provided to be a friendly one?

8 Communication – are customers kept informed about the service offered in the language they can understand? Do the providers of the service listen to what the customers have to say?

The *augmented service* refers to activities or additional services that are tangential to the physical transportation of customers from the point of departure to their destinations.

Question

In what ways might airlines offer an augmented service to customers? Can you think of any which are not currently offered?

PARADIGM SHIFT

> **A paradigm is a set of rules and regulations that guide our actions when solving problems.**

A paradigm is a set of rules and regulations that defines boundaries and helps us be successful within those boundaries, where success is measured by the problems solved using these rules and regulations. Paradigm shifts are different from continuous improvement. Examples include: going from donkey cart or horse drawn carriage to car or travelling long distances by aeroplane instead of by bus or ocean liner. Paradigm shifts have made it possible to send complex, accurate messages over great distances: they have facilitated moving from primitive methods such as shouting, smoke, fire, drum, flag signals to highly sophisticated mechanisms such as telegraph, telephone, fax, live video by wire, optical fibre, and communications satellite.

Paradigms have life cycles and towards the end of the life cycle, problem solving becomes more costly, more time consuming and less satisfactory (Figure 1.1). Solutions no longer fit the larger context because of changes that have occurred elsewhere. Nowhere is this better illustrated than in the case of needing to improve parts of the UK motorway network. The problems associated with the M6–M53 intersection, the Thelwall Viaduct connection and M6–M62 intersection in the north-west of England illustrate the point. Widening the M6 over the sections involved not only

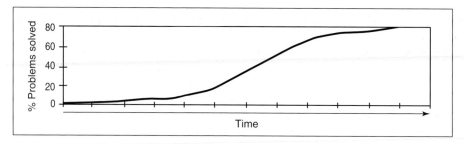

- Towards the end of the life cycle, problem solving becomes more costly, more time consuming and less satisfactory. Solutions no longer fit the larger context because of changes that have occurred elsewhere.

Figure 1.1 **Paradigm life cycle curve**

cost millions of pounds of taxpayers' money but placed an additional un-estimated burden on motorists in terms of long delays, excessive fuel consumption while negotiating the sections involved and psychological stress which is difficult to even estimate. The paradigm of widening busy stretches of motorways must surely be in the decline stages of its life cycle. A paradigm shift is required urgently.

Paradigm shifts require a change in perspective on the subject. Blinkered thinking associated with holding too rigorously to a paradigm can lead to missing opportunities and overlooking threats which may have a critical impact on a business. Two competitors may see the same opportunity or threat in different ways and the one which is able to make the best response can gain a sustainable competitive advantage over its rival.

The process of paradigm shift can be encouraged and effected early through the use of creative thinking. Creative thinking brings into place notions and ideas that would not normally be contemplated in the problem situation. Creative problem solving methods make extensive use of tech-niques and approaches that help to find solutions to recalcitrant open-ended problems.

FROM STEAM DRIVEN TO PETROL DRIVEN CARS

The steam car was a failure as a road vehicle for it proved too heavy and its control too difficult for this purpose. The electric motor seemed to offer one possible solution while other would-be inventors saw the gas-powered engine as providing a possible solution. Etienne Lenoir built an engine which used ordinary coal gas in 1863 and even made a car which he drove using his invented engine as the power source. Siegfried Marcus is credited with using petrol vapour for the first time in an engine to drive a car through the streets of Vienna in 1875. However, it was considered to be such a noisy vehicle that the police banned its further use on the public highways. Very much ahead of his time,

Edward Butler produced a petrol driven tricycle, with a two cylinder motor, a carburettor and ignition through a spark plug produced by a dynamo, in London in 1884. The 'Red Flags Laws' operated at that time in England restricting speed to 4 m.p.h. on the open road and 2 m.p.h. in built up areas. The laws laid down that a vehicle should be accompanied by a man walking before it carrying a red flag and warning people of the on-coming vehicle. They were a death sentence for all such inventions. In Germany, however, August Nikolaus Otto did much to advance the development of the gas engine in the 1870s – although it was powered from a mains supply.

Karl Benz gained acquaintance with the *boneshaker* bicycle at an early age and this prompted him to think of ways of mechanising road transport. He became interested in Lenoir's gas engine, made himself aware of recent developments in the field, and concluded that some petroleum derivative might be suitable as fuel. He also felt that this would be comparatively cheap since extensive oil reserves had been discovered in Pennsylvania in the 1850s.

In 1885 Benz produced his first car. It was a tricycle with a four-stroke engine using the Otto principle. He invented his own electrical ignition system and surrounded the engine with a mantle containing cold water for cooling. Transmission of the drive to the rear wheels was accomplished with chains and incorporated a primitive clutch.

Questions

1 In the light of the above, consider just how the paradigm shift (from horse-driven vehicle to mechanised road vehicle) occurred in this instance.
2 What lessons are to be drawn from this account?

CHARACTERISTICS OF CREATIVE THINKING AND CREATIVE THINKERS

Intelligence measures do not explain creative ability. Highly productive creative thinkers form more novel combinations than the merely talented. If one particular style of thought stands out about highly productive creative thinking, it is the ability to make juxtapositions between dissimilar subjects. It is a facility to see things to which others are blind.

It would be useful to understand the thinking processes which were involved in producing the *Mona Lisa*, as well as the ones that produced the theory of relativity. It would be more than useful to appreciate what characterises the thinking strategies of people such as Einstein, Edison, Leonardo da Vinci and Mozart.

Efforts have been made to establish the links between measures of intelligence and highly productive creative thinking, but intelligence measures themselves are insufficient to explain the latter. Psychologists reached the conclusion that creativity is not the same as intelligence.

A person can be far more creative than he or she is intelligent, or far more intelligent than creative.

Most people, given data or some problem, can work out the conventional response. Typically, people think *reproductively*; that is, on the basis of similar problems encountered in the past (see Chapter 3 for the development of this notion). When confronted with problems, we make use of previous experiences and apply a method or approach that has worked before. If there is more than one such approach we select the most promising and work within a clearly defined direction towards the solution of the problem. This can lead us to become too certain of the correctness of our conclusion and develop mind-sets (see Chapter 2).

Experience indicates that highly productive creative thinking is generated by thinking *productively*, not *reproductively*. When confronted with a problem, people thinking in this fashion look at a problem from many perspectives and search for many different ways of solving the problem. They come up with many different ideas, some of which are quite unconventional and often unique.

With *productive* thinking, the aim is to generate many different approaches. The least obvious must be considered as well as the most likely approaches. It is the willingness to explore different approaches that is important, even after a promising one is discovered. *Reproductive* thinking, on the other hand, can produce too rigid thinking. This can produce an inability to solve a problem that resembles past experiences only in superficial ways. Interpreting such a problem through the past experience will, by definition, not be productive. *Reproductive* thinking produces solutions which we have employed before and not original ones.

It is important to appreciate how highly productive creative thinkers generate so many alternatives and conjectures and why so many of their ideas are so rich and varied. Highly productive creative thinking is often produced by finding a new perspective that no one else has taken. The first step is to restructure a problem in many different ways. The first way one looks at a problem may be too biased by the way in which one usually views matters. Restructuring takes place by looking at a problem from one perspective and then moving on to another perspective and then still another. With each move, understanding deepens and one begins to understand the essence of the problem. In order to find creative solutions, one may have to abandon the initial approach that stems from past experience and reconceptualise the problem. By adopting more than one perspective, highly productive creative thinkers solve existing problems and even identify new ones.

It is possible that highly productive creative thinkers form more novel combinations than merely talented individuals. If one particular style of thought stands out about highly productive creative thinking, it is the ability to make connections or associations between dissimilar subjects. It is a facility to see things to which others are blind. Leonardo da Vinci forced a relationship between the sound of a bell and a stone hitting water enabling him to make the connection that sound travels in waves. Samuel Morse was trying to work out how to produce a telegraphic signal strong enough to be received coast to coast. One day he saw tied horses being exchanged at a relay station and forced a connection between relay stations for horses and strong signals. The solution involved giving the travelling signal periodic boosts of power. Nickla Tesla forced a connection between the setting sun and a motor that made the AC motor possible by having the motor's magnetic field rotate inside the motor just as the sun (from our perspective) rotates.

The ability to tolerate ambivalence between opposites or two incompatible subjects is thought to characterise highly productive creative thinking. Edison's invention of a practical system of lighting involved combining wiring in parallel circuits with high resistance filaments in his bulbs, two things that were not considered possible by conventional thinkers at the time. Because Edison could tolerate the ambivalence between two incompatible things, he could see the relationship that led to the breakthrough.

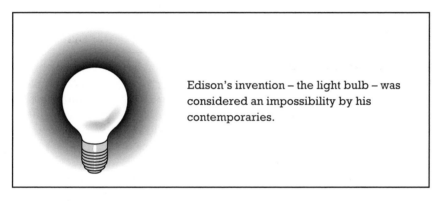

Edison's invention – the light bulb – was considered an impossibility by his contemporaries.

Qualities of a creative person

Creativity is a quality which exhibits itself in the way in which people conduct their lives. People who exhibit creative behaviour:

- challenge the *status quo*;
- confront assumptions;
- exhibit curiosity;
- like to investigate new possibilities;
- tend to take the initiative in most matters;
- are highly imaginative;
- are future oriented;
- tend to think visually;
- see possibilities within the seemingly impossible;
- are not afraid of taking risks;
- are prepared to make mistakes;
- are adaptable to different work environments;
- are adaptable to changing circumstances;
- see relationships between seemingly disconnected elements;

- distil unusual ideas down to their underlying principles;
- synthesise diverse elements;
- are able to spot underlying patterns in events;
- are able to cope with paradoxes;
- look beyond the first 'right idea'.

Acquiring creative problem solving skills

Research has shown continuously over the past fifty years that people can be taught, encouraged and coached or counselled to be more creative. Four basic creative strengths and skills can be easily taught:

1 Fluency – ability to produce many ideas (many of which may be fairly similar or having the same kind of theme).
2 Flexibility – ability to produce a varied mix of ideas (none, or few of which are similar or share the same kind of underlying theme).
3 Elaboration – ability to add detail, depth, mixtures of viewpoints or perspectives.
4 Originality – uniqueness, novelty, newness, creativeness (new) or innovativeness (improvement of existing).

Fluency can be developed by holding creative thinking sessions at which ideas for a hundred different uses for everyday objects (sponge, toothpick, eraser, brick, paper clip, etc.) should be generated. After reaching this number, one can then move on to working on work-related objects.

Flexibility can be improved by listing 50 different kinds of uses for everyday objects and then moving on to work on related challenges.

Elaboration can be developed by describing something (hobby, TV show, tree, cat, an athletic event, etc.) in considerable detail, using all the physical senses.

Originality can be learned by picking one common object and listing many new uses for it.

Regular practice in each one of the above activities can lead to the acquisition of improved creative skills.

---

exercise
─────

Fluency and flexibility and originality.

Think of a hundred uses, new use or types of uses for the following:

1 Scrubbing brush	7 Wooden pencil
2 Empty jam jar	8 Old hats (male and female)
3 Waste paper basket	9 Obsolete desk top computers
4 Disused railway track sleepers	10 Worn out carpets
5 Blunderbuss	11 Dead light bulbs
6 Bottle tops off empties	12 Sweat-shirts

Elaboration
Describe each one of the above twelve items in considerable detail, using all the physical senses.

QUESTIONS

1 Why should the modern day manager need to know about creative problem solving ?

2 Why is creative problem solving expertise an important asset for any business executive? How might executives improve their creative problem solving skills?

3 What is paradigm shift? How does it relate to creative problem solving?

4 What kinds of 'future shock' do you think the twenty-first century might have in store for us as: (a) workers, (b) consumers, (c) producers ? (d) managers?

5 Koestler said: 'True creativity often starts where language ends.' How would you interpret this statement in the context of business?

6 If we tend not think about what we think we know already, and existing ideas tend to make us myopic about new possibilities, how can we hope to get new insights into existing problems?

7 James March argues that: 'Organisations face a large number of problems of about equal importance, but only a few solutions. Thus the chance of finding a solution to a particular problem is small.' Does this mean that organisations must spend most of the time 'muddling through'? Why or why not?

8 John Harvey Jones said: 'Unless a company is progressing all the time, it is in fact moving backwards. It is quite impossible to maintain the status quo.' Can you account for John Harvey Jones's conclusion? Explain.

9 Growth and survival can be related directly to an organisation's ability to produce (or adopt) and implement new products or services, and processes (Van Gundy, 1987). How does one reconcile this suggestion with the fact that many products appear to have been around for many years (e.g. Mars bars) while others enjoy a revival (e.g. the Volkswagen Beetle car)?

10 Why should lack of agreement regarding goals and a lack of under-standing of cause–effect relationships give rise to a need for creative thinking?

11 *Fluency* (ability to produce many ideas); *flexibility* (ability to produce a varied mix of ideas); *elaboration* (ability to add detail, depth, mixtures of viewpoints or perspectives; and *originality* – uniqueness, novelty, new-ness, creativeness (new) or innovativeness (improvement of existing) are considered important creative skills. How might one introduce these skills into the management of meetings?

12 Differentiate innovation from creativity and invention.

CASES

Keeping prices competitive

John Holmes operates a clothes wholesale distribution business. Competition is strong and pricing is keen. Rising costs of distribution however are a constant problem and all competitors compete strongly on price. John is looking for ways of keeping prices competitive.

Question

How can John try to minimise price rises in the face of strong competition and at the same time still maintain profitability? (See Appendix 3 for some suggestions.)

Price and innovation

Sally Major owns a hi-tech company which produces assembled and part assembled components for a variety of industrial and consumer goods. Recently the technical department has achieved a major breakthrough in the production process which enables the firm to reduce the cost of producing all component assemblies and sub-assemblies by at least 50 per cent. As a general guideline to setting prices the firm usually adopts around a 100 per cent mark-up on the costings subject to this making the product competitive in the marketplace. Occasionally, where demand is high and there is no price consciousness, mark-up can be at least 150 per cent and still be in line with what competition is charging for similar products. There are only a handful of products where mark-up is less than 100 per cent and none where it is less than 80 per cent. In all cases, the firm makes sure that its pricing is in line with that of competitors. The firm adopts the role of market-challenger in all market segments. Market share varies from between 25 per cent and 40 per cent of the market segment.

Question

What action do you think Sally should now adopt with respect to pricing. (See Appendix 3 for comments.)

Anti-bacterium gel

Barbarossa dental research has invented a gel that when rubbed gently into the gums gives adequate protection from tooth decay and gum disorders for a period of about 6 months. The firm is pondering on how best to market the product or even whether to market it at all. If the product is marketed it is likely that dentists will no longer need to repair tooth decay in users of the gel and this will have a major impact on their business. Barbarossa relies on the dental trade for many of its other products and the prospect of dentists losing many customers means that Barbarossa, too, could also lose many of its customers (i.e. the dentists).

Question

How would you advise Barbarossa to proceed?

chapter
two

BLOCKS TO
CREATIVITY

INTRODUCTION

Creative thinking and problem solving is not an unfettered process. There are blocks to creative thinking and creative problem solving. The blocks are essentially of two varieties: individual and organisational. First we will look at the need to be ready for change and to deal with new kinds of problems. Next we will look at ideas about the problem solving process and what it involves. Then we will turn our attention to the various blocks that are encountered when trying to solve problems or think creatively.

First we will give attention to the blocks we experience as individuals and then we will turn to examining organisational blocks. In both instances we will consider what can be done to help overcome the various blocks which may hinder creative thinking and creative problem solving.

THE NEED TO BE READY FOR CHANGE

Executives must be ready for anything which requires having the necessary tools to proactively combat change. As Morgan (1989) states:

> Many organisations and their managers drive toward the future while looking through the rear-view mirror. They manage in relation to events that have already occurred, rather than anticipate and confront the challenges of the future.

If we were not at times 'blocked' in our thinking we would not need creative problem solving methods. In this chapter we will first consider the nature of problem solving before going on to examine *individual* and *organisational* blocks to creative thinking. In addition we will look at ways of dealing with both kinds of blocks. It is the existence of these blocks that gives rise to the need for a structured creative problem solving process and for training to help overcome particular mind-sets.

PROBLEM SOLVING

> **Successful problem solving involves a search for the best problem space as well as the best programme.**

Problem solving involves processing information. Conceptualising problem solving in this way Newell and Simon (1972) argued that this is a three stage process (see Figure 2.1):

1 *Recognising the task environment.* First, one perceives the events, interprets these invents and recognises the nature of the task – e.g. notice disquiet in the office and see that the task is to identify how the disquiet can be resolved.
2 *Transformation into the person's problem space.* Next one views the task in a specific way. Here one has to be quite specific about the goal – what has to be done, where one stands in relationship to the goal and what kinds of acts need to be carried out in order to reach the goal. For example, from experience one will know that one cannot jump to any quick conclusions about the source of the disquiet in the office but will know how to set about finding out the source of the disquiet.
3 *Processing the data and moving towards the goal.* Depending on how the problem space has been conceived, one uses various kinds of information given with the problem or drawn from memory to process the data so as to move towards the problem solution. For example, in the illustration one will have had experience, of diagnosing problems of unrest in the office and will be able to call upon this experience along with information noted which is specific to the current situation in the office.

In the course of working through the above steps – called 'following the programme' – the problem solver will notice whether any of the steps or series of steps he or she makes reduces the distance to the goal – i.e. resolving or solving the problem. If this seems to be the case then the problem solver will continue with that line of enquiry. If the steps do not seem to be productive then alternative steps will be followed. Progress and search for solutions are related to constant feedback of information obtained from people and objects in the problem situation. If the entire search programme fails to achieve the objective then the problem solver either quits, modifies the programme, or changes the problem space.

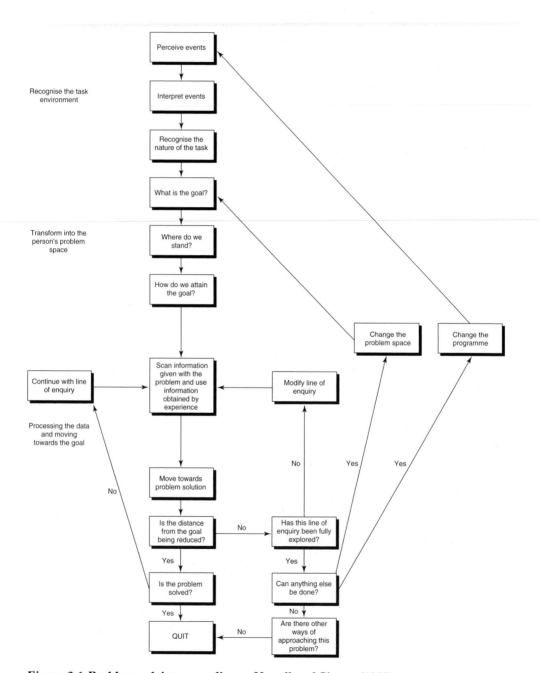

Figure 2.1 **Problem solving according to Newell and Simon (1972)**

The conclusion that might be drawn from the analysis offered by Newell and Simon is that problem solving involves the search for the most successful programmes. However, as Minsky (1974) argues, successful problem solving may not so much be a search for a successful programme as a search for the best problem space. It would seem, however, that both are required to increase the likelihood of finding good solutions to problems.

Isenberg (1984b) found that a number of key factors characterised the thought processes of executives:

- a feel for inconsistencies in information;
- an ability to build upon well learned patterns of behaviour;
- synthesis of isolated pieces of information;
- intuition to check on formal analysis;
- an understanding of the importance of interpersonal and organisational processes.

An inability to apply this mode of thinking effectively can lead to blocks occurring.

In addition, looking at the Newell and Simon model, blocks to finding solutions to problems can arise for the following reasons:

1 Incorrect perception of the task environment – negative mind-set.
2 Incorrect specification of the problem space – creative problem solving techniques may help to alleviate this problem.
3 Lack of relevant information or information overload. More or better information gathering procedures or the use of creative problem solving methods may assist in this case.

MIND-SET

WHERE MIND-SET EXISTS

We have always done it this way, why change?
There can only be one way to do it properly.
It's experience that counts – it's the only way to learn.
I learned to do it this way and it has never let me down.
Toy soldiers are for boys and dolls are for girls.
Televisions are for receiving information – not for two way communication.

Mind-set is a condition where an individual is over-sensitised to some part of the information available at the expense of other parts. Mind-set can be useful:

- It helps us to become sensitised to some important things and serves us well – for example, red lights act as warnings and alert us to impending danger.

- As a result of learning from experience, mind-set sensitises us to patterns that remind us of ways which have enabled us to solve past problems. We do not have to reinvent the wheel each time that we encounter the same problem. For example, if when dealing with an irate customer we have found an approach that seems to be satisfactory from the point of view of dealing with the situation, then when we subsequently encounter another irate customer we can deal with the situation using our acquired knowledge.

When mind-set blocks us

Luchins (1942) showed how mind-set under certain circumstances can produce fixation and stereotyping in problem solving behaviour. The phenomenon may show itself under conditions where the individual has discovered a strategy that initially functions well in solving certain tasks but later blocks the realisation of new and simpler solutions to similar problems. The effect reflects a dysfunctional consequence of the normal rational way of approaching problems that may block the establishment of a new perspective and more important lines of procedure in task environments that resemble those encountered before. Cyert and March (1963) observed similar behaviour among practising managers in real-life contexts. Typical managerial search is seen as simple minded and as over-emphasising previous experience, by selectively searching in areas close to where previous solutions have been found.

> **Mind-set is a condition where an individual is over-sensitised to some part of the information available at the expense of other parts**

Duncker (1945) investigated how past experience may block productive problem solving. He suggested the expression 'functional fixedness' to refer to a block against using an object in a new way that is required to solve a problem. Interesting real life examples of functional fixedness are provided by Weizenbaum (1984). According to the latter the steam engine had been in use for a hundred years to pump water out of mines before Trevithick had the idea of using it as a source of locomotive power – it had only been seen as a tool to help pump water out of mines. The computer, also, had been used for a long time as a calculator before its use as a general symbol manipulator was envisaged.

> **Typical managerial search is seen as simple minded and as over-emphasising previous experience by selectively searching in areas close to where previous solutions have been found. When stuck on a problem executives tend to follow their mind-set and this may be counter productive as far as previously unencountered problems are concerned.**

It would seem that while mind-set can provide us with substantial benefits, unfortunately there are times when it can stand in the way of progress. Mind-set can create difficulties for executives when they are facing new or novel problems. When stuck on a problem, executives tend to follow their mind-set and this may be counter productive as far as previously unencountered problems are concerned. Mind-set is often characterised by one-right-answer thinking, always looking for reasons why something will not work and an over-regard for logical thinking.

Executives may have learned from past experience that a particular way of dealing with a problem usually leads to a satisfactory solution. Constant successful application of the approach reinforces the belief that this way is the correct way to approach the problem, and even the only way to approach the problem. When a new problem arrives that defies solution by the learned approach executives becomes stuck and do not know what to do.

Negative or 'yet but' thinking arises out of executives' zeal to cater for contingencies. It is only natural that they should try to ensure that any project will stand a good chance of being successful, and good management practice advocates that executives should consider what may go wrong and make contingency plans. Every suggestion is therefore questioned and critiqued in order to make sure that the risk of failure is minimised. However, the process of criticism itself can stifle creativity by inducing a negative mind-set. Constructive criticism is required. Rather than making the comment 'yes but' one should use the phrase 'yes and'. For example, faced with the suggestion of making redundancies, the normal response might be: '*yes, but that will only lead to unrest on the shop floor and possible strike action*'. The better response would be: '*yes and wouldn't it be useful, since we can then find other jobs for those people within the company*'.

An over regard for logical thinking can also create a barrier to creative thinking. Some times we have to take steps into the dark, as it were, based upon hunch or intuition. We may have a feeling that what we are doing is the best course of action even though we cannot justify it in a traditionally logical way to ourselves. Perhaps the logical justification only becomes apparent post facto – we can see with hindsight that what we did was the right thing to do. Somehow we cannot perceive beforehand the logical justification – we have a perceptual block. The notion of perceptual blocks is discussed later in the chapter.

FORD MODEL 'T': THE MIND-SET OF HENRY FORD

Henry Ford's model 'T' remained unchanged for years, while General Motors (Chevrolet) was making changes – often using new technology.

Henry Ford said 'We'll give the customer any color he wants as long as it is black.' It was an arrogant statement by an arrogant man who had been on top so long he thought nothing could dislodge him from the number one position.

In the late 1920s Ford nearly went out of business as a result of this myopic approach. General Motors (Chevrolet) took over as number one in the US and Ford did not catch up until the late 1980s.

OTHER BARRIERS TO AN INDIVIDUAL'S CREATIVITY

> Some barriers limit an individual's creative output and are related to the people themselves. On the other hand there are those that emanate from the environment in which people operate.

Many researchers have attempted to address the phenomenon of barriers to creativity. These include Arnold (1962), Adams (1974), Jones (1987), and Majaro (1992). All have produced detailed lists of the various kinds of barriers to creative problem solving.

Some barriers limit individuals' creative output and are related to the people themselves. On the other hand there are those that emanate from the environment in which people operate. Personal barriers may be sub-divided into physiological barriers, such as the perceptual limitations of the senses or the brain's data handling capacity, and psychological barriers related to the person's behaviour or attitudes.

Arnold (1962) suggested:

1 Perceptual blocks, which prevent a person receiving a true, relevant picture of the outside world.
2 Cultural blocks, which result from influences of society.
3 Emotional blocks, such as fear, anxiety and jealousy.

Adams added a fourth category: intellectual and expressive blocks.

DEALING WITH AN INDIVIDUAL'S BLOCKS TO CREATIVITY

Jones (1987) initiated a study designed to find out more about the factors which inhibit creativity. In reviewing the literature on the subject he found that several authors included perceptual, cultural and emotional blocks within their taxonomies while others mentioned such factors as errors in thinking and personal fears. He identified four typologies of blocks. These were derived from cluster analysis of self-reported items. The typologies are:

1 *Strategic blocks*: 'one right answer approaches', inflexibility in thinking. These affect the approach taken to solve problems. They include the tendency to rely heavily on past experience or particular techniques without challenging their appropriateness; focusing on a narrow range of options for either problem definition or problem solving; and adapting an over-serious approach to problems which prevents the emergence of a playful, imaginative and humorous climate.
2 *Value blocks*: 'over-generalised rigidity influenced by personal values'. These occur when personal beliefs and values restrict the range of ideas

contemplated. Values co-exist and failure to reconcile them contributes to difficult personal and organisational dilemmas.

3 *Perceptual blocks*: 'over-narrow focus of attention and interest'. These arise from a lack of sensory awareness at a physical level and therefore contribute to lack of awareness of implications of situations.

4 *Self-image blocks*: poor effectiveness through fear of failure, timidity in expressing ideas, etc. These reduce effectiveness in advancing ideas assertively. They arise from a lack of self-confidence in the value of one's own ideas. Individuals may be reluctant to seek help and talk about personal feelings. This barrier seems to be the greatest impediment to the successful implementation of new ideas.

Jones's approach has resulted in training applications which centre on personal feedback and counselling, including suggestions for the most appropriate mechanisms for developing improved skills. Strategic blocks can be challenged through creative problem solving training. Values, however, are a more difficult problem, but creating an awareness of personal values in the individual offers some respite. Perceptual blocks can be freed through observation, and self-image blocks can profit from assertiveness training.

Blocks to creativity

- Strategic
- Values
- Perceptual
- Self-image

Figure 2.2 **Jones's blocks to creativity**

Creativity is a fragile business. It is stimulated by the right environment, self-image, and co-workers; it is inhibited by limiting beliefs, work situations and stresses. Awareness of the obstacles to creativity can help us push through our creative blocks.

Perceptual block

Look at the statement in Figure 2.3. How many times does the letter 'f' occur? See Appendix 3 for the answer.

Perceptual block

- Following the sinking of the old frigate *Ferdinand*, Nelson fought his way carefully around the cape in foul weather in the hope of meeting his foe again off the far side of the island. By the close of the day he found his adversary adrift and floating perilously close to the infamous granite rocks.

Figure 2.3 **Perceptual block**

MYOPIA IN THE WATCH INDUSTRY

The Elgin watch company has often been quoted as a classic example of a firm which exhibited acute symptoms of marketing myopia on its way to eventually going out of business. The company refused to adapt to the changing demands of the marketplace and failed to take account of the dwindling number of customers for its long established product – the classic high quality pocket watch with an anticipated long life-span.

Yet the case of Elgin was only one example of myopia in this industry. English watchmakers dominated watchmaking in the eighteenth and nineteenth centuries. The English verge escapement dominated world markets for many decades. Even when technological breakthroughs were sought for, it was the English watchmakers who led the way. Massey's work at the beginning of the nineteenth century led to the eventual use of the lever movement in watches which finally ousted the time-honoured verge. It also proved a better movement than the cylinder movements used on the Continent. However, the English watchmakers did not move with the times and their demise at the end of the nineteenth century was largely due to their lack of competitiveness with Swiss and American produced watches, which met the needs of consumers better.

It may seem rather obvious to us today that in order to survive in the marketplace a company should adapt its strategy to meet the changing wants and needs of its customers. However, the watch industry possesses a number of quirks and it doesn't necessarily always respond in the way one would expect. Nor does the unexpected always result in total failure.

The Swiss watch industry dominated world markets with its fine clockwork movements, elegant designs and 'quality' image for most of the twentieth century. Quality, elegance and accuracy are key features which people look for in a watch and some people are prepared to pay very high prices in order to obtain what they want. Up until 1970 watches were powered by clockwork movements and precision engineering dominated an industry where a key dimension of 'quality' reflected accuracy in time keeping. An 'Officially Certified Chronometer' certificate handed out by the Swiss authorities was a sure sign that a particular watch met with specific time-keeping standards. Watches carrying such certificates were eagerly sought after and could command high prices. Apart from accuracy features such as self-winding movements, elegance in design, gold metal casing and sometimes jewel adorned dials added to the desirability of a watch.

Firms such as Rolex, Patek Philippe, Jaeger, Breguet and Blancpain were world renowned for their ability to produce desirable watches of such a quality that only the better off people could afford to own them. A major breakthrough in technology, however, enabled the Swiss industry to invent the quartz movement which made it possible for accurate watches to be mass produced by anyone. The Swiss industry did not use the invention for fear that it would kill its existing market. However, watchmakers in the Far East grasped the quartz movement, and in a single year the sales of Swiss watches dropped by 25 per cent.

This is a case where mind-set coupled with paradigm shift spelt a disaster for a whole industry.

Why are 1996 coins worth more than 1984 coins?

Figure 2.4 **Why are 1996 coins worth more than 1984 coins? (See Appendix 3 for answer.)**

Is the aircraft flying towards you or away from you

Figure 2.5 **Is the aircraft flying towards you or away from you?**

> **Many people feel comfortable using conventional ideas and this is often one of the main barriers to creative thinking.**

Many people feel comfortable using conventional ideas and this is often one of the main barriers to creative thinking. There are many blocks to creativity and some are more destructive than others. Unless these barriers are released, then the usefulness of creative problem solving techniques and approaches will be lost. The particular blocks which are most destructive are the self-defeating beliefs, which state that:

(a)   Fantasy and reflection are a waste of time.
(b)   Problem solving is serious business; no fun or humour are allowed.
(c)   Feeling and intuition are bad.
(d)   Tradition is preferable to change.

There are many more blocks to creativity, as indicated above, but the above barriers need to be removed, as fantasy, originality, fun and change are definitely needed when we use the creative problem solving techniques. The rejection of conventional lines of thinking is of primary importance for a successful solution to the problem. Creative problem solving techniques require the user to have an open mind, which will allow the user to generate ideas – some of which will hopefully solve the problem which has arisen.

The broken clock problem

A clock face has roman numerals painted on its glass surface (Figure 2.6). One day the clock falls on the floor and an observer is about to pick up the four pieces of glass when she notices that on each piece the sum of the roman numerals comes to the same total. Can you work out what she saw?

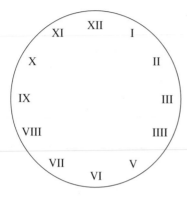

Figure 2.6 **The broken clock problem**

A version of the clock problem has been used in creativity training at Manchester Business School, by Tudor Rickards, and we are grateful for permission to share the puzzle. See Appendix 3 for illustrative solution.

BLOCKS TO ORGANISATIONAL CREATIVE THINKING AND WAYS OF DEALING WITH THEM

BLOCKS TO CREATIVITY IN ORGANISATIONS

People and organisations tend to fall into a variety of traps when trying to become more innovative.

1 Identifying the wrong problem.
2 Judging ideas too quickly.
3 Stopping with the first good idea.
4 Failing to get the support of key personnel in the organisation.
5 Failing to challenge assumptions.

Some of the major blocks are:

- Emphasis on managerial control – control can stifle creativity since autonomy and a degree of freedom are critical ingredients of creative thinking. Moreover, traditional financial controls are not appropriate for long-term innovation efforts.
- Short range thinking – there is a tendency to give priority to quick returns with financially measurable results.

- Analysis paralysis – ideas are often overanalysed and time is lost along with any competitive advantage.
- Rigid hierarchical structures – an unpredictable environment requires a responsive organisational structure and this is not characteristic of most organisations.
- There is a tendency to look for one project that is likely to generate a big payoff, rather than a number of smaller projects with small to medium payoffs. Good small projects can thus often be overlooked.
- Market versus technology driven product planning – there tends to be an overemphasis on market research, in line with the marketing orientation adopted by many companies. While the marketing orientation is very important it is often implemented at the expense of good ideas which come out of R&D and which never get off the ground.
- Pressure to achieve and do more with less resources – R&D departments are often penalised for cutting costs; the more the department saves one year, the less it has to play with the next. Paradoxically, the more companies have to cut back on expenditure, the more creative they must become.
- Lack of a systematic approach to innovation – a lack of real ideas about how to innovate.
- The belief that some people are creative and others are not.

Ways of dealing with blocks such blocks include:

- Encouraging prudent risk taking.
- Freedom of thought – some degree of autonomy.
- Linking rewards with specific performance.
- Encouraging different viewpoints on problems.
- Positive involvement of top management.
- Continual flow of ideas.
- Responding positively to new ideas.

ELEMENTS AND CONDITIONS OF CREATIVE ORGANISATIONS

One can divide the characteristics of organisational creativity into four distinct elements (the four Ps of creativity):

- People – teams or individuals.
- Processes – how ideas are developed and innovation accomplished.
- Place – creative environment.
- Product – the output of creativity.

One cannot treat each one of the four Ps in isolation from the others. They are inter-dependent. Perhaps the one to receive the least attention is 'place'. An organisation concerned with creating a climate that influences effective creative activity should provide at least the following:

- *Resources*: these should be appropriate and sufficient.
- *Security*: adequate salary and security of job tenure
- *Trust*: allow for mistakes.
- *Reward/recognition*: feedback, recognition and reward.

QUESTIONS

1 Why are people sometimes blocked in their thinking? How can they be helped overcome the various blockages that occur?

2 Why do people find it difficult to solve previously unencountered problems?

3 Differentiate between *individual* and *organisational* blocks to creative thinking. What can be done to cope with the difficulties created by these blocks or even help prevent these kinds of blocks occurring?

4 Tudor Rickards coined the phrase 'mental stuckness'. What exactly did he mean by this phrase and what is its relevance to the use of creative problem solving methods and techniques?

5 Morgan (1989) states: 'Many organisations and their managers drive toward the future while looking through the rear-view mirror. They manage in relation to events that have already occurred, rather than anticipate and confront the challenges of the future.' Assess the impact that this kind of thinking will have on creative thinking and problem solving in an organisation.

6 'If we were not at times "blocked" in our thinking we would not need creative problem solving methods.' What kinds of blockages to creative thinking, as individuals, do we encounter?

7 'Problems often don't stay solved, or solutions never quite work out as expected because the wrong problem was defined.' Comment on this apparent truism.

8 'The first good idea is never the best.' To what extent would you agree or disagree with this statement. Explain.

9 Picasso said, 'Every act of creation begins with an act of destruction.' How transferable is this notion to the domain of creative problem solving? Discuss.

10 How might making use of each of the following help overcome blocks to creative problem solving?:

- watching a magician at work;
- going to the theatre or cinema;
- family outings;
- visits to junk yards;
- mixing with or talking with different people – perhaps people whose value systems are different from your own;

- daydreaming to a sound effects record;
- free association to music;
- browsing around flea markets;
- scanning old science magazines;
- reading historical accounts;
- reading wants ads;
- indulging in or watching sports;
- studying new subjects through introductory level books;
- following the news – in the newspapers and television.

CASES

J.C. losing money

J.C. was unhappy–even worse, he was losing money. His advertising agency had beaten six other firms for the right to represent Ruby's Soap, but what once looked like a wonderful opportunity was turning out to be a major disaster. J.C. had scrapped Ruby's old campaign – which stressed the soap's cleansing powers – in favour of soft-soap testimonials. The new approach, which featured the caretakers of schools and churches talking about how wonderful Ruby's was, had been received well by everyone.

The advertisements differentiated Ruby's from its much larger competition. While competitors were tough on dirt, Ruby's became the one to use when you needed finesse, not muscle. J.C. had been a brand manager with a large fast-moving consumer goods firm for several years and was particularly pleased with this positioning of the appeal. It demonstrated the kind of know-how and expertise his agency could offer Ruby.

J.C. was constantly on the phone to Ruby's Soap headquarters suggesting marketing moves, promotions, and possible new products. But all of this time was costing J.C. money. He was getting paid just to do Ruby's advertising. While his ideas might be producing Brownie points, they weren't producing profits for his agency. The result was that what had started out to be a terrific account was quickly turning into a loser. J.C. wanted to renegotiate.

Jack Ruby hadn't asked J.C. to do anything except his advertising. While he valued J.C.'s ideas, he had made clear from the start exactly what he was buying from J.C.

Question

J.C. was losing money on the Ruby's account because he negotiated badly in the discussions that set the level of service the agency would provide. What could he do now?

New shoe company

The New Shoe Company, based in the English Midlands, is experiencing a fall in profits. The company measures profits in terms of the annual pre-tax return on capital employed.

The Sales Director says that falling profitability is a reflection of the current slump in the market. Total demand in the marketplace is much less than it was 12 months ago and the company has struggled to maintain its market share at the previous level as competition has intensified. Competition from European manufacturers has been sharpened by changes in the EEC trading regulations, and Spanish manufacturers in particular have taken advantage of their lower cost structure to make inroads into the British market. At the same time the New Shoe Company has failed to take full advantage of opportunities in Europe. It has not fully developed its market niching strategy where it can gain a competitive advantage. The Sales Director blames the firm's lack of competitiveness on the poor performance of the R&D team and the inability of the manufacturing departments to control costs.

The Technical Director claims that the firm's products are competitive with any that are produced world-wide. Indeed, in her view, the firm's products are by far the best available at the price offered. She points to the lack of marketing effort expended by the firm in the past year, pointing to the necessity to keep the firm's name before the public at all times, especially when competition is increasing in strength. At the same time she recognises that marketing effort requires financing and that this was not adequately provided during the period in question.

The Production Director points out that the company has been able to lower its manufacturing costs substantially through the introduction of new technology into the manufacturing process. However, he points out the accounting practices adopted by the firm distort the true picture. In his view, profitability has improved, though this is not truly reflected in the company's management accounts.

The Finance Director feels that the drop in profitability is attributable to recent acquisitions that the firm has made. Ventures into retailing have not been as profitable as had first been supposed. This might to some extent have been reflective of bad timing on behalf of the company, given the current recession, in making such acquisitions.

The Managing Director points out that clearly there is a problem and that perhaps one should pay particular attention to what competitors are doing and how the firm is responding from a marketing viewpoint.

Question

Consider the problems created by functional fixedness in this case. How might the situation be resolved?

The think-tank

Bolden Pharmaceutical, employing over 2,000 workers of all grades, welcomed its new chief executive Tim Hodges. Hodges had spent years working for petroleum companies anxiously exploring new avenues to extend their product market scope. Hodges felt that Bolden needed the same kind of treatment and that in addition to looking for new product market opportunities it needed to review its current operations and look for increased efficiency and savings which would help to cover the cost of new ventures.

As a first step Tim decided to set up a think-tank. The works was located close to open moorland on the Yorkshire–Lancashire border close to one of the many small towns that nestle in the valley bottoms. As part of the complex, but at a distance of roughly 400 yards from the main works, the firm owned an old house – at one time a rectory – which possessed fair sized gardens and an open aspect over the nearby moors. Tim thought that the building would provide an admirable place to locate the think-tank.

The building was quickly refurbished to provide ample accommodation for a think-tank team. The building allowed for the creation of a well fitted out conference room with overhead projector facilities, flip-charts, and an on-line desktop computer. In an open plan office, created by knocking down the wall between two adjacent first floor rooms, there was desk space for four people. A telephone which could take both internal and external calls was placed on each desk, along with an up to date PC and the basic office type software which goes with such equipment. Tim Hodges also agreed to finance any additional special purpose software that the team might require – up to a cost not exceeding £10,000 per annum. Secretarial support was provided by two part-time secretaries who between them covered the week 9–5 each day, Monday through Friday.

Four members of the middle management staff were seconded to the think-tank for a 12 month period initially. It was agreed that at the end of this period the situation would be reviewed and anyone wishing to return to their previous job would be able to do so. Temporary appointments were made to cover the work of the seconded executives during the year-long trial period. It was made clear that the seconded executives would not be available for their usual duties during this period but that they could be consulted from time to time by the temporary staff covering their work.

The team of four who made up the think-tank comprised one person with a background in the marketing operations of the company, one person from the finance and accounting area, one person from the R&D/ operations area and a member of the personnel team. The job of co-ordinating the team was to be rotated on a three-monthly basis with each person taking his or her turn at the helm.

The team were given no specific instructions as to how they should proceed with the task they had been give. Tim Hodges made it clear, however, through an internal memorandum to all members of staff – workers and managers – that the team would expect to receive full co-operation from staff at all levels in the organisation and that requests for help or information should be treated in the same way as if he himself had requested it.

Questions

1 What kind of blocks or hindrances do you think the team would be likely to encounter.
2 Given that think-tanks were at one time discarded as an outmoded way of thinking up new ideas, do you think that the team has any real chance of success? Explain.
3 In order to give itself the maximum chances of coming up with ideas, how do you think the team should define its mission? How should it operationalise its mission? How can it try to minimise being subsequently branded as a scapegoat for unsuccessful ventures?

The problem deputy

Bill was new to the job and it was also his first management post. He had taken over a department of 20 people and, although he had been looking forward to his new job with great enthusiasm, after two weeks in the job he now had worries and anxieties.

His problem was Kurt. Kurt was the deputy head of department and had been with the organisation for 11 years. He was 16 years older than Bill and secretly resented Bill's appointment. Kurt had not been appointed head of department because the other members of the department resented his management style, and the boss of the organisation had felt that although Kurt was an able man, the best interests of everyone would be served by appointing an outsider rather than confirming Kurt in the position of head of department.

Kurt had very strong views about his colleagues as Bill soon found out. There was much evidence to show that most of his comments had substance to them. He spent much of his time in Bill's office explaining why he thought most people in the department were lazy and needed 'a good whipping' to make them work. When Kurt was not running down his colleagues he would discuss classical music with Bill – an interest that was close to Bill's heart. Bill was secretly pleased when Kurt went off to get on with his normal work. While he found Kurt an interesting and stimulating fellow he did have reservations about him.

The departmental views of staff on the subject of Kurt were mixed. There was a faction that hated him and wished he would retire early. Kurt did have one or two friends, however, who were more sympathetic to his views and explained his aggressive manner away as justifiable frustration and disappointment. Bill was anxious to get off to a solid start in his new job and recognised that he lacked experience. He also felt that he needed to sort out the business of who was to be his deputy fairly quickly. Should he continue with Kurt in this role? Should he appoint someone else? Should he do without a deputy. Bill's boss wasn't much help in the matter. 'Well you have to manage with what you have', he said in a non-committal way. 'Kurt isn't a bad bloke at heart.'

Bill felt he couldn't think clearly in the matter. Something was causing a block to his thinking processes and he could not get to grips with it.

Question

Can you identify the main sources of blocks to thinking in this instance. What should Bill do?

Tunnel vision

The drive to complete the project was on. That was until local resistance was encountered. There seemed no way of getting round the problem. The locals wanted cash to get out of the way of the highway which was to be driven through their homes – more cash than the company was prepared to offer.

'If we pay up,' said Joe, 'everyone will get to know about it and everyone is going to want a cut. The project has enough on-costs. We won't pay up.'

'I guess we can re-route at little extra cost. It'll mean an extra couple of miles of highway and a tunnel but we won't have to meet the kind of resistance the locals are putting up here. It'll cost extra, more than we'd pay the locals, but heaven knows how much it would cost if we had to pay out to everyone who stood in our way.' Tom smiled.

'Sure agree with that,' said Joe, drawing on his cigar. 'Still we'd better analyse the figures in depth. After all we have to report on the change of plans to the board in due course and they will require justification for the change. How long do you reckon it will take to get the figures?'

Tom grimaced, 'Maybe a few days. If we have to get clearance from the board before we proceed that could add on several weeks. Also, of course, we'd have to pay the men while they were idle. Then there is the rent on the equipment; the interest on loans . . .'

'Hey hang on a minute. This could cost us a lot of money. Can't you get any rough estimates at all?', Joe scowled.

'Jupiter, Joe. All this takes time.'

'But we ain't got time. Before we know it the locals will have wind of the fact we are up to something and we'll have protesters, the government and the police breathing down our necks.' Joe wasn't pleased.

'Well we have to go through formal channels. The board meets once a month. The last meeting was three days ago . . .' Tom was interrupted.

'I think this calls for drastic action. There could be a big pay-off here if we just forge ahead one way or the other. Perhaps we ought just to pay up to the locals and hope for the best', Joe shouted.

'I think we ought to explore the lie of land. Get more information and find out what the locals are really up to', Tom said coolly.

'Every day that passes we have less resources. We cannot afford to do that. Anyway, I don't think it is necessary. What if we just let the locals cool their heels for a few days. We'll make them sweat. Then we'll offer them what we said we would. They'll see sense, I'm sure', Joe reflected.

Question

How do you think the problem should be resolved. What are the major blocks to thinking experienced by Tom and Joe.

chapter three

THEORIES OF CREATIVITY AND THE CREATIVE PROBLEM SOLVING PROCESS

INTRODUCTION

Notions about creativity and creative problem solving are complex. There is no one standard authority on the subject and information about these processes is therefore scattered and to be found in different disciplines. In this chapter I try to pull together some of the ideas which pertain to the subject in the hope of providing some background against which to appreciate the various steps of the creative problem solving process which are described in subsequent chapters. Figure 3.1 provides an overview of the main thread of the discussion which occurs in this chapter.

First we look at some general observations about the ideation process. Next we look at some of the ideas of those who think that creativity is explained best by the neuro-physiological functioning of the brain. Whole brain and two brain theories exemplify this latter approach. We will see a connection between the neuro-physiological functioning of the brain and the cognitive theory of creative problem solving discussed later in the chapter. Before looking at problem solving and creative problem solving, however, we give attention to two other important contributions to the theory of creative thinking. First we look at the notion of divergent and convergent thinking, and then we consider a suggestion that the conditions under which ideation takes place are very important.

The next parts of the chapter concentrate on creative problem solving itself. Ideas about problem solving are discussed and then creative problem solving is considered. Out of the several paradigms which it is thought may underpin creative thinking, the cognitive approach is selected as that being the most appropriate one to consider. Finally the chapter concludes by looking at the process of creative problem solving.

CREATIVE THINKING

Some observations on ideation

> Analytic planning has had little impact on how top management functions. Top management doesn't engage in solving isolated problems but deals with interconnected networks of problems and uses what it calls 'high intuition' (not guesswork) in which rapid pattern recognition takes place and solutions are generated and regenerated as new information is obtained.

Locke (1690) maintained that the source of all ideas is human experience and understanding. Ideas, as he saw them, sprang from knowledge, which in turn is derived from observation of the external world as well as awareness of our own internal ruminations on these observations. 'Knowledge' remains a somewhat vague notion, but implies more than remembered observations and includes some form of interpretation of these observations. Ideas may not merely come into and go out of our awareness like randomly displayed data elements, but instead can be consciously related to each other in ways that we begin to find useful, interesting, satisfying or even entertaining. Idea processing takes individual ideas and manipulates, synthesises and associates them with one another until they form a larger contextual pattern that we can consciously relate to some human concern or problem.

Idea processing does not rely on either mathematical algorithms or on other kinds of structured logical step by step solution methods. Many researchers have observed that the non-specifiable type of idea processing appears to be the more dominant approach of expert high-level decision makers. Mintzberg (1976), for instance, contrasts the analytical reasoning process of management science with the intuitive thought process of the manager and concludes that analytic planning has had little impact on how top management functions. Isenberg (1984a) reported that 'thought sampling' statements describing how senior managers think indicate that they do not engage in solving isolated problems but deal with interconnected networks of problems and use what he calls 'high intuition' (not guesswork) in which rapid pattern recognition takes place and solutions are generated and regenerated as new information is obtained.

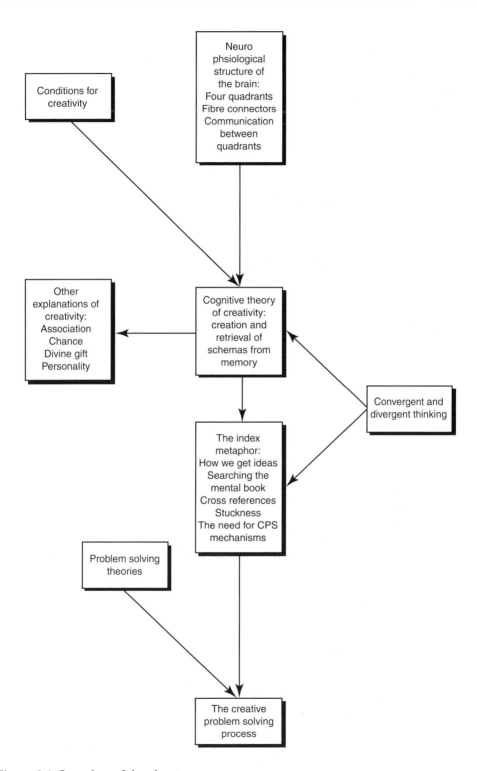

Figure 3.1 **Overview of the chapter**

THE BRAIN AS AN INFORMATION PROCESSOR

The brain has two *cerebral* hemispheres – a left and a right. The primary mental processes of these hemispheres includes vision, hearing, body senses, reasoning, language and non-verbal visualisation. Within each hemisphere is to be found one half of the *limbic system*. This is a control centre that governs such things as hunger, thirst, sleeping, waking, body temperature, heart rate, blood pressure and emotions. The limbic system plays an important role in transferring incoming information into memory. The two *cerebral* hemispheres and the two halves of the *limbic system* make up the four quadrants of the brain. The upper quadrants represent the *cerebral* hemispheres while the lower quadrants represent the two halves of the *limbic system*.

Fibres connect the two *cerebral* hemispheres and these fibres carry communications both within and between the two hemispheres. When solving complex problems or other intricate work, different thinking methods are required. The brain switches signals back and forth very rapidly between different areas within the two hemispheres via the fibre links. Switching thinking modes within the *cerebral* hemispheres (within each of the two upper quadrants) is simple, but switching between the two lower or upper quadrants is more difficult. Diagonal switching is most difficult because there are no fibre connections between diagonally opposite quadrants of the brain.

Left and right sides of the brain

> **There appear to be two modes of thinking, verbal and non-verbal, represented rather separately in the left and right hemispheres, respectively.**

During the 1960s, research on the brain caused scientists to conclude that both hemispheres are involved in higher cognitive functioning. It was found that each half of the brain produced different modes of complex thinking. The main argument to develop was that there appear to be two modes of thinking, *verbal* and *non-verbal*, which tended to be conducted separately by the left and right hemispheres, respectively. This in turn led initially to a number of 'brain' related theories concerning creative thinking, notable amongst which was Roger Sperry's Left Brain/Right Brain theory (see Le Boeuf, 1990). According to this theory the left brain is used for logical thinking, judgement and mathematical reasoning, while the right brain is the source of dreaming, feeling, visualisation and intuition.

The Whole Brain/Four Quadrant Model

Herrmann (1990) showed that it is possible to build a model of the human brain with two paired structures, the two halves of the cerebral system and the two halves of the limbic system. This permits one to differentiate between not only the more popular notions of left/right brain, but also the more sophisticated notions of cognitive/intellectual which describe the cerebral preference, and visceral, structured and emotional which describe the limbic preference.

Herrmann's *Whole Brain Model* also made use of the concept of *dominance*. Evidence indicates that wherever there are two of anything in the body, one of them is naturally dominant over the other. For example, we may be right- or left-handed. We can also be thought of as predominantly right- or left-'brained'. The implications of this for the way in which we prefer to do things are important. Indeed, sometimes our preferred way of doing things may well be counter-productive. Predominantly left-brained thinkers may experience more difficult relationships with colleagues than right-brained thinkers because they are not as sensitised to other people. On the other hand it may be that predominantly right-brained thinkers need to have goals and a schedule set for them to help them be more efficient.

The *Whole Brain Model* (Figure 3.2) presents four distinct thinking styles:

1 The upper (cerebral) left
   A   analytical, mathematical, technical and problem solving.
2 The lower (limbic) left
   B   controlled, conservative, planned, organised and administrative in nature.
3 The lower (limbic) right
   C   interpersonal, emotional, musical, and spiritual.
4 Upper (cerebral) right
   D   imaginative, synthesising, artistic, holistic and conceptual modes.

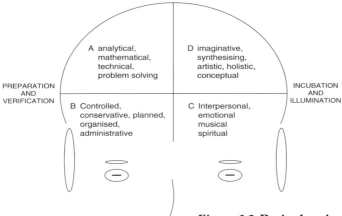

Figure 3.2 **Brain theories: the Whole Brain Model (Herrmann/Wallas)**

Among other things:

- Predominantly *A quadrant* thinkers prefer organising information logically in a framework, listening to lectures and reading textbooks, studying example problems and solutions, thinking through ideas, doing scientific/academic research, judging ideas based on facts, criteria and logical reasoning, dealing with reality and current problems.
- Predominantly *B quadrant* thinkers like finding practical uses for knowledge learned, planning projects, practising new skills, writing practical guides about how to do something.
- Predominantly *C quadrant* thinkers like to be very organised and precise in their work.
- Predominantly *D quadrant* like to take an overall view of new topics (not the detail), to take the initiative, ponder on possible outcomes of actions, use visual aids, solve open-ended problems, enjoy wild ideas, experiment, rely on intuition rather than logic, synthesise ideas, approach a problem from different angles.

From the point of view of undertaking creative problem solving activities, type D thinkers seem to have the most favourable frame of mind for this activity.

Wallas's model of the creative process

Graham Wallas (1926) set down a description of what happens as people approach problems with the objective of coming up with creative solutions. He described his four-stage process as follows:

1 In the *preparation* stage we define the problem, need, or desire, and gather any information the solution or response needs to account for, and set up criteria for verifying the solution's acceptability.
2 In the *incubation* stage we step back from the problem and let our minds contemplate and work it through. Like preparation, incubation can last minutes, weeks, even years.
3 In the *illumination* stage, ideas arise from the mind to provide the basis of a creative response. These ideas can be pieces of the whole or the whole itself, i.e. seeing the entire concept or entity all at once. Unlike the other stages, illumination is often very brief, involving a tremendous rush of insights within a few minutes or hours.
4 In *verification*, the final stage, one carries out activities to demonstrate whether or not what emerged in illumination satisfies the need and the criteria defined in the preparation stage.

The first and last stages are left brain (quadrants A and B) activities, whereas the second and third stages belong to the right brain (quadrants D and C).

It should be noted that Wallas's theory comes under criticism from

Weisberg (1986), particularly with respect to incubation. He details studies to substantiate his claim and believes that the role of incubation in creative problem solving is ambiguous and may in fact have little function. Research quoted by Weisberg suggests that none of the four stages can be said to have any supporting evidence. He argues that it is the conscious mind that is creative.

CONVERGENT AND DIVERGENT THINKING

> **Divergent thinking processes and convergent thinking processes are related to creativity.**

Guilford (1967) claimed and cited evidence to support the view that divergent thinking processes, as opposed to convergent thinking processes, are related to creativity. Divergent thinking involves a broad search for decision options with respect to a problem for which there is no unique answer. In the divergent processes, the generation of alternatives involves finding many combinations of elements that may provide many possible answers. Fluency of thinking and originality characterise a divergent search for alternatives, rather than a rigorous adherence to prescribed steps and criteria for finding some uniquely 'correct' result. In a convergent search, the opposite is true; that is, it is a unique solution to meet the prescribed criteria that is sought. As Guilford (1975) points out however, these two modes are not necessarily used in isolation and can be intermixed in so far as a divergent approach can be used on the way to a convergent solution. The extent to which the whole process can be characterised as divergent or convergent is relative rather than absolute and depends on the degree of limitations imposed on the answer. We might thus conclude that both divergent and convergent thinking contribute to the gaining of creative insights.

Guilford, as discussed by Dacey (1989), argues that a major impediment to effective convergent thinking lies not in the use of a problem solving paradigm but in the selection of a good one. Dacey (ibid.) has referred to Edward De Bono's theories of divergent thinking which combine vertical and lateral dimensions. De Bono states 'vertical thinking digs the same hole deeper; lateral thinking is concerned with digging a hole in another place' (Dacey, ibid.). Seemingly, if that hole is in the wrong place, then no amount of logic is going to put it in the right place. Therefore, although the Creative Problem Solving Method (CPSM) requires these dual thought processes, the model will not be constructive unless the 'digger' is on the right track.

It is argued that the function of divergent thinking is to 'broaden out' the thought process and thus reject mind-set and disregard constraints on problem solving. Convergent thinking applies a greater degree of judgement and narrow focus. The argument is, however, the subject of some criticism. Weisberg (1986) considers that divergent thinking is not in fact an important aspect of creativity and that studies have shown that creative ability is not related to divergent thinking ability. He argued that novel solutions to problems can in fact be achieved without it. He feels that creative problem solving does always require a fresh perspective. Weisberg in fact is critical of creative problem solving methods. However, one should bear in mind that his evidence for such a claim is based upon only two illustrations.

THE CONDITIONS OF CREATIVE THINKING

Mary Henle (1962) outlined what she considered to be the necessary conditions for creativity thinking (Figure 3.3). There were five such conditions: receptivity, immersion, seeing questions, utilisation of errors and detached devotion.

Receptivity

> **Receptivity involves detaching oneself from one's current activities and simply paying attention to the ideas that arise.**

The generation of creative ideas requires us to hold a certain attitude. It is thought that receptivity involves detaching oneself from one's current activities and simply paying attention to the ideas that arise. The attitude is present in those who have experienced and reported mystical or near mystical experiences.

Immersion

> **Our knowledge may work against our creative thinking, for we tend not to think about what we know. Existing ideas tend to blind us to new ones and it seems that creative ideas do not occur to us unless we spend a great deal of time and energy engaged in just the activity which makes their emergence most difficult. The paradox is not easy to solve.**

Newton arrived at the law of gravitation by always thinking about it, and similar feelings were reported by Poincare (1952). Wertheimer ([1945] 1959) writes that Einstein tried for years to clarify the relation of mechanical movement to electromagnetic phenomena. Moreover, as Humphrey (1948) indicates, Gauss had been trying in vain to prove a theorem for four years, when the solution suddenly came to him. In

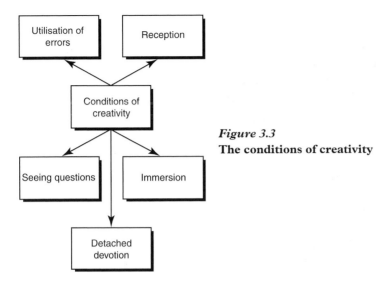

Figure 3.3
The conditions of creativity

general, the mathematician tends to get good ideas in mathematics, the musician in music, the psychologist in psychology. Creative thinking arises more easily in fields and in relation to problems that we know a good deal about. However, there is a paradox here, for our knowledge may work against our creative thinking – we tend not to think about what we know. Existing ideas tend to blind us to new ones and it seems that creative ideas do not occur to us unless we spend a great deal of time and energy engaged in just the activity which makes their emergence most difficult. The paradox is not easy to solve.

Seeing questions

> **A question requiring an answer can in fact limit creative thinking since it is unlikely that in our thinking we will go beyond the question before us.**

It is argued that a question requiring an answer can in fact limit creative thinking since it is unlikely that in our thinking we will go beyond the question before us (Langer, 1942). While a question often limits the kind of answer we obtain it may be also argued that the really creative aspect of problem solving may be more precisely to pose a question rather than to answer one. Alternatively, the task may be viewed as to revise a problem with which we are confronted in order to see it in a new way or in a broader context. As Wertheimer ([1945] 1959) said: 'Often in great discoveries the most important thing is that a certain question is found.'

Utilisation of errors

Error can present a new problem and thus stimulate thought.

While the goal of problem solving may well be correct solutions we must recognise the role of error in helping us arrive at better solutions. In science wrong hypotheses increase our knowledge just as much as correct ones. Error can present a new problem and thus stimulate thought.

Detached devotion

Very intense motivation to solve a problem may well impede the problem solving process.

Creative work is full of paradoxes, and none more than the need of the creative thinker to be both immersed in the problem yet at the same time sufficiently detached from it to consistently see it afresh. One must recognise that very intense motivation to solve a problem may well impede the problem solving process. Concentrating on the goal to the exclusion of other relevant aspects of a problem often prevents solution of a problem. The creative thinker must stand back from the problem so that it can be critically examined and evaluated. It is possible that a function of the incubation period suggested by Wallas (1926) enables one to achieve that sufficient detachment.

PROBLEM SOLVING

Not all problems require the use of a Creative Problem Solving process. In some cases a CPS process would not be as useful as an existing routine or ready-made solution. These kind of solutions generally exist for recurring problems, and when it is possible to use one it is often much quicker and more practical.

Van Gundy ([1981] 1988: 3) believes 'a problem can be defined as any situation in which a gap is perceived to exist between what is and what should be'. Based on this definition, a problem solving process is one whereby a situation that is not as it should be is changed into one that is as it should be.

However, it should be noticed that not all problems require the use of a CPS process. Indeed, in some cases a CPS process would not be as useful as an existing routine or ready-made solution. These latter kind of solutions generally exist for recurring problems, and when it is possible to use one it is often much quicker and more practical.

A problem exists when an individual has a goal and a choice of means by which it might be achieved, but does not know how to proceed immediately. The psychology of problem solving deals primarily with intellectual problems: those that can be solved mentally or by manipulating symbols. It uses three principal methods: (1) examining what scientists, mathematicians, and others have said about their own activities; (2) presenting test problems to experimental subjects, noting the effect of various conditions on the likelihood that the problems will be solved; (3) asking individuals to 'think aloud' as they solve problems, and devising theoretical models to explain the sequence of steps that typically appears in such reports.

The processes of problem solving are not entirely open to consciousness.

The testimony of scientists and others indicates that the processes of problem solving are not entirely open to consciousness. One may begin by reasoning consciously and deliberately, but the solution often comes in its own time, suddenly and 'out of nowhere'. As noted earlier, Graham Wallas (1926) described such a problem solving sequence as consisting of four stages: *preparation*, in which the individual defines the problem for himself or herself and explores various possibilities; *incubation*, when attention is turned to other things, and the problem disappears from consciousness; *illumination*, when the solution suddenly appears; and *verification*, in which the new solution is checked to see if it will work. Of course, this sequence does not apply in every case. Moreover, Duncker (1945) noted that every phase of a solution is essentially a productive reformulation of the original problem.

The mathematician Gyorgy Polya introduced the idea that there are general techniques for solving problems, which he called 'heuristics': procedures that often help though they cannot guarantee success. One useful heuristic is working backward from the solution: if the answer were known, what characteristics would the problem possess? Another important heuristic is to establish subgoals: think of some situation from which it might be easier to obtain the solution, and work toward that situation first. Still another is means–end analysis: establish lists of methods that are useful for attacking various kinds of goals or subgoals, and work through the list systematically.

Recent research on problem solving has involved computer programs that enable a computer to solve difficult problems. If the sequence of steps taken by the machine is similar to the sequence reported by human subjects who think aloud, the program itself can be regarded as a theory of the problem solving process. The programs developed go through the same sequences of steps (and make the same sorts of errors) as people who are thinking aloud; thus they probably incorporate many of the principles that govern human problem solving.

THEORIES OF CREATIVE PROBLEM SOLVING

There are a number of schools of thought as to the origin of creativity (Henry, 1991): grace, accident, association, cognitive, personality.

Grace

Creativity is something of a mystery, drawing forth images of wonderful insights, imaginative efforts, illumination and intuitions that come from nowhere. It seems the work of magic. The idea of genius may add force to this notion since creative artists, musicians, etc. seemed to be endowed with superhuman potential. Creativity in this sense is seen as a divine gift.

Accident

This is the opposite of it being a divine gift. It rises by chance. Holders of this view offer various types of accidental discoveries such as those of immunisation arising from an interruption in work, radioactivity from the wrong hypothesis and the smallpox vaccination from observation.

Association

This is the most popular and suggests that applying procedures from one area to another gives rise to novel associations, and that such associations form the bedrock of creative ideas. The notion was popularised by Koestler under the term 'bisociation', and it underlies the justification for many divergent thinking techniques, such as lateral thinking and brainstorming.

Cognitive

> **Creativity is a normal human activity. It uses cognitive processes like recognition, reasoning and understanding.**

Creativity is a normal human activity. It uses cognitive processes like recognition, reasoning and understanding. Many inventors work at a problem for years. Research has concluded that ten years of intense preparation is needed for significant creative contributions. Deep thinking about an area over a long period leaves the discoverer informed enough to notice anomalies that might be significant. Highly creative people are strongly motivated and seem able to concentrate over a long period.

Personality

Creativity is a state of mind which can be learnt. Some people seem to have a facility for it while others do not, but they can improve with practice. Mental barriers to creativity have to be removed to allow innate spontaneity to flourish. Creative acts are not isolated acts of perception, they require an emotional disposition, too, for any new idea replaces and in effect destroys the previous order. It takes courage and persistence to brave the resistance that any change seems to engender.

The five perspectives make some valid points but here we pay particular credence to accident, association and cognitive.

ACCIDENT AND THE GAINING OF CREATIVE INSIGHTS

After the death of his collaborator in research Niepce, Daguerre, a decorator and diorama showman, worked on alone in the search for finding ways to capture images obtained through cameras, permanently. By the autumn of 1837 he had realised that silver compounds such as silver nitrate and particularly silver iodide possessed the kind of properties for which he and Niepce had been searching.

He had put a few plates, which he thought were spoiled because he had not exposed them long enough, into an old cupboard. After a few weeks he took them out with the intent of washing them and using them again. To his complete surprise the pictures on them were clearly visible. What had occurred? How could the plates have developed by themselves? He cleared out everything he had stored in the cupboard until it was empty. There was nothing there to provide any explanation. His curiosity was piqued, however, and he argued to himself that there must have been something in the cupboard to account for the apparently inexplicable phenomenon. Getting down on his hands and knees he explored the recesses of the cupboard in detail. There he discovered, in the narrow fissures at the bottom of the cupboard, a number of glittering balls of mercury which had escaped from a broken bottle. Immediately he recognised what must have occurred. The silver iodide plates had been developed by the chemical reaction of the mercury vapour!

Daguerre tested his theory by exposing a new plate for a short time and heating it over a bowl of mercury in a dark room. The picture appeared as if by magic. Fixing the plate in sodium sulphate, which dissolved the silver halides, he peered at the first 'daguerreotype'.

Question

'Accident' obviously had its role to play in this discovery but there were other factors too. Can you identify these other factors?

DISCOVERIES

Velcro is a Swiss invention dating from 1948. Returning from a day hunting, the engineer Georges de Mestarl noticed that burdock seed heads clung to his clothing. Under the microscope he discovered that each of these heads was surrounded by minute hooks allowing them to catch onto fabrics. It then occurred to him to fix similar hooks on fabric strips which would cling together and serve as fasteners.

Eight years were needed to develop the basic product: two nylon strips, one of which contained thousands of small hooks, and the other even smaller loops. When the two strips were pressed together , they formed a quick and practical fastener. The invention was named Velcro: from the French *velours* (velvet) and *crochet* (hook).

THE COGNITIVE THEORY OF CREATIVITY

Cognitive processes have been a much disputed topic for many years. Various schools of psychology, the Psychoanalytical, Gestalt and Associative, all have their various perspectives on the subject. When reading the following it is important to bear in mind the earlier sections of this chapter which looked at the neuro-physiological structure of the brain and its relationship to thinking modes.

At the core of the thinking process is memory. It is thought that there may be both long term and short term memory. Short term memory can hold only a small amount of information at any one time. Long term memory, on the other hand, has a vast information storage capacity. If we paid attention to all the things our senses are reporting at any particular moment and took them all into consideration it would be very hard for us to decide what to do. We can only hold a few items in our short term memory and that is what enables us to focus on what is important and to act quickly.

Long term memory may be thought of as being filled with all the images, sounds, odours and other types of sensory data in an assembled form and which we hold as a symbolic picture of our remembered information. Information itself is learned from our experience and stored in chunks ('chunking') along with cues associated with the information.

We can often recall the wanted material by recalling the unwanted accompaniment. The learned material and the cues form complex networks of information. Thus when we are trying to think of objects that might resemble 'red faces' we might find it easier not to concentrate our minds upon 'faces' but rather to make connections with similar images – beetroots, the setting sun, etc. From a creativity point of view it is how we make the connections along and across the networks that is of interest.

According to the connectionist, or parallel distributed processing model, proposed by McClelland (1981), information about people, events and objects is stored in several interconnected units rather than in a single location. The strength of the connections between these units increases as a result of learning. Subsequent retrieval of information about a particular person, event or object, involves gaining access to one or more of the relevant units, followed by a spread of activation to other relevant units.

One of the general characteristics of connectionist or parallel distributed networks is that they provide an explanation of the fact that we seem to possess both episodic (or autobiographical) memories and semantic (or knowledge based) memories. By way of illustration, we possess information about several cars with which we are familiar and we also have knowledge of the general concept of the car. According to McClelland and Rumelhart (1986), the stimulus word 'car' leads to the activation of several units referring to specific cars, and averaging process indicates the typical features of cars in general.

The brain as a human information processing system

The process of thinking effectively means accessing very large volumes of information in long term memory via a bottleneck memory space, which takes the form of short term memory. While the speed of access to long term memory is extremely rapid it appears possible to consider only small amounts of information at a time. Bottlenecks are symptomatic of inefficient operation and usually result in a slow down or cessation of operation if they become overloaded or choked. This view of the human information processing system points to limitations in terms of its efficiency. In problem solving or trying to think creatively, we immediately come up against these limitations. Creative problem solving aids need to help us circumvent these difficulties if they are to be useful aids to thinking.

Not only is the efficiency of the human information processing system constrained by its own structure, it is also affected by how people use it. It is thought that through a process of selective perception or filtering we pay attention to only certain features of things we sense. The concept of a perceptual filter is important because of the factors that constrain it – for instance, beliefs, attitudes, etc. Mind-sets may occur because of the various beliefs and attitudes we hold and the impact they have on our perceptual filter.

How knowledge is stored in memory

Understanding how knowledge is thought to be stored in human memory enables us to appreciate how long term memory may be organised and how the search of long term memory may be conducted. Among the earliest ideas on representation were those of Quillian (1968) who introduced the notion of the semantic network. This maintained that knowledge can be represented by a kind of directed, labelled graph structure in which the basic structural element is a set of interrelated nodes.

Semantic network theory has a place in the structure of representation, but it does not allow one to structure knowledge into higher order representational units. Nevertheless, externalising this form of representation can be employed effectively in facilitating creative thinking – see, for example, mind maps (Figures 9.11, 9.12 and 10.4).

Schemas

It is the major function of schemas to add a structure which allows for the encoding of more complex relationships among lower level units (see Rumelhart and Norman, 1983). Schemas are learned as a result of experience and reside in memory to be called upon at any time. Schemas are packets of information in which there is a fixed part, representing those characteristics which are always true of exemplars of the concept, and a variable part, which need not always be true. The schema for the concept of 'elephant' would contain constant parts such as 'elephant has a trunk' and variable parts such as 'elephant can be found in a zoo'. Variables have default values if the incoming information is unspecified. Thus the concept of 'pensioner' might have as its fixed part 'is retired from his or her former occupation', but unless the variable 'age' is specified this would default to 'old'. Schemas can also be embedded within one another so that a schema consists of a configuration of subschemas and so on.

According to schema theory, schemas influence the way that new information is processed in a number of ways. The schema that is currently activated guides the selection of what is to be encoded and stored in memory, so that information relevant to that schema is more likely to be remembered than non-relevant information. The schema provides a framework within which the information can be stored and which can be used at retrieval to guide search processes.

Scripts, deltacts and MOPS

Workers in the area of Artificial Intelligence have made important contributions to cognitive science. This perspective suggests that we make use of special types of schemas known as *scripts* and *deltacts* (Schank and Abelson, 1977) in dealing with problems. Scripts allow people to make inferences about a situation and are assembled from smaller data elements called MOPS (memory organisation packets). MOPS serve to organise experiences around essential similarities, enabling people to recognise old situations in new guises and to draw conclusions.

Scripts are stereotyped responses based on experience. It is argued that in trying to cope with a new situation or problem, people try to recall previous ways in which they have dealt with similar problems: they try to recall a script. A script is an organised memory structure that describes a suitable sequence of activities to deal with a particular problem or situation. Scripts guide what people do, think and say. Retrieving an appropriate script from memory allows people to deal with a situation or a problem in an effective manner.

Schank and Abelson (1977) suggested that people undertake 'goal directed behaviour' to cope with problems or situations where a relevant script cannot be retrieved (i.e. because they have never learned one in the first instance). Discovering the goal may be part of the process and sometimes the goal may have to be implied from several aspects of a description.

In addition, one has to find a set of ways in which to satisfy the main goal. These take the form of subgoals and associated plans which Schank and Abelson (ibid.) termed 'deltacts'.

Schank and Abelson (ibid.) argued that higher level structures, which they termed *themes*, serve as nuclei around which *goals*, *plans* and *scripts* are organised. In trying to solve a problem it is suggested that we organise our thoughts around a theme. For example, imagine that the boss has decided to remove the opportunity of earning extra money from people working in an office. There are various possible responses that workers could take to this action, but one theme that could emerge is that of challenging the boss's authority to prevent people earning extra money. Scripts, deltacts, etc. would be organised around the theme of 'challenge authority' and as a consequence, solutions to emerge might be such things as 'appeal to a higher authority in the organisation' or even, if it were possible, 'flout the boss's authority'.

HOW WE GET IDEAS: THE INDEX METAPHOR

Building on the concept of schemas, scripts, deltacts and themes we can develop a metaphor to show how ideas may be generated and the role that creative problem solving aids can play in helping the ideas to emerge. This is the *index metaphor* (Figure 3.4).

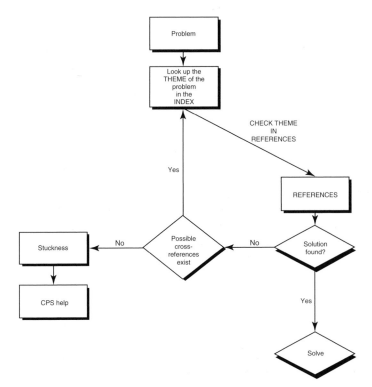

Figure 3.4 **The index metaphor**

The index metaphor supposes that we store all our information, knowledge and experience in a huge 'mental book' which has an index and cross-referencing facilities. How we deal with a problem is influenced by our perception of it. We take our perceived problem, identify the main theme and look it up in the index of the 'mental book'. The index provides us with a number of references to entries regarding the information we have related to the subject of the problem (schema or scripts). It may also be that we do not have any references with respect to the particular problem. Assuming in the first place that there are such references, then we look up each of these references in turn to see whether it provides us with the kind of information that we require to solve the problem. Sometimes we may be lucky and find that a reference (the schema or script) enables us to find an exact solution to the problem. This is either because we have previously successfully tackled and solved the same problem or because we have, at some time, learned and stored information on how to solve this particular kind of problem.

At other times, when an exact fit cannot be found, there may be cross-references under various headings (MOPS) in the mental book which enable us to put together sufficient information (a new schema or script) to solve the problem. The new information (schema or script) subsequently becomes embedded in memory for future reference. In order to make use of the cross-references (MOPS) and formulate the new approach (script or schema) we need to be absolutely clear on what it is we are trying to achieve in terms of solving the problem (the main goal) and what constraints (deltacts) we are working under.

The huge mental book is, of course, being constantly updated with new material and adjustments made to the index. New cross-references (MOPS) are also entered. A cross-reference (MOP) may be entered every time two apparently unrelated, weakly related or unrelated events seem to have a particular bearing on a particular matter. The cross-references (MOPS) may fade with time if they are not subsequently reinforced with evidence to support their usefulness.

Working through the 'mental knowledge book' enables us to solve many of the problems we encounter. Moreover, the speed of access through the index can be very rapid. However, there are occasions when the use of the 'mental knowledge book' may fail us. In the first instance we may be unable to find any entry in the index which is helpful. Second, the complexities of the cross-references may be so large that they exceed the capabilities of our information processing capacity. In either case we may become stuck on a problem.

It is at this point that creative problem solving aids can be extremely useful. They force us to look up entries in our 'mental knowledge book' which we would not normally consider relevant in the search of the index. For these entries there are no existing recognisable cross-references or, alternatively, the cross-entries are so far down the line of 'looking up' that it would take an immense amount of time and effort to find them.

PROBLEM SOLVING MECHANISMS

A schema develops because it is a useful and efficient mechanism for solving problems. If there is no problem to be solved there is no need to give conscious attention to the processing of information and consequently little need to establish memory links among salient features of the current experience. A schema is a goal oriented cognitive mechanism. The goal is to solve the problem.

A problem can take on a vast number of shapes. It might be a standard problem of the type one commonly observes in educational settings (find this or find that). It might be an internally created problem 'How can I get to the grocery, the bank and the cleaners before 5 p.m.?' For each problem some action needs to be taken, and in many instances a set of goals or subgoals needs to be established and procedures need to be identified for achieving them. Obviously some problems are more difficult than others and will require elaborate interfacing of multiple schema.

The problem solving function of a schema is supported by the componential structure of the storage mechanisms. As reported by various researchers, there are many aspects to problem solving and these include recognising the problem, making a mental model that fits the problem to some internal representation, forming plans for solving the problem, and carrying out the solution. To solve a problem one must ask several questions, such as:

- What exactly is the problem?
- Do I have a frame of reference for it?
- Is it unique?
- Have I solved any problems that are similar to it?
- Have I noted all of its critical features?
- What will I do first to solve it?
- Do I know how to solve it?
- How will I know when I have found a good solution?

ANALOGICAL REASONING

In order to make use of the abstractions and prior instances that make up a schema, the individual typically must engage in analogical reasoning. An elemental requirement for using analogical reasoning is that the pieces must fit together in a cohesive pattern. Thus, the cohesion and connectivity of the schema must come into play.

Analogical reasoning allows the individual to map the current experience onto a template that has been derived from previous experiences. This template develops as part of the elaboration knowledge of the schema. The abstractions that are part of the schema make up a basic part of this template, and the individual either consciously or unconsciously will attempt to match each of these with some aspect of the current experience. If the abstractions are not well developed, some or all of the mappings may occur between the memory of a specific previous problem, rather than the more general abstract details, and the current problem.

AN ARTIST'S VIEW OF CREATIVITY

'The method of awakening the Mind to a Variety of Inventions . . . a new kind of speculative invention, which though apparently trifling and almost laughable, is nevertheless of great utility in assisting the genius to find variety for composition. By looking attentively at old and smeared walls, or stones and veined marble of various colours, you may fancy that you see in them several compositions, landscapes, battles, figures in quick motion, strange countenances, and dresses, with an infinity of other objects. By these confused lines the inventive genius is excited to new exertions.'

Leonardo da Vinci *A Treatise on Painting*

THE PROBLEM SOLVING PROCESS

Bransford and Stein (1993) proposed a model for improving problem solving skills. It is based on research in the field of problem solving by such people as Wertheimer ([1945] 1959), Polya (1957) and Newell and Simon (1972). The components of the approach are represented by the acronym IDEAL. Where

        I = Identify problems and opportunities.
        D = Define goals.
        E = Explore possible strategies.
        A = Anticipate outcomes and act.
        L = Look back and learn.

Identify problems and opportunities

The argument is that one should identify potential problems and treat them as opportunities to do something creative. It is just as important actively to look for problems than simply to respond to them when they become critical or when they are noticed. Actually identifying problems and then treating them as opportunities in the dimension of strategic management can lead to the establishment of a strong competitive advantage – namely, the creative use of the TOWS matrix (see Chapter 4).

Bransford and Stein (1993) quote the example of a friend who for years had never questioned the fact that he often got splattered with grease when he fried bacon. One day while looking through a mail order catalogue he found a device which protects cooks from hot, splattering grease – effectively a fine wire mesh with handle to place over the frying pan during cooking. What impressed their friend more than anything else was not the invention itself but the fact that someone had actually identified the problem in the first place and viewed it as an opportunity. The friend had never thought explicitly about the fact that splattering grease signified the existence of a problem that once identified might be solved.

Defining goals

Different goals often reflect how people understand a problem. For example the problem of lack of strategic direction in the business could be identified. All concerned might agree that it could represent an opportunity to do something creative. However, people could disagree on what the goals should be. Some people might argue that the objective of the business should be growth in one direction while others might argue for growth in another. In each instance the goals clearly reflect how different groups perceive the same problem. Defining the goal is thus a crucial step in moving towards a solution to a problem.

In practice, people often do not consider alternative goals but move straight to the exploration of strategies. Under these circumstances strategies may well be generated which lead to the solution to a given problem, but deciding which one to choose then becomes a difficult problem. Moreover, if goals have not been specified then solution strategies which are generated may not provide acceptable answers to a problem. A simple illustration is found in the case of a small firm wanting to appoint a replacement secretary for the owner of the business. The former incumbent of the position decided to retire after many years of service. The problem identified itself to the owner and he placed an advertisement in the local newspaper for a replacement secretary. This was done and in due course six candidates with good secretarial qualifications were interviewed for the position. None of them could be appointed because none of them appeared to be able to do what the managing director was looking for. What he wanted was someone who could really deputise for him when he was away on business – clearly not the job for a secretary but, because of years of experience and a willingness to take responsibility, one which the previous holder of the post had taken on! What he really wanted was a deputy and a secretary! Had he defined the goal as having someone who could deputise for him while he was absent then the solution would have been obvious.

Exploring possible strategies

This involves reanalysing goals and considering options or strategies that might be employed to achieve those goals. In many instances it is easy to consider all the relevant information without experiencing a strain on short term memory capacity. As problems increase in complexity this becomes more difficult to do. Experienced problem solvers often keep track of information by creating external representations. Rather than trying to keep all the information in their heads they write it down on paper – or some other medium. This allows them to think more freely about the problem they want to solve. There are many ways of recording and analysing a problem – graphs and Venn diagrams are examples – see also mind maps in Chapters 9 and 10. The most effective way to represent information depends on the nature of the problem. Hayes (1989) and Halpern (1989) suggested that some problems are more readily solved if one uses verbal representation whereas others may be better represented visually or even mathematically. Other additional general approaches include: working a problem backwards, or focusing on a simpler, specific situation – building scale models or performing experiments that simulate certain characteristics of a real world environment, are good examples.

Although there are general strategies for solving problems, specialised knowledge is often necessary to solve some problems. For example, we may know how to set about gathering market survey data but the actual designing of a questionnaire which will enable the data to be collected requires expert knowledge and skill to construct.

Anticipating outcomes and acts

Following the selection of a strategy, contingency plans should be drawn up and the strategy implemented. Often, an active role in testing strategies has to be taken before possible outcomes can be anticipated. The building and testing of a prototype, for example, can often help anticipate the outcomes of particular strategies.

Look and learn

The last component of the IDEAL model is to look at the effects of the particular strategy and learn from the experience.

When trying to solve a problem the emphasis should be on finding the *first* step rather than in trying to find a complete solution immediately. Having tried out the first step and learned from the experience one can then proceed to work through subsequent steps. Test marketing is a case in point, where the launch of a new product is done on a gradual basis. Any aspects of the introduction which are less than satisfactory are corrected before the next stage in the roll-out process. Writing and debugging computer programs follows a similar process.

THE PROBLEM SOLVING PROCESS AND THE CREATIVE PROCESS

The capacity to identify problems and opportunities is one of the most important steps in the creative process. The art of defining and redefining one's goals is particularly important since different goals suggest different lines of thought and have a powerful effect on the solution strategies that are considered. The anticipate and act phase of the IDEAL model can help us uncover inappropriate assumptions that may be limiting the creativity of our thinking. Functional fixedness and mind-set prevent people from solving a problem because they assume it requires routine thinking. Long term efforts to enhance creativity will not be successful unless one looks at the effects of one's actions and tries to learn from them.

THE SIX STAGES OF THE CREATIVE PROBLEM SOLVING PROCESS

The six stages are 'objective finding, fact finding, problem finding, idea finding, solution finding, acceptance finding'. Within each stage both divergent and convergent thought processes are used; essentially this is the search for data and then the narrowing down of data. During the convergence, 'one looks for material which is either very close to the point of issue or close enough to warrant further consideration'. Specific items that are identified as important or relevant to a particular stage are known as 'hits'. Clusters of 'hits', which are related to one another, are known as 'hotspots'.

The objective finding stage essentially involves divergent thinking to generate a list of problems. Convergence is then used to identify the most relevant problem areas for further exploration. 'Hits' and 'hotspots' are identified by questioning ownership (is one motivated to solve it), priority (how important is the problem), and critical nature (how urgent is it to solve this problem).

Next is the fact-finding stage, where overall comprehension of the problem is increased by collection of relevant information. This also helps new ideas to be generated. 'Hits' and 'hotspots' can assist convergence here. The previously identified problem(s) may now be seen from a new perspective.

Problem finding essentially uses the previous stage 'hits' to identify the most productive problem definition possible.

Idea finding helps to structure the search for potential solutions. Mainly divergent activity is used to generate many ideas using a variety of idea-generation aids.

Solution finding is basically the choice of ideas that can be transformed into workable solutions.

The final stage of acceptance finding is primarily a divergent activity that helps to implement solutions successfully via:

1 listing potential implementation obstacles and ways to overcome them;
2 developing both preventive actions and contingency plans; and
3 generating an action plan to implement a solution.

THE CREATIVE PROBLEM SOLVING PROCESS

It is generally accepted that the creative problem solving process can be broken down into six stages (Figure 3.5). These six stages are:

1 Objective finding – define the problem area.
2 Fact finding – gather information.
3 Problem finding – define the problem correctly.
4 Idea finding – generate solutions to the problem.
5 Solution finding – evaluate and choose between possible solutions.
6 Acceptance finding – implement chosen ideas correctly.

Each of these stages involves activities that first require divergent thinking and then convergent thinking. When thinking in a divergent way,

the task is to generate as many ideas and solutions as possible. There should be no limits to the ideas that are formed at this stage. Once a satisfactory level of ideas has been reached, convergent thinking must take place. The purpose of this thinking is to focus on obtaining solutions to the problem based on the ideas from the divergent thinking. These activities can be thought of as filling a funnel with ideas that go through a filter. Plenty of ideas are poured in, but only those that are useful and relevant come out.

The six-stage process may be further extended by the addition of further stages:

- constantly analysing the environment;
- specifying assumptions;
- controlling to ensure that objectives are achieved post implementation.

The extended process is shown below.

Figure 3.5 **The creative problem solving process**

A NINE-STAGE PROCESS FOR CREATIVE PROBLEM SOLVING

1 Constantly analysing the environment to find potential problems.
2 Objective finding – define the problem area.
3 Fact finding – gather information.
4 Problem finding – define the problem correctly.
5 Specifying assumptions.
6 Idea finding – generate solutions to the problem.
7 Solution finding – evaluate and choose between possible solutions.
8 Acceptance finding – implement chosen ideas correctly.
9 Controlling to ensure that objectives are achieved *post implementation*.

It is not always necessary to execute the entire process. Each stage is individual and in many circumstances some of the stages need not be implemented. For instance, it is very often the case that we are presented with a problem without having to look for one, or sometimes the best solution is easily apparent without the need to evaluate all the ideas.

A complete worked example of the creative problem solving process using illustrative methods is to be found in Appendix 1.

QUESTIONS

1 'There are no theoretical underpinnings to the creative problem solving process.' Discuss.

2 Explain how the *whole brain theory* of creativity is linked to the four stages of gaining creative insights suggested by Graham Wallas.

3 What is meant by receptivity, immersion, seeing questions, utilisation of errors and detached devotion as being the conditions necessary for the gaining of creative insights?

4 How would you reconcile the different theoretical perspectives – grace, accident, association, cognitive and personality – on creative problem solving?

5 How is the *index metaphor* a reflection of the cognitive approach to creative problem solving?

6 Discuss the similarities between the IDEAL problem solving model and the nine identified steps of the creative problem solving process. Explain the major differences.

7 How is the concept of the brain as an information processor reflected in:

(a) the whole brain theory;
(b) schema theory.

How can these two theoretical frameworks be interlinked?

8 Differentiate between divergent and convergent thinking. What role do both play in the creative problem solving process?

9 Critically evaluate Mary Henle's *conditions of creative thinking*. Are they supported anywhere else in other theoretical perspectives? Explain.

10 How relevant is analogical reasoning to creative problem solving? Explain.

CASES

The quest for innovation

Technical achievements do not appear out of the blue. Apart from the incentive to the inventor and the possibility of putting inventions to practical use there is the development of craftsmanship which plays a decisive part. The steam engine depended on a high standard of boiler making, which in turn demanded that the craft of riveting had to be well developed. In the field of watchmaking the main achievement of Peter Henlein, the Nuremburg locksmith who lived at the beginning of the sixteenth century, was not that he invented the watch but that he was able to produce springy strips of steel which were elastic enough to permit them to be bent tightly into coils. Anyone could have thought of making a pocket version of a clock of course, but to make it so portable, a suitable main-spring was necessary.

Leonardo da Vinci described many technical ideas in his books, both in words and drawings. These included a power loom, a wheel-lock pistol, a flying machine, a revolving stage, a pendulum driven pump, and several devices for utilising the motive power of steam. These ideas had to remain dreams for a few more centuries because there was no practical possibility of realising them. In his time Leonardo only carried out the construction of harbours, canals and fortifications. The passage of time between getting the inkling of an idea and its eventual fruition as something useful to mankind can be enormous. Thales of Miletos, the Greek philosopher who lived around 600 BC was the first to notice that rubbing pieces of amber attracted straw, feathers and other light material. More than 2,000 years passed by after Thales' observations without any research work being done in the field. It was not until William Gilbert, physician to Elizabeth I, experimented with amber and lodestone and found the essential difference between electric and magnetic attraction that the impetus was given to the quest for harnessable electricity.

Innovations seem to be the product of different people's ideas, often over a period of time. Alexander Graham Bell is often credited with the invention of the telephone, but what exactly was his role in the creation of this device? In 1860 in Frankfurt am Main, Germany, Philipp Reis succeeded in inventing an apparatus that enabled him to convert audible sounds into visible signs and with which sounds of every sort might be reproduced by the galvanic current at any distance. He called it a telephone. A few years later he died at the age of 40 without ever having the chance to develop his machine to its full potential. Somehow one of the Reis telephone sets found its way to the natural science department at Edinburgh University where Alexander Graham Bell was working (Larsen, 1961). Bell took a special interest in the machine, developed it and, as is well known, eventually obtained a patent for a telephone. This is not to suggest that Bell's contribution was any the less but merely to point out how ideas arise and are progressed.

Question

Consider how the different theoretical perspectives outlined in this chapter may throw light on the various concepts about innovation discussed above.

The steam turbine

Many inventors, engineers and scientists played a role in the development of the steam turbine. However, it was left to one man – Charles Algernon Parsons – to turn this concept not only into a reality but also into a widely applicable concept that could be used for other kinds of turbine based devices.

The prototype of the steam turbine was Giovanni Branca's seventeenth century engine. Trevithick produced a 'whirling engine' in 1815 which revolved at 300 revolutions per minute, but it failed because it could not produce enough power. Most of those who dabbled with the concept of the steam turbine did not appreciate that it would have to rotate at an enormous speed in order to be efficient. It appeared that only Watt had any appreciation of the problem involved. In answer to Boulton's suggestion that such an invention would put his reciprocating engines out of business, Watt is said to have replied: 'Without God making it possible for things to move 1,000 feet per second, it cannot do much harm' (Larsen, 1961: 68).

Others worked on the concept of the steam turbine during the nineteenth century. De Laval made substantial inroads into the problem of developing the concept. In the 1880s he produced a turbine wheel which could rotate at up to 40,000 r.p.m. He geared an electric generator to the turbine after succeeding to reduce the speed of rotation to 3,000 r.p.m. but the capacity of the system seemed limited and was unsuitable for use in large scale power stations.

Parsons had left university life at Cambridge at the age of 22 to become an engineering apprentice in Newcastle upon Tyne. He soon came to appreciate that in order to build large scale power stations something better than the conventional reciprocating steam engine would be required. The latter was not nearly efficient enough for the purpose of generating electricity. Steam leaked out all over the place and there were limits to the size to which it could be built. In addition he also noted that the time had arrived for the development of large scale power stations. All these factors provided a motivation for him to find a workable solution to the problem.

While ruminating on the problem he perceived that the stumbling block which no one so far had managed to overcome was the fact that steam travels at high speed and unless the wheel of the turbine could be made to rotate at least at half the speed of the steam acting upon its blades efficient use of energy could not transpire. Parsons sought to reduce the steam pressure and speed without reducing efficiency and economy. He eventually succeeded in doing this by causing the whole expansion of the steam to take place in stages so that only moderate velocities would have to be reached by the turbine wheels.

Parsons put his ideas into practice in a model he produced in 1884. Parsons experienced a good deal of opposition to his ideas from those who had vested interests in the reciprocating engine and, although he began to build portable turbo-generators, he could find no buyers. His fortunes were changed when the Chief Constable of Gateshead asked Parsons to illuminate a pond with electric lights powered by one of his portable generators. The pond had frozen over in the winter of 1885–6 and a local hospital had decided to raise funds by getting young people to skate on the ice, charging them for admission. The event proved a great success and received considerable subsequent publicity in the press. As a result of the publicity the future of the steam turbine was assured.

Question

Consider how the various theories suggested in this chapter are reflected in this short account of the development of the steam turbine.

chapter
four

OBJECTIVE FINDING, FACT FINDING AND PROBLEM FINDING/ DEFINITION

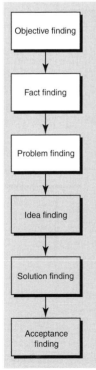

INTRODUCTION

Establishing and defining the problem is probably the most important stage of the creative problem solving process, for unless the problem is correctly defined it is unlikely that a truly satisfactory solution to it can be found. Einstein is reputed to have said that if he had one hour to save the world he would spend fifty-five minutes defining the problem and five minutes finding the solution (Wilson, 1997).

The objective finding stage essentially involves 'divergent thinking to generate a list of problems one is facing'. Convergence is then used to identify the most relevant problem areas for further exploration. 'Hits' and 'hotspots' are identified by questioning 'ownership' (is one motivated to solve it); priority (how important is the problem); and critical nature (how urgent is it to solve this problem).

Next is the fact finding stage, where overall comprehension of the problem is increased by collection of relevant information. This also helps new ideas to be generated. 'Hits' and

Figure 4.1 **Position of this chapter within the CPS process**

'hotspots' can assist convergence here. The previously identified problem(s) may now be seen from a new perspective.

There are a variety of problem definition mechanisms. They can be considered as either redefinition approaches or analytical approaches. First we look at redefinition approaches. The techniques we consider here include *laddering, goal orientation, boundary examination, progressive abstractions* and *the 'why' method.* Under the heading of analytical methods we look at *decomposable matrices* and *cause and effect diagrams.*

Stressing the importance of objective finding, fact finding and gaining different perspectives on a problem can itself sometimes alleviate blocked thinking. The problem we start off with is not necessarily the one which we should try to solve. It is quite possible that if we try to solve the problem as we initially perceive it then either it won't be solved to our satisfaction or the solution we implement will only provide temporary relief to the problem. Quite often we are apt to treat symptoms rather than getting to grips with the real problem itself.

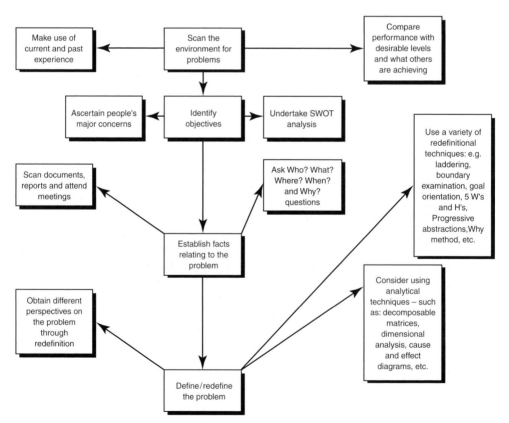

Figure 4.2 **Overview of objective finding, fact finding, and problem finding/definition**

OBJECTIVE FINDING

Constant environmental analysis and problem recognition

Executives and managers have to be constantly on the lookout for problems and might be able to identify them in one of a number of ways:

1 By comparing current experiences with past experiences.
2 By comparing current experiences with current objectives or plans.
3 By comparing performance with models of desirable outcomes.
4 By comparing performance with that of other organisations or sub-units.

(Pounds, 1969)

Pounds noted that the most commonly used approach was the first and that the third and fourth were rarely used. Some business problems require extensive study because they seem likely to uncover the possibility of producing profitable marketing opportunities or, conversely, sizeable losses. Some will require immediate attention while others may be less urgent.

Problem identification and objective finding

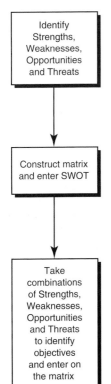

One possible approach involves using SWOT analysis. One first identifies various strengths, weaknesses, opportunities and threats. One then looks as various combinations of strengths–opportunities, strengths–threats, weaknesses–opportunities and weaknesses–threats to identify potential objectives.

In Figure 4.4 a toy manufacturer is reviewing its marketing position and strategies. A more general approach to objective finding involves asking the group to defer judgement and list some major concerns in the company or business.

Next one identifies 'hits'. This is a subjective process and varies from company to company and from person to person. Clusters of hits can be grouped into hotspots and more generic or succinct objectives formulated. To do this they use the criteria of ownership, priority and critical nature. After reviewing the hits and applying the criteria, decide on the problem statement. One is then ready to move on to the next stage – fact finding.

Figure 4.3 **Objective finding**

	Strengths (S)	Weaknesses (W)
	1 Strong existing contacts with outlets 2 Well established company name and image	1 High production costs 2 Seasonal sales
Opportunities (O) 1 Film spin-offs 2 Holidays approaching	How to win major toy contracts using outlets and company name (O1, S1, S2)	How to advertise products so that they will sell all the year round (O2, W2)
Threats (T) 1 Competition from abroad 2 Kids now want electronic gizmos	How to use the company name to develop electronic toys to appeal to 'techno' kids (T2, S2)	How to reduce costs to compete with threats from foreign competition (W1, T1)

Figure 4.4 **A toy manufacturer reviews its marketing position and strategies**

FACT FINDING

The purpose of this stage is to generate relevant data to improve understanding of the problem (Figure 4.5). This in turn allows you to consider different problem perspectives. The six honest serving men method (Parnes *et al.*, 1977) is perhaps most useful in the fact finding stage, although it can be applied usefully at other stages. The technique involves asking such questions as:

> Who will be . . .?
> What will they . . .?
> Where will they . . .?
> When should it be . . .?

The steps are as follows:

1 State the problem in the format . . . In what ways might . . . ? (IWWM . . .?).
2 Write down separate list of Who? What? Where? When? Why? and How? questions relevant to the problem.
3 Examine responses to each question and use as a stimulus to generate problem redefinitions.
4 Record problem redefinitions generated in (3) above.
5 Select the best redefinition for ideation purposes.

Much of this kind of information can be obtained from scanning documents and reports and attending meetings. In addition many of those involved in problem solving will have this information in their heads. It is necessary to get the information out into the open.

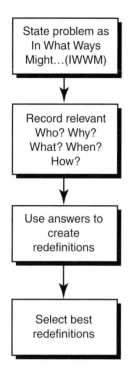

Figure 4.5 **Fact finding**

Example

The problem concerns low staff morale in a super-market chain.

1 IWWM we improve staff morale?
2 Who are the people concerned?
   Shop service counter staff.

   What is low morale?
   Lack of motivation to do a good job and present a friendly interface with the customer.

   Where does the problem seem to persist?
   In all city centre locations.

   When is the problem most in evidence?
   At weekends.

   Why should one try to raise morale?
   To improve the customer–service interface and encourage more customers to shop at weekends.

   How can morale be heightened?
   By finding out how best to satisfy the wants and needs of staff.

The foregoing might produce the following problem redefinitions:

IWWM we satisfy the wants and needs of week-end retail counter staff in city centre stores?
IWWM we seek to improve the friendliness of the customer service interface?

DIMENSIONAL ANALYSIS

This is a useful method for producing a checklist for use during pre-problem solving (Jensen, 1978). It also acts as a general guide for prefacing the use of some other analytic method. Defining the limits or boundaries and dimensions of a problem are important. The method examined here considers a problem from five different dimensions: substantive, spatial, temporal, quantitative and qualitative. The following steps should be followed:

1 State the problem.
2 Write down separate descriptions of the problem in terms of What? Where? When? How much? How serious?
3 Answer questions relating to each of the five dimensions.
4 Assess the answers provided in terms of their significance for solving the problem.
5 Select those areas most pertinent to the problem for further analysis.

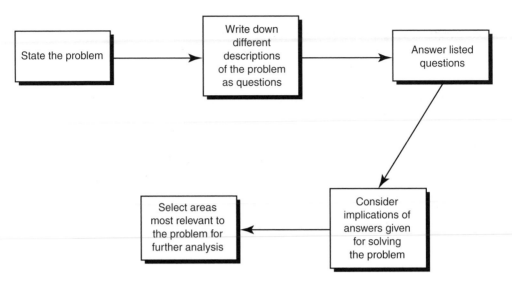

Figure 4.6 **Dimensional analysis**

Example

1 Shop-floor productivity is declining.

2 What aspects of shop-floor productivity in particular are declining?
Where is the decline in productivity occurring (most)?
When is the productivity declining (most)?
How much decline in productivity is involved?
How serious is the decline in productivity?

3 (a) *Substantive*
   (i) Commission/omission – does something need to be done, stopped or modified?
   (ii) Attitude or deed – is the decline due to attitudes or observable behaviour?
   (iii) Ends or means – is it a cause or an effect? Is it a symptom of an underlying problem?
   (iv) Active or threatening – is it threatening or just irritating?
   (v) Visible or invisible – is the real problem apparent?
   (b) *Spatial*
   (i) Local/distant – is it limited to a specific location?
   (ii) Isolated or widespread – how extensive is it?
   (c) *Temporal*
   (i) Long-standing or recent – how long has the problem existed? If solved will it lead to more problems?
   (ii) Future implications – can it develop into something more serious?
   (iii) Persistent nature – is there a pattern in its incidence of occurrence?

(d)   *Quantitative*
    (i) Single or multiple – are the causes one or many?
   (ii) Many or few people – how many people are involved?
  (iii) General or specific – does it apply generally or only to certain subgroups?
  (iv) Simple or complex – does it comprise only a single element or is it made up of many interlocking elements?
   (v) Affluence or scarcity – is it due to a scarcity of something?

(e)   *Qualitative*
    (i) Deep-rooted or surface problem – is the problem deep-rooted?
   (ii) Survival or enrichment – is it a matter of survival or does it merely bring into question the quality of a situation?
  (iii) Primary or secondary – is it perceived to be of primary importance?
  (iv) What values are being violated – what is wrong?
   (v) To what degree are values being violated – is it serious or trivial?
  (vi) Proper or improper values – should the values be honoured?

PROBLEM FINDING/DEFINITION

The problem finding stage encourages one to consider a variety of problem perspectives. Restating the problem might unlock a new viewpoint that can lead to many creative solutions. To create these viewpoints, the group examines the information obtained during fact finding to generate possible problem redefinitions. A systematic approach to problem definition can help and direct staff in their efforts to obtain relevant information. In addition, it is also informative to all those people in the organisation who will be affected by the findings and recommendations.

Problem definition must take into account the situation of the company and its ability to take sound action. Poorly thought-out decisions can cause major problems, sometimes with disastrous consequences. Many things can go wrong and many opportunities can be missed. The executives in the firm need to anticipate and prevent as many of these as possible and in each case the first action should be a precise definition of the problem (see Figure 4.8).

Problems arise all the time in business. Some are vitally important problems and concern sales, profits, and the general welfare of the business. A well-planned statement of the problem has to be thought through. Since different executives may have different perspectives of the problem, and hence different views as to its precise nature, there is a need to consult everyone concerned before the problem is finally fully specified. Each individual must contribute his or her thoughts to the problem definition before a valid, useful study of the problem can be properly undertaken.

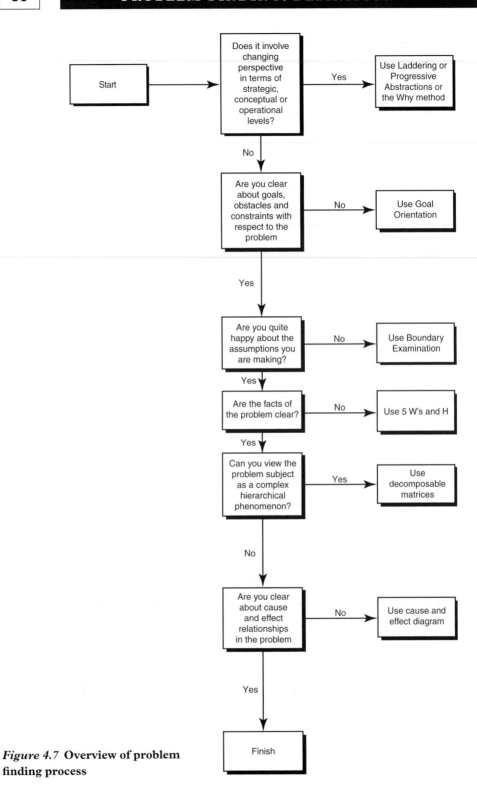

Figure 4.7 **Overview of problem finding process**

- **SSUEPVEERNMALRETKTEETRS**

- In the above line cross out seven letters so that the remaining letters, without changing their sequence, will spell out a well known English word. See appendix 3 for the answer.

Figure 4.8 **Defining the problem**

THE DELIVERY COMPANY THAT COULD NOT DELIVER

A private parcel delivery company had many hundreds of parcels reported missing by angry customers. Most of these parcels turned up within a few days but none of the delays did much to promote the efficient next day delivery image of the company. The firm undertook to appoint one its senior managers to investigate the matter and to report to the directors of the company on his findings.

After much information gathering the manager reported that there seemed to be too many people working on the sorting of the parcels and that many of them did not seem to know what to do. This, he felt, was producing considerable confusion with the result that some packages were being put onto the wrong vans while others were temporarily stored in corners of the sorting room because staff did not know what to do with them.

1 Suggest perspectives on this problem.
2 What action do you think might be taken to solve the problem?

See Appendix 3 for what the firm did.

REDEFINITION APPROACHES

There are a number of methods which come under this heading. The main idea behind these approaches is to enable the problem solver to gain new perspectives on the problem.

Getting perspectives on a problem

Two useful approaches to problem definition are suggested by Rickards. The first involves the practising of getting different perspectives, while the second, a technique called 'laddering' provides a useful method for gaining perspectives on actual problems.

Practising perspective getting

Generate a wide variety of scenarios which are readily 'visible in the mind's eye'. Try to make the scenarios ambiguous in nature. Describe the scenario in three or four sentences and then get people to suggest some possible problem perspectives.

Example

Sam is early for work.
He is searching his desk.
The desk is very untidy.
He repeatedly examines the drawers.

Possible problem perspectives:

How to find whatever is missing.
How to tidy the desk.
How to arrange things in the office so nothing gets mislaid.

An alternative approach, suggested by the author, is to use pictures where the situation is ambiguous and ask people to identify problem perspectives. Have a go at the ones in Figures 4.9 to 4.13.

REDEFINITION APPROACHES: LADDERING

Perspectives can come in varying degrees of complexity. One can think of them as occupying different heights on a ladder. It is often useful to consider where you are on a ladder and whether it would be worthwhile going up to higher levels of generality or down to levels of specifics. The ladder can have many rungs, but we can think of the ladder has having a top portion, a middle portion and a bottom portion. At the top we find the *strategic* or *conceptual level*, in the middle we find the *operational* and *managerial level*, while at the bottom we find the *immediate* and *fix-it-quick level*.

For any situation with which one is familiar it should be possible to find all three levels on the ladder. Asking the question *Why?* moves one up the ladder while asking the question *How?* helps one to move down the ladder.

Example

Consider some perspectives faced by a sales manager trying to expand sales:

How to improve sales techniques (high level).
How to provide sales training (middle level).
How to produce a sales manual (low level).

Laddering is useful for exploring and resetting perceived boundaries of a problem investigation. It helps to avoid too narrow a band of perspectives.

Figure 4.9 Problem situation 1

Figure 4.10 Problem situation 2

Figure 4.11 Problem situation 3

Figure 4.12 Problem situation 4

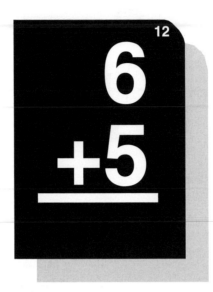

Figure 4.13 **Problem situation 5**

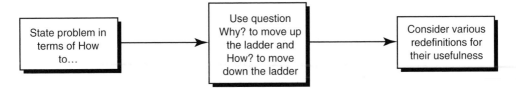

Figure 4.14 **Laddering**

THE PYJAMA COMPANY

A pyjama manufacturer faced resistance from employees to frequent changes to job and work methods that developments in the product and production methods had forced on them. To tackle this problem the company decides to make use of the creative problem solving process. The stages of the process are: objective finding, fact finding, problem finding, idea finding, solution finding, acceptance finding. Here we will review how the company set about the first three of these stages.

Objective finding involves stating what the company wanted to achieve. Here the company wanted to overcome the resistance from employees to new methods of operation. The problem concerned employee satisfaction and grievances. The problem of resistance needed to be solved in order to increase the motivation of employees and thence productivity and efficiency.

Fact finding involves stating the facts of the situation. Here output standards had been set for all the jobs in the factory. Each employee's output was calculated daily and the performance of all workers published in a daily list. The best performers were at the top of the list and the worst performers at the bottom. A bonus was paid according to each person's productivity. High output led to better financial rewards and higher status with management. Most of the employees' grievances related to the fact that as soon as they learned a particular job and started to earn high bonus payments that came with experience they were transferred to another job. Management was thus resented by the workforce since workers were constantly frustrated by their loss of earnings.

Problem finding is concerned with identifying the problem. Many problems seemed to be apparent: lots of complaints about pay-rates, absenteeism, high turnover of personnel, low standards of efficiency, marked aggression against management, etc.

Redefining the problem: the boundary examination technique was used to restructure the assumptions of the problem and produce a new perspective on it. It involved the following steps:

1 The problem was initially considered to be 'in what way might the company overcome resistance to new tasks?'
2 To overcome this resistance, further ways of rewarding workers in addition to financial incentives needed to be found. This could have resulted in employees being more favourably disposed towards transfers between tasks/jobs.
3 The problem was redefined as: 'how might employees be encouraged to be more positive towards the transfers?'

REDEFINITION APPROACHES: GOAL ORIENTATION

Goal orientation is a redefinitional technique which assists us in obtaining a correctly defined problem. It has five stages the first of which is to work out a general outline of the problem. Suppose that the problem with which we are confronted relates to falling sales experienced after the entrance of a new competitor into the market. In this case we might accept this as the general statement of the problem. The second step is to work out what the goal is: where the organisation wants to be after solving the problem. This might be to regain the previous level of sales that had been experienced. The next steps are to work out what obstacles and constraints the organisation must face in order to reach the goal. An obstacle might be that only limited funding is available from within the firm to put an idea into practice. A constraint might be that the existing prices of products need to be maintained since cuts or rises in prices are not considered to be practical considerations for competitive reasons. The final stage is to come up with a new problem statement. This might be:

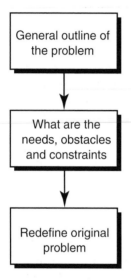

Figure 4.15 **Goal orientation**

'How to get more people to buy our products without reducing or raising prices or being reliant on funds from within the firm?'

Once the problem is correctly defined we can move on to the next stage of the process – idea finding.

REDEFINITION APPROACHES: BOUNDARY EXAMINATION

Boundary examination (de Bono, [1970] 1971) encourages one to take a fresh look at the assumptions one is making with respect to a problem. Through re-examining the assumptions one can gain a new perspective on a problem. The process is as follows:

1 One writes down an initial statement of the problem.
2 Important words and phrases in the statement are highlighted and examined for any hidden assumptions.
3 Important connotations of assumptions are identified, without considering the relevance of assumptions.
4 Any new problem definition that is implied is recorded.

Example

A firm wants to reduce costs of producing and marketing its goods so as to be more competitive in the marketplace.

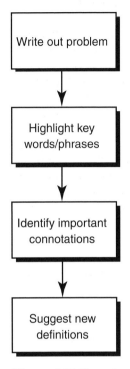

1 In what ways might the company reduce costs of producing and marketing its goods so as to be more competitive in the marketplace?

2 In what ways might the *company reduce costs* of *producing and marketing* its goods so as to be *more competitive in the marketplace*?

3 (a) *company reduce costs* – assumes that the firm can reduce costs and it is necessary to do so.

   (b) *producing and marketing* – assumes that the focus of the problem is production and marketing.

   (c) *more competitive in the marketplace* – assumes that the firm is not competitive enough in the marketplace.

4 (a) *company reduce costs* and (b) *producing and marketing* were taken as the key assumptions. It was felt that the real problem lay not in reducing costs or in more efficient production and marketing but in making the product more attractive to customers. This led to the redefinition: *How to make the product more attractive to customers?*

Figure 4.16 **Boundary examination**

Boundary examination can produce thought provoking problem definitions. However, there are no clear guidelines for indicating how boundary assumptions should be examined.

---

exercise

Try to formulate new perspectives on the following problems by using the boundary examination technique:

- A firm wants to get office staff to work weekends to reduce the backlog of unfilled orders, but staff are reluctant to do so.
- A firm is reconsidering relocating its distribution depot to another site and hiring new staff because of the problems caused by wild-cat strikes at the present site.
- Absenteeism is creating nursing shortage problems in an NHS Trust hospital.
- Trains on inter-city journeys are persistently late in arriving at their destinations.
- Demand for holiday travel to a particular destination is falling year by year.

REDEFINITION APPROACHES: PROGRESSIVE ABSTRACTIONS

The method was suggested by Geschka *et al.* (1973) and allows one to make different problem definitions by employing progressively higher levels of problem abstraction until a satisfactory definition of the problem is attained. It is similar to the laddering technique mentioned earlier in the chapter. In essence it relies on repeatedly trying to identify the essential problem through a series of abstractions from problem redefinitions. The steps are:

1 Write down a general statement of the problem.
2 Generate possible problem solutions by asking the question: what is the essential problem?
3 New problem definitions are developed from the answers produced at (2).
4 (2) and (3) are repeated until the solutions begin to exceed existing skills and technological resources and/or until the solutions are outside one's sphere of influence.
5 Select a satisfactory problem definition for the purpose of generating ideas.

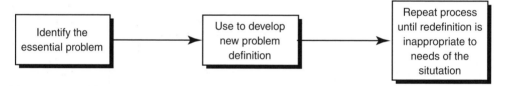

Figure 4.17 **Progressive abstractions**

Example

1 How to improve meetings.
2 IWWM we improve meetings?
   (a) have at the most convenient times;
   (b) circulate agendas well in advance;
   (c) have better structured meetings.
3 IWWM we schedule meetings at the most convenient times for people?
   (a) use diary facilities on email to find times when people have other recorded commitments;
   (b) invite only people for whom the meetings are highly relevant.
4 IWWM we invite only people for whom the meetings are highly relevant?
   (a) keep a detailed list of people's interests and update regularly on the network.

The abstractions are continued until either a working solution or number of solutions can be found or until answers seem to be impractical. In the above example it will be noted that only a part of the possible progressive abstractions have been illustrated. At stage (3) for example, one could ask 'IWWM we have better structured meetings', and of course there are also other possible progressive abstractions at stage (1) than the one selected for illustration.

REDEFINITION APPROACHES: WHY METHOD

This method really reflects the 'why' dimension of the laddering technique mentioned earlier in the chapter. The method again relies on changing the level of abstraction and was suggested by Parnes (1981). As we noted earlier changing the level of abstraction leads to new perspectives. The method is useful for broadening out a problem and exploring its various boundaries. It also helps the user to appraise basic goals and objectives. The following steps should be followed:

1 State the problem.
2 Ask why it is that one wants to do whatever is stated in the problem.
3 Answer the question posed in step (2).
4 Use the answer to redefine a new problem question.
5 Repeat stages (2) and (3) until a high level of problem abstraction is achieved.

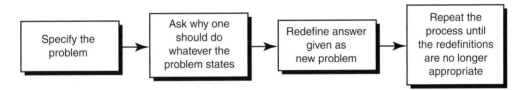

Figure 4.18 **'Why' method**

Example

IWWM we improve the performance of car tyres?

Question: why do we want to improve the performance of car tyres?
Answer: to improve tyre road handling under adverse conditions.
Redefinition: IWWM we improve tyre road handling under adverse conditions?

Question: why do we want to improve tyre road handling under adverse conditions?
Answer: to make cars safer to drive.
Redefinition: IWWM we make cars safer to drive?

Question: why do we want to make cars safer to drive?

At this point we have gone too far with the level of abstraction. We could redefine the problem as:

How can we improve the performance of car tyres to make cars safer to drive?

ANALYTICAL TECHNIQUES: DECOMPOSABLE MATRICES

If it is possible to view the subject of a problem as a complex hierarchical system then this form of analysis can be employed (Simon, 1969). It involves breaking down the system under study into its various subsystems. The method employed is as follows:

1 Establish that the subject of the problem can be viewed as a hierarchical set of subsystems – organisations, groups of people, the human body, many different products, production processes, marketing strategies, etc. can be viewed as such systems.
2 List the major subsystems and their components.
3 Enter the subsystems and their components into a diagonal matrix such that it is possible to identify cells representing the interaction of one subsystem with another.
4 Use a five-point scale to represent the importance of the interaction or strength of the relationship between and within the subsystems.
5 Select the highest weighted interactions for further analysis or generation of ideas.

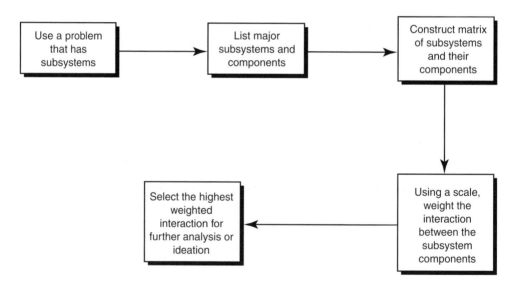

Figure 4.19 **Decomposable matrices**

Example

Problem: how to improve the design/performance of a motor car.

1 Motor car is suitable for this form of analysis – it is a complex hierarchical system comprising a number of subsystems.
2 The major subsystems and their components are:

The finished product:
(a) economy;
(b) comfort;
(c) reliability;
(d) acceleration;

(e) road handling;
(f) durability;
(g) carrying capacity.

Power subsystem
(a) engine;
(b) transmission;
(c) fuel;
(d) gearbox;

(e) electrical;
(f) brakes;
(g) clutch.

Lubrication subsystem:
(a) oil and grease material specification;
(b) servicing requirements.

Electrical subsystem:
(a) alternator;
(b) battery;
(c) ignition system;
(d) lighting system;
(e) windscreen wipers;

(f) doors;
(g) radio;
(h) instruments;
(i) wing mirrors.

Chassis subsystem:
(a) body;
(b) seats;
(c) windscreen;

(d) interior finish and fittings;
(e) wheels;
(f) tyres.

Note: all the subsystems form part of the hierarchy but not all the subsystems form part of the same branch of the hierarchy. Finished product, power and lubrication form a branch, for example, but electrical forms part of another branch incorporating finished product and power. It is useful to draw a tree diagram to identify the hierarchies (Figure 4.20).

3 Matrix

Here, for reasons of space, we will consider interactions between the first three subsystems only – finished product, power and lubrication.

Scores of 5 within the same subsystem are show in bold (**5**), while those of 5 between subsystems are show in bold italics (*5*). Where high scores at the interface between subsystems occur these will be seen as of great interest and key areas for further exploration. For example gearbox (power subsystem d) and oil and grease material specification (lubrication subsystem a) and servicing requirements (lubrication subsystem b) are picked out as very important.

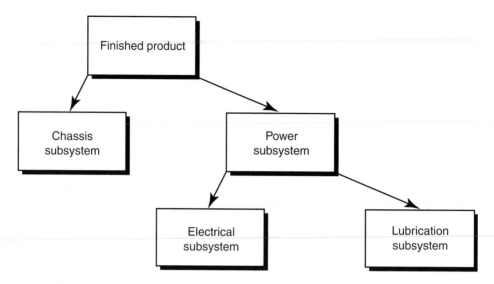

Figure 4.20 Hierarchical subsystems of a motor car

		Finished product							Power							Lubrication	
		a	b	c	d	e	f	g	a	b	c	d	e	f	g	a	b
F	a	–	3	2	5	3	1	4	5	4	5	4	1	2	1	4	4
P	b	–	–	2	2	4	2	4	3	3	1	1	2	1	2	1	1
	c	–	–	–	1	1	1	1	5	5	2	5	5	5	5	4	5
	d	–	–	–	–	4	1	4	5	5	5	5	2	1	3	3	2
	e	–	–	–	–	–	1	4	3	5	2	2	2	4	3	1	1
	f	–	–	–	–	–	–	1	5	5	5	4	4	5	5	5	5
	g	–	–	–	–	–	–	–	5	3	2	2	2	4	3	1	1
P	a	–	–	–	–	–	–	–	–	5	5	5	3	4	5	5	5
	b	–	–	–	–	–	–	–	–	–	1	5	2	2	5	5	5
	c	–	–	–	–	–	–	–	–	–	–	1	1	1	1	1	1
	d	–	–	–	–	–	–	–	–	–	–	–	1	1	5	5	5
	e	–	–	–	–	–	–	–	–	–	–	–	–	1	1	1	1
	f	–	–	–	–	–	–	–	–	–	–	–	–	–	1	1	1
	g	–	–	–	–	–	–	–	–	–	–	–	–	–	–	1	1
L	a	–	–	–	–	–	–	–	–	–	–	–	–	–	–	–	5
	b	–	–	–	–	–	–	–	–	–	–	–	–	–	–	–	–

Figure 4.21 A decomposable matrix
Notes: FP = finished product
P = power
L = lubrication

ANALYTICAL TECHNIQUES: CAUSE AND EFFECT DIAGRAMS

The problem first identified here is the high absenteeism rate. We look for causes, effects and associations and produce a map or diagram (Figure 4.22). The next stage involves picking out those causes and effects which seem to be central to the problem under study. If something is too far removed from the central problem then it is discarded. In Figure 4.22 the boxes relating to orders and repeat sales are peripheral to the central problem and so are discarded. The remaining boxes, however, may be taken either as suitable redefinitions of the original problem or as starting points for further exploration (see also the *Decision Explorer* (formerly known as *COPE*) in Chapter 12).

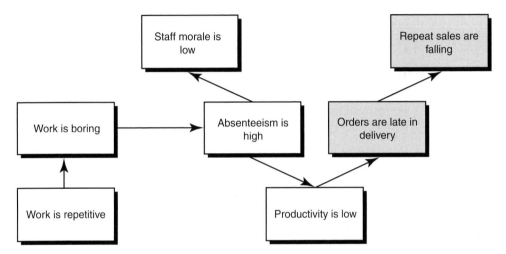

Figure 4.22 **Cause and effect diagram**

QUESTIONS

1 Why is problem redefinition important? Describe *two* different mechanisms which can help with the task of defining and redefining problems.

2 'The solution to a problem lies in its definition.' To what extent would you agree or disagree with this statement? Why?

3 A firm is concerned with improving productivity in the office. Illustrate how *two* different problem redefinition methods can help bring about new perspectives on such a problem.

4 How can one try to make sure that one has correctly defined a problem?

5 Why is it often desirable to undertake problem redefinition when trying to find solutions for a problem? Take any management problem which you consider has many possible solutions and outline two methods which might be used to help redefine the problem.

6 A civil engineering project involves constructing a road through a crocodile infested swamp. Experience to date shows that the crocodiles present a considerable hazard to human life and threaten the completion of the project within the time schedule. Failure to complete within the scheduled time period will incur penalties of the order of £1 million pounds per day. Suggest different perspectives on the problem using the laddering technique.

7 In order to define a problem it is first necessary to recognise that a problem exists, to identify objectives and establish facts relating to the problem. Illustrate how you would do this with regard to a problem of your own choice.

8 Show how dimensional analysis might be used to define the limits, boundaries and dimensions of a problem relating to inroads being made into your markets by competition.

9 Using a management problem of your own choice show how you might use the following methods to help with defining the problem:
   (a) goal orientation;
   (b) boundary examination;
   (c) progressive abstractions;
   (d) Why method.

10 Illustrate with a suitable example how you might use decomposable matrices.

11 Consider how you might use cause and effect diagrams in dealing with previously unencountered problems. What are the main difficulties you might expect to encounter?

CASES

Keeping up with demand

A firm was faced with the problem of keeping up with the demand for its products. It had only limited resources available in terms of workforce and machinery and demand for its products was far in excess of what it could produce. In order to try to generate some insights into the problem the firm felt that it might be a good idea to try and get a different perspective on the issues involved. Accordingly it decided to use the first stages of the creative problem solving process for this purpose. The steps it took are outlined below:

1   How to increase production in order to keep up with demand?

2–3 What are the factors of production? In what ways can we reduce production times? In what ways can we encourage the workers to work faster? In what ways can we increase the possible capacity of production? In what way can we speed up the production process?

4   Could be redefined as: How can we reduce production times?

The problem has now been redefined as a more precise problem. The focus is now on the production time rather than just on production itself. The problem has now been identified and defined in a precise enough way that the next stage can be carried out.

The second stage is that of fact finding. It is during this stage that the overall comprehension of the problem is increased. The idea is to collect all relevant information which may help one to see the problem from a new perspective.

Production times are made up of two main different factors. These factors are: employee performance and machine performance. These two factors can be broken down again into more factors.

Employee performance is related to experience, time of day, time of week, training, machine using. The more experienced and more trained the employee, the quicker they work. At the beginning of the week or day, employee performance is at its lowest, at the end of the day or week, it is at its highest. The quality of the machine the employee uses effects how motivated they are. The better the machine, the more motivated the employee.

Machine performance is related to age of machine, make of machine and type of machine. The older the machine, the slower it is and the more frequently it breaks down. Some of the machines are of an inferior make to other machines. These machines are also slower and more prone to failures. Different machines are used for different parts of the production line. The more complex the process, the more complex the type of machine, the slower the production rate.

The location of the production plant and its available space is such that expansion of the production line is not possible. However, excess storage space is available for finished goods and raw materials. The factory runs on a daily single 9–5 shift for five days a week.

A new competitor has recently started building a production plant within the local area. The area suffers from a lack of a skilled labour pool and the competitor will be looking to employ workers from the local area as it has no workers as of yet.

After the fact finding stage, the information revealed is used at the problem finding stage. In this, the third stage, this newly revealed information is used to develop the best product or problem definition possible.

At the end of the fact finding stage, the problem can be redefined as: '*How can we increase the daily production levels?*'

Question

Critically evaluate what the firm did. Can you reach different conclusions by using a different approach? Illustrate and explain.

Quillian Pens

Quillian Pens carried out the following SWOT analysis on its products:

Opportunities
1 Growth in developing markets.
2 Growing number of pen collectors.
3 Increasing interest in high tech pens.
4 Small but growing corporate gift market in many countries.

Threats
1 Increasing competitive activity at lower price points.
2 Imitation of own products by competitors.
3 Competitive brands achieving strong consumer identity.
4 Growth in secondary brands and own brands.

Strengths
1 High consumer awareness.
2 Brand names.
3 Global recognition.

Weaknesses
1 Too many old products in the range.
2 Lack of innovative products.
3 Somewhat 'boring' image.
5 Insufficient range of pens in the low price category.

Question

Identify the problem objectives that the Quillian company might seek answers to.

Catalogue selling

The management team of catalogue sales has problems with filling the increasing amount of orders sent in to them and hence are beginning to fail to satisfy all their customers. Clearly the company wants to find ways of filling orders and hence satisfying customers. Increasing productivity is an obvious area for investigation.

Until now the management team has been making rapid progress. Over the past 12 months sales have risen steadily and so has net profit. The marketing team has done its job and the company is awash with fresh orders. However, in the past few weeks the company has found that weather-related delays and over-runs in the cost of building new warehouse facilities will preclude the possibility of expanding inventory storage or taking on more staff for at least six months.

Question

Using the first three stages of the creative problem solving process suggest how the problem may be redefined for the purpose of generating insights into the situation.

Reducing wear and tear

Motorways wear out with use. The wearing out process is gradual and uneven. At regular intervals resurfacing becomes necessary and this involves costly repair work which can create huge traffic jams in high density use areas.

As a first step to finding ways of reducing the costs, creativity consultants have been called in to gather information relating to the problem and to obtain different perspectives on it so as to subsequently facilitate ideation.

Questions

What redefinitions of the problem might they consider?

Production problems

The Ebonite Company produces car batteries. Recently it has been experiencing production problems. The firm operates a standard production line and the operations manager has for a long time been considering introducing an alternative method of working. However, both bosses and employees appear to be resistant to the new idea. As things stand the operations manager has noted the following trouble-spots:

- Many defective items.
- High staff absenteeism.
- Low productivity.
- Raw materials and finished inventory levels too high.

Question

Consider the kind of fact finding activities that the operations manager needs to undertake in order to define the real problem or problems in this instance.

chapter
five

MORPHOLOGICAL ANALYSIS AND RELATED TECHNIQUES

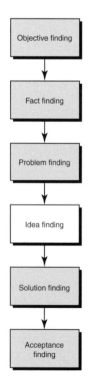

INTRODUCTION

In this chapter the techniques we look at are essentially systematic structuring mechanisms designed to facilitate the gaining of insights into the problem. A variety of techniques are considered including checklists, listing, morphological analysis, force-fit triggers, the heuristic ideation process and component listing. If the subject of a problem has one or more easily identifiable dimensions then most of these techniques may be useful tools for helping to generate ideas.

Figure 5.1 **Position of this chapter within the CPS process**

CHECKLISTS

This is the use of questions as spurs to ideation. The simplest set of questions comes from the six basic questions:

1 Why is it necessary?
2 Where should it be done?
3 When should it be done?

4 Who should do it?
5 What should be done?
6 How should it be done?

Example

How to create a friendly atmosphere at work:

Why?: to make it easier to communicate with colleagues and get work done.
Where?: especially in meetings where staff of all grades are present.
When?: prior to the meetings taking place.
Who?: the departmental manager.
What?: tell all staff how a meeting should be conducted and what is expected of them.
How?: a booklet or leaflet circulated to all staff for guidance purposes.

The following questions might also be usefully applied to problems in general:

- Adapt?
- Modify?
- Substitute?
- Magnify/maximise?

- Minimise/eliminate?
- Rearrange?
- Reverse?
- Combine?

Example

A desk.

Adapt?: make it convenient for different sizes of people.
Modify?: make it portable.
Substitute?: make it of metal instead of wood.
Magnify/maximise?: make the drawer space larger.
Minimise/eliminate?: get rid of protruding handles.
Rearrange?: rearrange the location of the drawers and integrated trays.
Reverse?: have a detachable/reversible glass/plastic top to the desk.
Combine?: combine with chair into an integrated unit.

The following might also be applied:

- Add or subtract something.
- Change colour.
- Vary materials.
- Rearrange parts.

- Vary shape.
- Change size.
- Modify design or style.

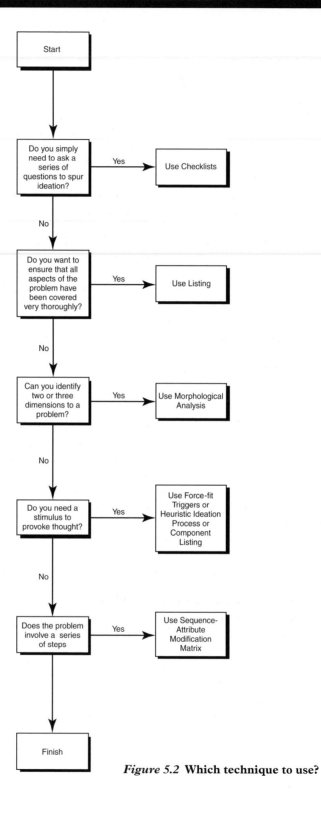

Figure 5.2 **Which technique to use?**

Example

A wrist-watch.

Add/subtract something: add a compass.
Change colour: have multicoloured cases.
Vary materials: make cases out of fibreglass.
Rearrange parts: have the hours running from 12 to 1 instead of 1 to 12 and make the watch hands move backwards.
Vary shape: triangular, hexagonal, octagonal, square, round, etc.
Change size: have many different sizes.
Modify design or style: have frequent updates on style and have designer type labels linked to well known fashion houses.

The technique facilitates idea generation by having one prepare a list of items related to a problem and checking the items against certain aspects of the problem. It can be used both as a problem delineation list and as a solution finding list. The purpose of the former is to provide a direction for the idea search, to make sure that no ideas have been overlooked, and to evaluate the applicability of ideas borrowed from a previous problem. Checklists used for possible solutions are concerned with developing new ideas. The most common use of checklists involves identifying new product ideas by making alterations to existing products.

Example

The problem encountered in a knitwear garment business is that because the market is a seasonal one, in summer it is not appropriate to produce thick jumpers or cardigans. The business is therefore looking to design a new product or modify an existing one which utilises the same system of production as the thick jumpers and cardigans. The problem is thus how to develop a new product by modifying an existing one that will be suitable for summer sales.
The checklist considers such things as:

1 Producing short-sleeved jumpers and cardigans instead of long-sleeved ones.
2 Using synthetic materials instead of wool.
3 Using thinner materials.
4 Using lighter material and not wool.

Problem solution checklists are a simple method of preventing the oversight of obvious solutions to a problem. They also enable previous solutions to be adapted to current problems. In order to be effective the technique is best used as a supplement to more open-ended techniques.

ATTRIBUTE LISTING

Attribute listing is a good technique for ensuring that all possible aspects of a problem have been examined. Attribute listing involves breaking the problem down into smaller and smaller bits and seeing what can be discovered as a result.

Example

Let's say you are in the business of making torches. You are under pressure from your competition and need to improve the quality of your product. By breaking the torch down into its component parts – casing, switch, battery, bulb and the weight (the attributes of each one) – you can develop a list of ideas and you can improve each one (Table 5.1).

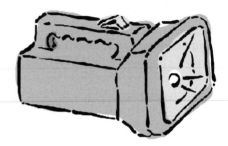

Figure 5.3 **Attribute listing for a torch**

Table 5.1 **Attribute listing: improving a torch**

Feature	Attribute	Ideas
Casing	Plastic	Metal
Switch	On/off	On/off/low beam
Battery	Consumable	Rechargeable
Bulb	Glass	Plastic
Weight	Heavy	Light

Attribute listing is a very useful technique for quality improvement of complicated products and procedures for services. It is a good technique to use in conjunction with some other creative techniques, especially idea-generating ones like brainstorming. This allows you to focus on one specific part of a product or process before generating a whole lot of ideas.

Example

Saw.

Attributes:

- central blade unit;
- vertical cutting process;
- constant cutting speed;
- cuts light metals and light to medium woods and plastics.

Improvements to central blade unit:

- possible alterations to the diameter of the blade;
- alter the number of teeth of the blade;
- different types of blade for cutting different materials.

Improvements to vertical cutting process:

- horizontal cutting;
- circular cutting;
- circular trimming.

Improvements to constant cutting speed:

- automatic variable speed;
- manual variable speed;
- cutting speed controlled by locking device.

Material to be processed:

- wood;
- plastic;
- steel.

Example

A firm wants to change the style of its toffee-apple sticks. The attributes of the sticks are:

- made of wood;
- used to hold toffee apples;
- need to be disposed of properly once the product has been consumed.

Once the list has been fully completed each attribute is studied in turn. The following processing of the information obtained was conducted:

Made of wood:

- Could it be made of other materials?
- Would other materials be more reasonable to purchase and work with, thus reducing the production cost?
- Could the material used be a substance that can be recycled – or even a biodegradable substance?

Usage:

- Currently hand-held, could it be changed to a free standing toffee apple?
- Could it be flavoured to produce more taste for the consumer?

Disposability factors:

- Could the stick be made edible so that it would obviate the need to dispose of it and avoid the potential creation of litter?

COMPETITIVE REPOSITIONING OF A PRODUCT

There are a number of different ways of positioning a product in the minds of consumers in order to differentiate it from competitive offerings. The positioning may be based on:

1 Product features – such as the low calorie content of some foods.
2 Product benefits – e.g. a particular model of car as 'the most economical way to get to work by car'.
3 Associating the product with a use or application – e.g. 'the wine you have on special occasions'.
4 User category – associating the product with a user or class of users – e.g. 'the car for the business executive'.
5 With respect to competition – e.g. 'an IBM compatible microcomputer'.

In addition to the five methods of positioning highlighted above there are also many less common ways.

A product or service will require its positioning adjusting from time to time. This is referred to as repositioning and can become necessary if:

(a) a competitor's new product or service has been positioned next to the brand and this is having an adverse effect on the product or service's share of the market;
(b) consumer preferences with respect to the product or service have changed;
(c) new customer preference clusters have been pin-pointed that suggest promising opportunities;
(d) the original positioning was incorrect.

Exercise

Take each one of the five methods of positioning mentioned above and assume that the producer of the goods in each case wishes to reposition the product for one or other of the four reasons mentioned above. Using attribute listing identify features, benefits, associated applications, or competition related factors – as appropriate – to suggest ways of repositioning either the products listed in the examples or other products of your own choice.

MORPHOLOGICAL ANALYSIS

The technique originated in the complex technological world of astrophysics and rocket research in the 1940s and was the work of a Swiss astronomer Fritz Zwicky (1948). It is only in recent years that Zwicky's analytical technique has emerged from the depths of research establishments and been recognised as being applicable to a wide range of situations.

Morphological analysis is a tool which can help generate a vast number of ideas. It works best as a visual aid. However, this can prove difficult in circumstances where the problem is complex. Ideally, the problem should have two or three dimensions to permit the construction of two-dimensional or three-dimensional grids.

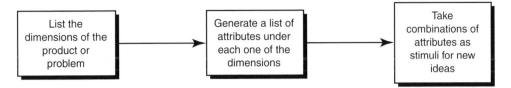

Figure 5.4 **Steps in morphological analysis**

First, possible dimensions are listed which describe the problem or system being studied. No more than three dimensions can be represented diagramatically, and they must be relevant and have a logical interrelationship. For example, if an organisation decides to alter its product in response to changing requirements it may consider product shape and the material out of which the product can be made as two such dimensions. In this case the dimensions would be represented on a two-dimensional grid (or cube for three dimensions) and a list of attributes is then generated under each dimension. Free-wheeling and off-beat ideas are encouraged.

The next step is to examine combinations of attributes across the dimensions, however unusual or impractical they may seem. For example, a cross may be put in a box if the combination is used at present and a nought if it is a potential one worth pursuing. Promising ideas are then subsequently evaluated for their suitability.

The technique may be used by an individual or a group. If it is used by a group then, ideally, the group should consist of six to eight experienced people who each record their own ideas. There should be a leader who collects the ideas and who must be able to communicate enthusiastically while keeping a steady momentum going. A warm-up session is customary prior to problem solving and this provides an opportunity to select and discuss the dimensions of the problem. It is helpful to express the problem in generic terms, to make much use of imagination, and to ensure that the dimensions and attributes are independent.

A session begins with the problem being revealed and placed where it can be seen easily. Each member of the group is asked to define its dimensions and then to read them out. A discussion then ensues on which dimensions should be used. Each member is then given a diagram on which they have to complete the items, and then, as with the dimensions, to read them out. The same process is then repeated with a larger diagram. Once this has been completed the leader has to try to collate all the items onto an overhead projector transparency. Having agreed on a final joint diagram the group can carry out other activities such as listing the five most exciting ideas, or identifying the five worst and trying to improve them.

When considering more than three dimensions, a variation called *morphological forced connections* may be applied. This uses a two-dimensional grid with the dimensions written across the top columns and the attributes, or ways that they can be accomplished, written in the cells beneath. A combination is represented by a line linking a cell from each column.

Morphological analysis is ideal for generating a large number of ideas of an opportunity-seeking or exploratory nature in a logical way. It is also a powerful tool for broadening an individual's horizons with respect to a problem situation. However, it is unsuitable for problems where one must focus on a narrow band of options or where a problem only has a single dimension.

Example

Suppose a firm wants to generate ideas for a new educational toy for toddlers. The first stage is to identify suitable categories of ideas to use as axes of a matrix, bearing in mind that one is seeking to discover opportunities rather than come up with an immediate solution. The chosen dimensions must be relevant to the problem and have some logical interrelationship. However, the items listed under each dimension can be as offbeat as one wants. The morphology identifies the dimensions which describe the toy and then identifies lists of attributes under each dimension (see Table 5.2 for example).

Table 5.2

Material	Where used	Educational purpose
Felt	Cot	Alphabet
Rubber	Pram	Numbers
Plastic	Play Pen	Shapes
Wood	Beach	Sounds
Transparent perspex	Car	Colours
Wool	Bath	Textures
Metal	Garden	Co-ordination
Inflatable plastic	Holidays	Smell
Luminescent		Construction

In the example given in Table 5.2, the attributes of each dimension can be combined with each other, thus giving $9 \times 8 \times 9$ (648) possibilities. Sometimes it may be necessary consider three or even four dimensions, but this makes the task of evaluating ideas laborious and so the two or three most important dimensions are usually chosen.

Example

Suppose the problem is how to cope with seasonal workloads. Let us assume there are two dimensions to this problem: time and money (Table 5.3). Under each of the two headings we might list attributes as they apply to the problem. There are $3 \times 3 = 9$ combinations we can consider, and we consider every combination. For example, we can take 'insufficient time' and 'cheap to hire temporary staff' as an example. This in fact suggests one possible way of solving the problem.

Table 5.3

Time	Money
Irregular hours	Expensive to pay overtime
Unsociable hours	Cheap to hire temporary staff
Insufficient time	Lack of positive cashflow

Example

A footwear manufacturer wants to extend its range into more specialised and unusual products. In this case the axes used were type (the type of footwear worn by people) and age group (the age range that might use the footwear) (Table 5.4).

Table 5.4

Type of footwear								
Age range	Boot	Slipper	Trainer	Sandal	Casual shoe	Work shoe	High heels	Dance shoe
Baby								
Toddler								
Pre-school								
Child								
Adolescent								
Adult								
Retired								

Example

The problem is how to encourage new readers to a newspaper by producing a supplement which will be funded by advertisers. Chosen dimensions are the intended market, the type of articles and the type of advertiser (Table 5.5).

The SCIMITAR system

Somewhat allied to the concept of morphological analysis is the SCIMITAR system developed by John Carson (Figure 5.5). In the 1980s,

Table 5.5

Type of article	Intended market	Advertisers
Sport	Pet owners	Cosmetic surgery
Cooking	Housewives	Music clubs
Cartoons	Business women	Book clubs
Cars	Female teens	Dating agency
Holidays	Male teens	Records/music
Make-up	Children	Perfume
Problems	Business men	Clothes
Horoscopes	Pensioners	Sports goods
Stories	Families	Make-up
Puzzles	Gardeners	Toys

Carson developed a method for searching for new products (Carson and Rickards, 1979). Its idea generation mechanism is a three-dimensional model of the company which is systematically searched to find multiple answers to the question: market needs + corporate means = ? The three dimensions are markets, processes and raw materials.

SCIMITAR has been used widely in many firms and has never failed to yield valuable new product ideas.

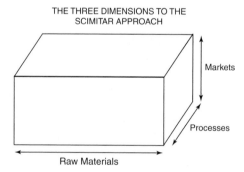

Figure 5.5 **SCIMITAR**

FORCE FITTING TRIGGERS

Providing visual stimuli to help spark off ideas in people's minds can be a very useful technique. Here the idea is to force fit combinations of attributes that one associates with an unrelated object to the problem with which one is preoccupied. All one needs is a set of trigger cards on which are depicted pictures or drawings of well known objects and a flip chart onto which one records the attributes generated and the subsequent implications for the problem itself.

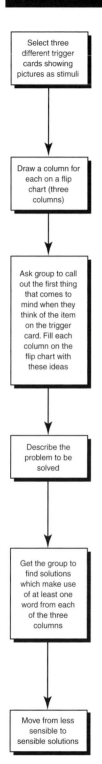

Select three different trigger cards showing pictures as stimuli

Draw a column for each on a flip chart (three columns)

Ask group to call out the first thing that comes to mind when they think of the item on the trigger card. Fill each column on the flip chart with these ideas

Describe the problem to be solved

Get the group to find solutions which make use of at least one word from each of the three columns

Move from less sensible to sensible solutions

The procedure is as follows:

1 Choose three different trigger cards showing pictures like those shown in Figure 5.7 and draw a column for each on a flip chart (three columns).
2 Ask the assembled group of individuals to call out in turn the first thing that comes to mind when they think of the item on the trigger card. Fill each column on the flip chart with these ideas.
3 Describe the problem to be solved. Get the group to find solutions which make use of at least one word from each of the three columns.
4 Move from less sensible to sensible solutions.

Figure 5.7 **Force fit triggers 1**

Imagine that one is working on the problem of improving interdepartmental communications and that the three pictures in Figure 5.7 have been selected to help come up with ideas. First one lists attributes or associations for each picture:

Bull:

- Spain;
- fighting;
- dangerous;
- powerful;

- has horns;
- steer;
- part of the food chain.

Figure 5.6 **Force fitting triggers process**

Aircraft:

- jet powered;
- bomber;
- fast;
- flies high;

- used in war;
- destroys enemies;
- has a pilot and crew.

Mother and child:

- safe and secure;
- loving relationship;
- warm;

- friendly;
- caring;
- lasting relationship.

(1) Has horns + flies high + warm and friendly

Stress the powerful effect and importance of making sure that all organisational units communicate with one another in a warm and cordial manner.

(2) Steer + has a pilot and crew + lasting relationship

Need to provide written guidelines or training to enable employees to develop durable and lasting good practice methods of interdepartmental communication.

---

exercise

Using combinations of three of the trigger cards shown in Figure 5.8, suggest insights, ideas or solutions for each of the following problems:

1. How to get greater commitment to the organisation from employees.
2. How to deal with difficult customers.
3. How to recruit high calibre management staff.
4. How to increase productivity on the shopfloor.
5. How to reduce thefts from supermarkets.
6. How to close a sale in a selling situation.

Figure 5.8 **Force fit triggers 2**

HEURISTIC IDEATION TECHNIQUE

This technique provides an interesting variation in the approach to suggesting new product ideas. In principle the technique reflects those suggested by Tauber (1972).

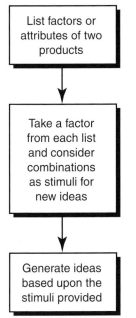

List factors or attributes of two products

Take a factor from each list and consider combinations as stimuli for new ideas

Generate ideas based upon the stimuli provided

Figure 5.9 **Heuristic ideation technique**

The approach breaks down the structure of existing products into lists of factors or attributes. A desktop computer, for example, could be broken down into such items as monitor, mouse, keyboard, processor, etc. The next step is to take another product and to break that down into its elements as well. Lists of the two sets of components are then arrayed next to one another and different combinations (one from each list) are taken as stimulation for thought.

Example

An out of town holiday hotel is looking for ideas of augmenting its service to guests; a hospital is used as the other product:

Hotel (factors: accommodation, entertainment, eating facilities, transportation).
Hospital (factors: nurses, doctors, diagnostic equipment, operating theatres, ambulances).

Various combinations are listed and numbered:

 1 accommodation: nurses;
 2 accommodation: doctors;
 3 accommodation: diagnostic equipment;
 4 accommodation: operating theatres;
 5 accommodation: ambulances;
 6 entertainment: nurses;
 7 entertainment: doctors;
 8 entertainment: diagnostic equipment;
 9 entertainment: operating theatres;
10 entertainment: ambulances;
11 eating facilities: nurses;
12 eating facilities: doctors;
13 eating facilities: diagnostic equipment;
14 eating facilities: operating theatres;
15 eating facilities: ambulances;
16 transportation: nurses;

17 transportation: doctors;
18 transportation: diagnostic equipment;
19 transportation: operating theatres;
20 transportation: ambulances.

All kinds of possibilities are suggested by these combinations. For example combinations 1 and 2 suggest a resident doctor and nurse. Combination 3 suggests the installation of different kinds of diagnostic equipment (of a non-medical nature) to help guests with their problems – e.g. an information desk, a computer terminal with an expert system that help with the most common queries, etc. Combination 5 suggests a free daily transportation system into the town – returning later in the day at specific times to pick up guests and return them to the hotel. There are many more interesting possibilities that can be found by looking at the various combinations and using a little imagination.

The method presents a systematic way of generating a relatively large quantity of ideas. Careful attention however has to be given to ensure that all the relevant important factors are included.

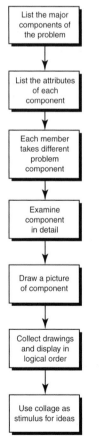

COMPONENT DETAILING

The method, suggested by Wakin (1985), makes use of some of the features of both attribute listing and morphological analysis. It is a technique suitable for use with a group of investigators. The procedure is as follows:

1 The major components of the problem are listed.
2 The attributes of each component are identified and listed.
3 Different problem components are allocated to different group members for study.
4 The components and their attributes are studied and noted in detail.
5 A picture is drawn of each component, including as much detail as possible.
6 Drawings are collected and displayed where they are visible to all those involved in the exercise. The pictures should be displayed, paying attention to their logical ordering.
7 The collage is reviewed for possible ideas.

This method is useful when one is looking for ways to improve a product, service or process. The technique helps people to see a problem from new perspectives by using drawings that vary in size and drawing style. While

Figure 5.10 **Component detailing**

it is obviously most useful for dealing with tangible products or processes, most services do have tangible aspects and these might be depicted pictorially. Abstract representations can also be effective and provide interesting and thought provoking insights.

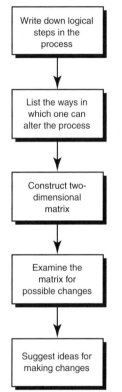

SEQUENCE-ATTRIBUTE MODIFICATION MATRIX

This is a useful method to adopt when examining a problem that comprises a logical sequence of steps. It makes use of aspects of attribute listing, checklists and morphological analysis (see Brooks n.d.). It also requires the user to apply forced relationships in order to stimulate ideas. The steps involved are as follows:

1 Enumerate the logical steps involved in the problem under consideration.
2 Indicate ways in which the process can be altered (e.g. eliminate, substitute, rearrange, reverse, combine, increase, decrease, magnify, etc.)
3 Construct a two-dimensional matrix such that the steps appear vertically along the left-hand edge of the matrix and the modifications horizontally along the top of the matrix.
4 Examine the matrix cells for instances where change seems to be promising or where further study would be productive.
5 Suggest ways of introducing the changes identified.

Figure 5.11 **Sequence-attribute modification matrix**

Example

Problem: poor record of recruitment of sales office staff. Staff turnover high and average length of stay less than three months. Personnel and the line manager recruit and appoint staff.

1 Steps followed in the process:
   (a) Keep records of all jobs in the sales office and their job specifications.
   (b) Update and modify job specifications from time to time.
   (c) Place advertisement in the media when a vacancy arises.
   (d) Send out details of job specifications to all applicants for posts.
   (e) Short-list suitable applicants for interview.
   (f) Conduct face to face interviews with applicants.
   (g) Take up references for those who appear to be interesting.
   (h) Send out offer to successful candidate.

2 Substitute, rearrange, combine, increase, decrease, improve, eliminate.

3 Construct matrix using the following abbreviations for steps in the process:

(a) Keep records.
(b) Update records.
(c) Place ads.
(d) Send job details.

(e) Short-list.
(f) Interview.
(g) References.
(h) Offer.

4 Construct two-dimensional grid (see example below).

	Substitute	Rearrange	Combine	Increase	Decrease	Improve	Eliminate
Keep records						x	
Update records				x			
Place ads			x	x		x	
Send job details						x	
Short-list				x			
Interview			x				
References							
Offer	x						

Observations:

- The way in which job descriptions are kept and the frequency with which they are updated might be improved. More frequent updates and a review of the kind of information included in the job descriptions might be productive.
- When jobs are advertised in the media they might be combined with other job vacancies so that a bigger display can be purchased in the press. This might catch the attention of more prospective employees. It could be good policy also to increase the number of outside media in which a job is advertised and also to advertise it internally as well. The number of times an advertisement appears might also be increased. Generally, the quality of the advertisements needs to be looked at. This will be particularly the case if the switch to advertising more than one type of job in the same advertisement is adopted. Professional advice of an advertising agency would be useful in this matter.

- The quality of the information given out to prospective applicants also needs to be re-examined. After all, such material is part of the internal marketing operations of the company and it needs to sell itself to prospective employees. Good applicants may be deterred from applying if they are not convinced that the job represents a really good opportunity.
- The policy of how many candidates to interview needs to be reviewed. It is possible that the firm should consider short-listing more applicants than has been the practice in the past.
- A single interview lasting half an hour may not be adequate for this type of post. Other selection and screening methods need to be considered. Prospective applicants could be invited to meet staff in the office over coffee and to spend some time in the office in order to get some idea of the kind of work that is being undertaken. This could be combined with the formal half-an-hour interview.
- When it comes to making offers the current practice is to make an offer on the day. It might be better practice to ring the successful candidate on the day following. If there is a good alternative candidate and the first candidate declines the offer then an appointment can still be made without incurring additional cost or missing out on an opportunity altogether.

QUESTIONS

1 What are the principles that lie behind morphological analysis? Illustrate how you might use the technique on a problem of your own choice.

2 Evaluate the use of checklists from the point of view of aids to ideation.

3 How would you use a checklist to find improvements for the following products?:
   (a) hair rollers;
   (b) washing powder (clothes);
   (c) shoes;
   (d) new edition of a textbook.

4 Suggest how you might use attribute listing to find improvements for the following:
   (a) desktop computer;
   (b) wedding;
   (c) funeral;
   (d) checking in at an airport;
   (e) fun fair.

5 Use the force fit images in the text to find insights into the following problems:
   (a) how to improve the customer service level in a bank;
   (b) how to make money on the stock exchange;

(c) how to reduce scrap level when producing machine parts/components;

(d) how to reduce employment turnover of staff.

6 Use a method which would enable you to come up with ideas about adding utilities to a comb.

7 Illustrate how the heuristic ideation technique might be used to come up with ideas for improving the level of customer service in restaurants.

8 Illustrate how you might use component detailing to tackle the problem outlined in question 7 above.

9 Illustrate how you might use the sequence-attribute modification process on a problem of your own choice. What are the limitations of this method?

CASES

Getting more involvement in church affairs

The local church is looking for ways of encouraging parishioners to be more involved in church matters. It always seems to be the case that the same few people do most of the organising of events while the large majority participate by attending whatever has been organised for them. The vicar feels that some creative thinking is called for and someone mentions to him that there is a creative problem solving technique called morphological analysis which might help them to come up with some ideas.

Question

Identify what you consider to be the main dimensions to this problem and generate a list of attributes under each heading. Which combinations, in your opinion, seem to be pertinent to the vicar's needs in this case?

Delta Engineering

Delta Engineering manufacture circuit boards for use in desktop personal computers. At the present time it supplies one standardised board – without any sub-assemblies or attachments – to a number of different producers of desktop computers.

The firm is looking to expand its product-market scope and recognises that tailor-made circuit boards or other partly assembled boards may be possible avenues for exploration. However, it also recognises that circuit boards are used in many other products and may well differ in terms of specification for different market segments. In addition there are obviously other factors which have an important bearing on what the firm might do.

Question

Assess the usefulness of morphological analysis in this case in terms of assisting the firm to come up with ideas or insights into the problem.

Kay's café

Northport is to get a facelift. Many millions of pounds, donated by the EU, are to be spent on turning a reasonably prosperous seaside resort into a trendy, desirable location for families, singles and even the aged.

Kay's café is half way along a side street which leads directly onto the main promenade. Some 100 yards further inland is the more prosperous Noble Street, tree-lined and populated with high class retailers for may different products, as well as some dozen or so high class cafés and restaurants. Kay's café is run by Gemma along with Nora and Stoker (the waitress and waiter, respectively). Gemma spends all her time behind the till, while Nora and Stoker take it in turns to wait on or rustle up the food and drink.

The café has been there for more than twenty years and attracts a regular clientele of passers-by as well as some seasonal trade from holidaymakers in the spring and summer. Tea, coffee, fruit drinks, sandwiches and cakes make up the menu. With the exception of the sandwiches and the coffee and tea, which are made on the premises, the other items are bought in. Cakes are delivered each morning to the shop by a local baker.

The promised change to Northport was reported at length in the local newspapers, along with the notice that retailers might be able to qualify for a grant to modernise and revamp their premises if they could argue a sufficient case with the holders of the money. Gemma, the proprietor of the café, was most enthusiastic about this possibility and immediately went into raptures about how they would profit well from this development. Stoker, in his usual guarded way, pointed out, however, that they would need to come up with some pretty good ideas if they were to stand any chance of qualifying for the money. 'After all,' he said, 'it will take more than home made sandwiches and plastic seats and table-cloths to show that the café is going to be one of the star attractions of the new Northport.'

Question

Illustrate how morphological analysis, or one of the other techniques described in this chapter, can help Gemma and her colleagues to come up with good ideas for how they might develop the café.

chapter
six

BRAINSTORMING
AND ITS VARIANTS

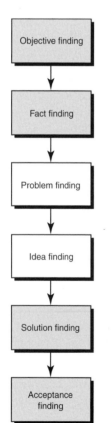

Objective finding

Fact finding

Problem finding

Idea finding

Solution finding

Acceptance finding

INTRODUCTION

The chapter reviews some of the more popular forms of brainstorming. These include classical brainstorming, wildest idea variant, round robin brainstorming, Gordon–Little variant, trigger method, brainwriting and brainlining (brainstorming on the Internet).

CLASSICAL BRAINSTORMING

Brainstorming is a technique that dates back to before the present century. A form of brainstorming was practised in Asia over 3,000 years ago; however, in modern times its popularisation has been attributed to Alex Osborn in the 1940s and 1950s (Rickards, 1988). Most brainstorming techniques fall into two categories: unstructured and structured. Unstructured brainstorming is not guided by any agreed-upon set of procedures. The result is often an unproductive session. A good example of structured brainstorming is *classical brainstorming*. It is based upon a few major principles and was originally recognised and used from the early 1950s.

Figure 6.1 **Position of this chapter within the CPS process**

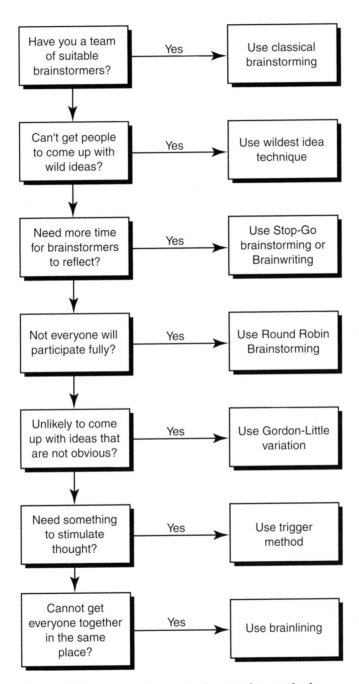

Figure 6.2 **Overview of some brainstorming methods**

Osborn (1953) advocated the virtue of 'deferment of judgment' as an aid to creativity. Later work at Buffalo in the United States by Parnes (1963) supported Osborn's claims that through the deferment of judgement principle, more and more good ideas could be produced in unit time. Osborn had four basic rules for brainstorming:

1 Criticism is not permitted – adverse judgement of ideas must be withheld.
2 Free-wheeling is welcome – the wilder the idea the better. One should not be afraid to say anything that comes into one's mind. This complete freedom stimulates more and better ideas.
3 Quantity is required – the greater the number of ideas, the more likelihood of winners.
4 Combinations and improvements should be tried out. In addition to contributing ideas of one's own, one should suggest how ideas of others can be improved, or how two or more ideas can be joined into a still better idea.

Brainstorming can be used to help find solutions to many different kinds of open-ended problems. For example, trouble-shooting problems (how to reduce downtime on the production line; how to reduce shop lifting in the store) and problems where a large number of ideas are required (identifying new product concepts; new market/segment concepts; names for products or companies). Unsuitable problems might include those which require technical or professional expertise beyond the capability of the members of the group or those which have only one answer.

The term 'brainstorming' has become a commonly used word in the English language as a generic term for creative thinking. The basis of brainstorming is generating ideas in a group situation based on the principle of suspending judgement – a principle which scientific research has proved to be highly productive in individual effort as well as group effort. The generation phase is separate from the judgement phase of thinking.

Good brainstorming is part of a creative cycle of expansion and contraction. The first phase, expansion, relies on unleashing one's creativity. The second, contraction, demands the use of judgement to focus on the best or most relevant ideas.

Rules of brainstorming

Brainstorming is a tool to generate ideas, and some ground rules are needed to maintain order. Following four rules will maximise productivity:

- Evaluate later;
- Go for quantity;
- Encourage wild ideas;
- Build on other ideas.

Evaluate later

One does not have to defend or explain ideas. Evaluating or explaining interrupts the process and can make it hard to generate ideas. All ideas put forward are equally valuable and people are apt to hold back their ideas if they feel they may be ridiculed.

Go for quantity

The generation of many ideas opens up a wide range of possibilities. This quantity has two dimensions: *flexibility* and *fluency*.

Flexibility is a range of different classes of ideas. Imagine one is brainstorming for frozen items to sell in a store. The list might include ice cream, microwave dinners, concentrated fruit juice and desserts. This shows flexibility; the variety of types of products is high.

Fluency reflects variety of ideas clustered around a common theme. Returning to the frozen food, the list may contain several kinds of ice cream, including Raspberry Ripple, Rum and Raisin, Vanilla and Chocolate. The fluency of ice cream related ideas is also high.

Encourage wild ideas

Everyone can think of wild ideas. For example, one should look beyond trying to satisfy the customer. One should try to create ideas that can:

- Dazzle the customer.
- Leave them feeling breathless.

Build on other ideas

Ideas that are shared during brainstorming can inspire even more ideas. Osborn believed that modifying or combining ideas could lead to new and even better ones. These ideas come from people with the creative skill of elaboration. They are able to expand an idea or take it in a new direction. Elaboration may happen spontaneously. Combining two ideas that might not seem closely related can produce a better idea. It will certainly produce a wild one.

Brainstorming is a traditional approach to creative thinking. The whole idea of brainstorming is that people's thoughts act to stimulate one another and produce a chain reaction of ideas. There are many variants to brainstorming.

THE PROCESS OF BRAINSTORMING

A brainstorming session needs to be well planned and those who take part as group members need to be well briefed beforehand on how the sessions are to be conducted and on the rules they will be expected to apply. The brainstorming group should comprise 10–12 people: a leader, a scribe, and 8–10 regular and guest members. Ideally, it should take place away from the everyday place of work. The room needs comfortable chairs, flip charts, blu-tack and marker pens.

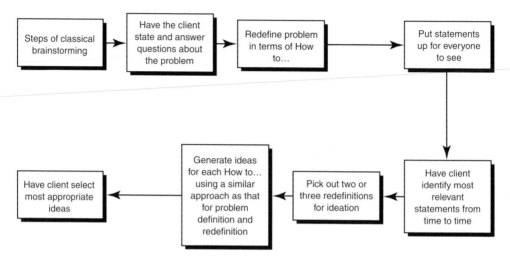

Figure 6.3 **Classical brainstorming steps**

There are a number of stages to brainstorming:

1 The client should be asked to state the problem and clarify any aspects which appear confusing to the group members.
2 The problem is recorded along with any redefinitions produced by the group.
3 The client picks the most useful redefinitions which are then used for idea generation.
4 Ideas are then generated.

A formal statement of the problem is given by the client. The brainstorming group then attempts to interpret the goals or objectives of the situation. A good technique for understanding goals is to use the 'how to' approach. For example, when looking for good new product ideas the problem might be variously defined as:

• how to introduce new products which are winners (problem as given);
• how to identify winning new products (sub-problem);
• how to satisfy customers' wants and needs (looking at the problem in a new way);
• how to get the horse first past the post (metaphorical approach).

The client is invited to indicate those redefinitions to be most useful, and redefinitions continue focusing on what the client has indicated as a fruitful direction. Finally, the client selects one or more redefinitions for ideation purposes and the group then begins to generate ideas for each one of the selected problem redefinitions in turn.

Example 1

Problem as given:

• How to decrease production times.

Redefinitions:

• How to increase the use of computers.
• How to improve the efficiency of the workforce.
• How to generate flexibility.
• How to replace batch production with continuous production.

Problem taken:

• How to improve the efficiency of the workforce.

Ideation stage:

• Job sharing between departments.
• Introduce performance related pay.
• Encourage social outings.
• Give workers super powers.
• Get rid of lunch breaks.
• Discuss how to achieve common goals.
• Bring in organisational consultants.
• Replace workers with computers.

Example 2

Problem as given:

• How to make the manufacture and marketing of cartons more profitable.

Redefinitions:

• How to identify new and profitable uses for a carton.
• How to satisfy customer wants.
• How to be the early bird and catch the worm (gain entry to new markets).

Problem taken:

• How to identify new profitable uses for a carton.

Ideation stage:

• shoe boxes;
• folders;
• boards for notices;
• videocassette and tape box;

- components for picture frames;
- advertising material;
- hardware packaging;
- pencil cases;
- theatre stage decor;
- dress models;
- drawing and painting pads;
- egg holder;
- envelopes;
- wrapping material;
- chocolate packaging;
- perfume box;
- paper bin;
- desk organiser.

Example 3

Problem as given:

- A clothes manufacturer is facing resistance from employees to the frequent changes to job and work methods that developments in the product and production methods have forced upon them.

Redefinitions

- How to make employees more enthusiastic to new methods.
- How to make new methods more welcome.
- How to make the rewards more appealing.
- How to determine what kind of rewards to give.
- How to achieve the appropriate balance between new methods and rewards.

First redefinition taken:

- How to make employees more enthusiastic to new methods.

Ideas:

1 Give them incentives.
2 Make them co-operate.
3 Ask them what would please them.
4 Make the new methods appear challenging.
5 Introduce benefits with each new method introduced.
6 Reduce negative responses towards new tasks.
7 Train the employees to become more flexible.
8 Alter the inspection routines.
9 Show them that co-operation will be to their benefit.

Second redefinition taken:

- How to make rewards more appealing.

Ideas:

1 Ask the employees themselves.
2 Look at a crystal ball.

3 Give them non-monetary rewards.
4 Make them offers they cannot refuse.
5 Offer holiday trips and parties.
6 Tell them what they will lose if they do not co-operate.
7 Ask someone who knows.
8 Show them the punishments.

The answer seems to lie in reducing or eliminating the hostility towards the new ways of performing jobs or tasks. Employees may be persuaded to have a more positive attitude if some kind of reward is offered with each new method that they learn. This way new methods will appear challenging rather than threatening. For example, learning a new method might be rewarded with token points. After collecting a certain number of points employees might be offered a special reward such as three days additional paid leave.

Brainstorming is used most frequently to generate as many solutions to a particular problem as possible because quantity is favoured over quality. The product of a brainstorming session is ideally a wide range of possible ideas that can be presented to a client. The basic assumption is that 'two heads are better than one' and that together, in groups, innovative solutions can be found.

Most of the problems faced by organisations are not well structured. They do not have any obvious steps or parts, and there is no obviously right or wrong answer. Such problems are referred to as 'poorly structured'. Creative thinking is required to make decisions on poorly structured tasks. For example, a company deciding how to use a new ingredient in its consumer products is facing a poorly structured problem. Other poorly structured problems might include coming up with a new product name, image or logo, or finding new or original uses for familiar objects like a coat hanger, paper clip or brick.

WILDEST IDEA VARIANT

Getting really good insights into a problem can often be greatly assisted by participants introducing wild ideas into the proceedings. It is the leader's responsibility to ask the participants to make this kind of contribution. Wild ideas may not be productive in themselves but they can spur others on to think of more practical ideas.

Sometimes, however, the group may experience difficulty in generating wild ideas – this is often the case with less experienced groups. In such an instance the leader may suspend the normal session and introduce a variant of brainstorming which encourages people to speculate. When this is done, members of the group are actually asked to write down a fantasy or dream-like solution to the problem. Next, the various suggestions are collected and written on the flip chart. Each fantasy idea is then brainstormed until a realistic idea is found.

Example

PROBLEM: reducing the amount of paperwork in the office.
FANTASY SOLUTION: do without all the paperwork in the office.
PRACTICAL SOLUTION: use email for everything, except where paperwork is absolutely essential.

STOP AND GO BRAINSTORMING

The procedure here is similar to classical brainstorming except for the fact that the session is divided up into segments. Rest periods are introduced every 3–5 minutes or so to allow participants to gather their thoughts and peruse the ideas that have been recorded up to that point.

ROUND-ROBIN BRAINSTORMING

Here again the rules are the same as those for classical brainstorming, but instead of the participants being encouraged to shout out ideas at random, each person in turn is asked to make a contribution. The 'round' is repeated several times until it appears that ideas have dried up or until a fixed period of time as elapsed.

GORDON–LITTLE VARIATION

This variation was suggested by William Gordon while he was working for the Arthur D. Little organisation. Gordon noted that participants in brainstorming sessions often look for ideal or obvious solutions and once these have been found suspend their really creative thinking. To obviate this problem he suggested a procedure that initially avoids presentation of the problem to be solved. Instead the leader guides the group in focusing on the underlying concept or principle of the problem. Only gradually does the leader reveal more and more information as different ideas are developed.

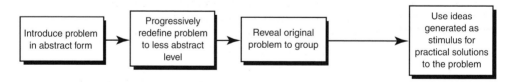

Figure 6.4 **Gordon–Little variation**

The steps involve the following:
1 Introduce the problem in an abstract form and ask participants to suggest ideas for solving the problem in this abstract form.
2 In the course of the ideation process the leader introduces key pieces of information associated with the problem. As a result of this information the problem is progressively refined to a less abstract level.

3 The leader eventually reveals the original problem to the group.
4 Using previously generated ideas as stimuli, the group generates ideas with regard to the specific needs of the original problem.

Example

Suppose the real problem is to do with implementing change in the workplace:

1 The problem is first introduced in an abstract form – e.g. how to get something off the ground. Suggestions might include 'attaching it to a balloon'.
2 After ideas have been exhausted at this level the leader might suggest that the problem involves getting a new project off the ground. Suggestions at this stage might include 'extensive consultation with everyone involved in the project'.
3 When the problem is eventually revealed, the suggestions at stages 1 and 2 might be usefully modified to produce novel insights into the real problem.

The Gordon–Little variation is an interesting one, but one of its drawbacks of course is that it doesn't readily allow for problem definition – unless, of course, the method itself is used to define the problem. Using it in the latter way will unfortunately preclude its use for generating ideas for the same problem.

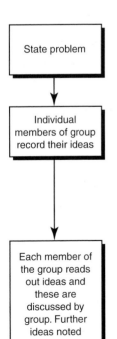

TRIGGER METHOD

The trigger method is often used in conjunction with classical brainstorming (see Bujake, 1969). The procedure adopted is as follows:

1 Read out a statement of the problem to the group.
2 Ask each member of the group to record ideas in silence (allow five minutes for this).
3 One member of the group is then asked to read out his or her ideas to the rest of the group.
4 The ideas read out are then discussed by the rest of the group for about ten minutes with the objective of developing variations on the ideas or even new ideas.
5 The procedure continues until all ideas have been discussed.

Figure 6.5 **Trigger method**

PROBLEMS WITH BRAINSTORMING

There are problems with brainstorming. It is 'still hopelessly misunderstood and badly executed by managers who assume that any discussion of ideas is automatically brainstorming' (Rickards, 1985: 55). The term is frequently used incorrectly, and success depends on the experience and skills of the group leader. Moreover, brainstorming is a thought skimming technique and not always enough to help staff grappling with 'stuckness' on an issue, or with strategic decisions (Rogers, 1993).

According to Hicks (1991), brainstorming as a creative problem solving tool has its limitations. While it is useful for acquiring large numbers of ideas, it is better suited to conceptually simple problems, as opposed to the more complex development of those ideas. Brainstorming also relies on random association and therefore does not always produce original solutions. Brainstorming is not a suitable technique for a number of situations, including those with a high technical content, people motivation and problems requiring the consideration of written material.

BRAINWRITING

Brainwriting is used by individuals or a group to put ideas in writing. Each person writes their ideas down on index cards, self-adhesive notes or slips of paper. Large groups find it helpful because everyone gets to express their ideas completely and quickly. Individuals can write their ideas down in a private, quiet place and share them later. To use it by oneself is easy:

1 Get a stack of index cards, self-adhesive notes or slips of paper.
2 Pick or be asked a question that requires a new, fresh answer.
3 Sit down, relax and write down every idea on a separate card and initial it. One uses the rules of brainstorming and the skills needed to make them work.

BRAINLINING

Peter Lloyd on the *Compuserve* creativity forum has been active in promoting brainstorming over the Internet – hence the term 'brainlining'. The word combines the words 'brainstorming' and 'online', which describes fairly well what is meant by brainlining. The word also refers to live, real-time, online sessions directed by him, incorporating special techniques, and focused on generating ideas for solving specific problems.

With the growth of online services, the process of exchanging and building upon the ideas of groups of people has occurred spontaneously. Online forums, for example, can be thought of as ongoing brainstorming sessions to the extent that they allow for the free flow of ideas.

On *Compuserve*'s creativity forum, several scheduled online sessions have been staged in which people trained to brainstorm online have worked on generating ideas to solve specific problems. These brainlining sessions make use of games designed for the peculiar dynamics of online idea generation. Brainlining games stimulate the flow of ideas, encourage humour, and make the process fun.

Brainlining is extremely efficient. It allows all participants to enter ideas simultaneously. All ideas are visible, everybody can see every idea, and all ideas are recorded and available to all participants after the session has ended.

Brainlining also introduces the leadership of a trained moderator who conducts each session and introduces special stimulants during the session – the kind used in top-level live brainstorming sessions, but designed specifically for brainlining.

The most important feature of brainlining is cross-pollination. Online services such as *Compuserve*'s creativity forum, provide a vast, cross-disciplinary congregation, world-wide in scope, which provides the most diverse, intelligent, and unique global think-tank imaginable.

Brainlining sessions increase in effectiveness to the degree that they enlist people of divergent interests and expertise.

General rules

1 The Moderator is in charge; one has to follow the Moderator's directions.
2 Only the Moderator types in ALL CAPITALS and only when giving directions.
3 The games are played with intensity, mutual support and fun.

Alphabet soup game

1 The Moderator states the problem and announces a letter of the alphabet.
2 All Brainliners make Suggestions using the given letter.
3 Play continues until the Moderator gives a new letter or stops the game.

Example (hypothetical illustration)

Moderator: HOW DO WE GET MORE PEOPLE TO BRAINLINE? THE LETTER IS 'M'.
Jazz: Do it to *music*.
Classic: Offer *more* free time on the Net.
Pop: Stress the *magic* of it.
Rock: Show them it is a way of *meeting* people.
Jazz: *Magnify* their need to join.

Rock the boat game

1 Moderator announces the problem and makes a Suggestion.
2 Any Brainliner makes an Opposing Suggestion.
3 All Brainliners pitch in with Opposing Suggestions and continue until the Moderator calls a stop to the game.

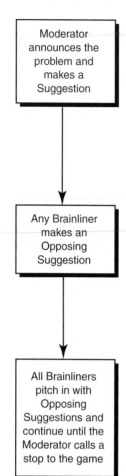

Figure 6.6
Brainlining process

Example

Moderator: HOW DO WE MAKE SURE WE ARE NEVER LATE FOR APPOINTMENTS? Make sure we don't go to meetings.

Jazz: Make sure we always go to meetings – early.

Rock: Make sure meetings don't start before we arrive.

Classic: Ask for meetings to be held up until we can attend.

Hot potato game

1 Moderator announces the problem, makes a Suggestion, and names a Brainliner.

2 The Brainliner named builds on the Moderator's Suggestion, names another Brainliner, and continues to build and name.

3 Moderator and all named Brainliners continue to build and name other members until the Moderator calls a stop to the game.

Example

Moderator: HOW DO WE MAKE MONEY ON THE STOCK MARKET? ANALYSE MARKET TREND. JAZZ

Jazz: Predict future trends. Rock.

Rock: Only for shares which have upward trends at current time. Moderator.

Moderator: Get information from experts. Classic.

Classic: Find out who are the experts. Pop.

Pop: Approach a financial consultant. Jazz.

QUESTIONS

1 What advantages and disadvantages do the different variants of brainstorming have in comparison to conventional brainstorming?

2 A department is experiencing problems of getting certain of its members to participate fully in departmental activities. How might brainstorming be used to come up with possible solutions to such a problem? Illustrate your answer.

3 Show how you might use the Gordon–Little variation to redefine a problem of your own choice.

4 Suggest ideas of your own about how brainlining might be developed.

CASES

Reducing wear and tear

The problem has been defined has how to compensate for the fact that vehicles tend to travel in each other's 'tracks' and cause excessive wear at certain points on the surface of a motorway.

Question

Suggest solutions to this problem (see Appendix 3).

Inefficient office juniors

Most departments in the firm always employ an office junior to help with the routine chores of the office. The firm feels that it is showing a degree of social responsibility by providing employment to people who might otherwise be unemployed. At the same time it reckons that it is also providing on the job training for people so that they can gain experience and take on more responsible jobs in due course. Office juniors are usually school-leavers, although occasionally older staff are appointed to such positions; juniors can be of either sex.

The office junior has the lowest status of any white collar job in the business and is generally poorly paid. Incumbents of these positions are at the beck and call of all members of a department and are generally treated as skivvies or messengers. They seldom have the opportunity to develop skills which will enable them to progress to more responsible posts in the organisation.

Generally, office juniors are treated as being something of a nuisance by their colleagues. There is a feeling that one has to give them something to do otherwise they will become bored and hang about the office and cause minor disruptions to the important work that is being undertaken. Moreover, as one person in the Accounts Department put it: 'You have to give them something to do to keep them out of trouble. But if you give them something to do they will probably get it wrong and you will have to do it all over again. It is best to give them things to do that they cannot possibly get wrong. This usually amounts to running errands for you.'

It is not surprising, therefore, that there is a high turnover in office juniors. If an office junior stays for more than a couple of months that is considered to be good going.

Question

Use brainstorming or one of its variants to come up with ways in which this problem might be resolved.

Sorting out acquisitions

A large company has grown to its present size through a series of acquisitions. This has enabled the firm to diversify considerably from its initial product-market scope. So far the procedure following an acquisition has been to leave the acquired firm still in the hands of the previous managers and simply treat it as a subsidiary of the main firm.

These subsidiaries have their own board of directors and have unfettered power with respect to policy making. The main company, however, does own the majority of the shares in them and therefore has effective control via the medium of voting power at shareholder meetings.

Recently, some subsidiaries have shown inefficiency in setting their marketing policies with the result that loss of market share and fall in profitability have ensued. In addition there has been some degree of cannibalisation taking place as a result of some of the subsidiaries, whose product-market scope is not too different from one another, putting new products into the market which compete with one another in the same market segments. Then there is of course the not unusual problem of duplication of facilities offered by the subsidiary companies.

Question

What options might the main company pursue to resolve all the identified difficulties? What other difficulties do you think there are? Use brainstorming or one of its variants to come up with some ideas.

Coolers

The Coolers company produces home refrigerators and has successfully marketed these products for a period of ten years. In recent years, however, the market has become more and more competitive with new entrants from abroad making sizeable inroads into the market. Not only has Coolers' market share been substantially eroded but its return on capital employed has also begun to slide downwards. Its pre-tax return fell from an all time high of 27 per cent just over three years ago to 18 per cent in the last financial year.

Some of the competitors have patented improvements to refrigerator design that the company cannot duplicate. The firm has not tried to reposition its products in the minds of customers, but even if it did it feels that it might be difficult (though of course not impossible) to do so. However, the firm does not know which direction repositioning might take or what the consequences of such action might be. It is becoming more and more difficult to get business and there is considerable under-utilised capacity in the industry at home.

The company is considering diversifying its product market scope through acquisition or some form of strategic alliance. In the course of considering this line of action the following questions have become apparent:

- What business is the firm really in?
- What customer wants and needs are really being met by the firm?
- How are the current trends in the marketplace likely to influence the developments of the markets in which the firm is currently operating?
- What products are likely to be required by customers in the markets currently served by the firm?
- What other product-market opportunities exist?
- What products should the firm seek to add to its product lines?

Question

How can brainstorming techniques help in this case. Use brainstorming or one of its variants to come up with some ideas on how to solve some of the above problems.

Computers Incorporated

The Chief Executive of Computers Incorporated believes that there must be a market for portable personnel computers that are used on the move in remote locations for long periods of time.

'There are many itinerant professionals and similar people who travel about all over the world, operate in remote regions and need a portable computer to help them with their work', he says.

Most of the executives in the firm agree with this point of view, but as the Technical Director points out, computers need power and batteries have limited capacity and need frequent recharging. As long as there is an electricity supply close by then there is no problem. However, travellers in the remote regions of continents often do not have access to such power.

The company feel that this is a problem which requires further investigation and decides to:

(a) try to establish the true extent of the potential demand for a suitable product
(b) come up with some ideas of providing a technical solution to the problem of powering portable computers under such operating conditions.

Question

Use brainstorming or one of its variants to come up with solutions to problem (b) above.

More quality from work?

Management was concerned about work performance on the shopfloor. Output was down on previous years and there were more rejects than ever on the production line. The operations manager decided to hold a brainstorming session with the foremen. The following summarises what took place.

PROBLEM AS GIVEN: Employee output down and more rejects on production one.

PROBLEM RESTATEMENTS: How to . . .

1 increase performance levels;
2 get a better trained workforce;
3 improve work quality;
4 make employees work harder;
5 motivate workers to higher performance;
6 reward good performance;
7 improve working environment;
8 achieve job enrichment;
9 get hold of improved machinery;
10 encourage workers to work longer hours.

Restatement 5 was take as the basis for idea generation and the following ideas were illustrative of those produced:

1 increase wages;
2 vary job routines;
3 provide on the job training;
4 improve housekeeping;
5 give workers more responsibility;
6 better incentives;
7 performance related pay;
8 give feedback on individual or group performance;
9 competitions.

A couple of wild ideas were thrown into the session as well:

1 eliminate the need for work;
2 offer employees millions of pounds as an incentive.

Questions

1 What use, if any, could the above ideas be to helping in solve the problem.
2 Can you build on the ideas produced in any way so as to improve them.
3 Try using some of the other problem restatements to produce insights into the problem.

Thoughts on back-stabbing

'Why aren't there more murders in business?' John asked.

There was silence in the room.

'I mean, everybody has it in for someone at some time in their life and there is a lot of metaphorical "back stabbing" going on in most organisations. I am sure the thought of committing murder must go through many people's minds.'

'Are you being serious?', Sally asked, looking up from her work and resting her pen on the end of her nose.

'Of course', John replied. 'And anyway most crimes are never solved – or do not even come to light. So perhaps there are lots of murders taking place every day in the business world.'

'Oh, don't be absurd!', Jayne interjected. 'You really do have the weirdest ideas.'

'Well, what do you think people do about people they can't deal with?', John asked.

'I really have never had time to consider it', Jayne retorted. 'I know people get pretty angry with one another at work sometimes, but never enough to want to murder one another.'

'So what do they do?', John asked.

'They keep quiet about it for one thing', Sally interjected impatiently.

'Yes, perhaps they do', said John, thoughtfully.

Question

Imagine someone was creating a lot of problems for you at work. Perhaps they saw you as a threat to their own prospects for advancement in the organisation. How would you deal with threats of this nature? (Hint: brainstorm the kind of problems that they might create for you. Next brainstorm how you might deal with such problems.)

chapter seven

LATERAL THINKING AND ASSOCIATED METHODS

INTRODUCTION

Edward de Bono coined the term 'lateral thinking' and has been actively promoting it for the past 30 years. Essentially lateral thinking is not just one technique but a number of different ways of making oneself open to creative thinking and problem solving. On closer examination it will be seen that lateral thinking has many overlaps with synectics (see Chapter 8) and several other well known methods as well. Edward de Bono has written extensively about the process of lateral thinking – the generation of novel solutions to problems. The point of lateral thinking is that many problems require a different perspective to be taken in order to solve them successfully.

The chapter intersperses a variety of additional mechanisms suggested by various writers with the main ideas expressed by de Bono about lateral thinking. Lateral thinking can be categorised under the headings of *awareness*, *alternatives* and *provocative methods*. The chapter considers each of these aspects of lateral thinking in turn.

Awareness concerns the way in which people look at a problem; under this heading we review such things as *dominant ideas*, *tethering factors*, *polarising tendencies*, *boundaries put around problems*, and *assumptions*. With respect to the last of these we also look at a number of techniques to help us get to grips with the assumptions we hold. We consider *assumption smashing, challenging assumptions* and *assumption reversal*.

Alternatives refers to alternative ways of viewing a problem and we look at such things as *avoidance devices, rotation of attention, change of entry point, quota of alternatives, concept challenge, keyword omission,* and *fractionalisation and bridging*.

Lateral thinking does advocate some ideation methods and these come under the heading of provocative techniques. They include *random stimulus, intermediate impossible, reversals, distortion and exaggeration, exposure, cross fertilisation, problem switching* and the use of the term *po*. An introduction to thinking in terms of metaphors and analogies is also presented as well as thoughts about the *discontinuity principle*.

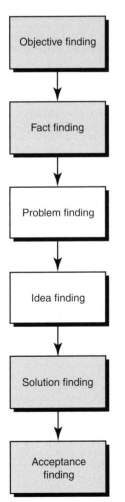

OVERVIEW

Lateral thinking is about moving sideways when working on a problem to try different perceptions, different concepts and different points of entry. The term covers a variety of methods, including provocations to get us out of the usual line of thought. Lateral thinking is cutting across patterns in a self-organising system, and has very much to do with perception. The term 'lateral thinking' can be used in two senses:

- Specific: a set of systematic techniques used for changing concepts and perceptions, and generating new ones.
- General: exploring multiple possibilities and approaches instead of pursuing a single approach.

Lateral thinking is a way of thinking that requires people to look at things in an unconventional manner and requires them to be aware of the limitations of their normal frame of reference. For example, the assumptions people make are not always justifiable under given circumstances and there is a tendency to view situations as having either this solution or that solution, with no other alternatives. Lateral thinking also demands that we should be aware of the other ways in which a situation can be viewed.

Figure 7.1 **Position of this chapter within the CPS process**

De Bono identifies four critical factors associated with lateral thinking:

1 recognising the dominant ideas that polarise perception of a problem;
2 searching for different ways of looking at things;
3 relaxation of rigid control of thinking;
4 use of chance to encourage other ideas. This last factor has to do with the fact that lateral thinking involves low-probability ideas which are unlikely to occur in the normal course of events.

Lateral and vertical thinking

Differences between lateral and vertical thinking:

- Vertical thinking is selective; lateral thinking is generative.
- Vertical thinking is analytical; lateral thinking is provocative.
- Vertical thinking is sequential; lateral thinking can make jumps.
- With vertical thinking one has to be correct at every step; with lateral thinking one does not have to be.
- With vertical thinking categories, classifications and labels are fixed; with lateral thinking they are not.
- Vertical thinking follows the most likely paths; lateral thinking explores the least likely.
- Vertical thinking is a finite process; lateral thinking is a probabilistic one.

De Bono ([1970] 1971) envisages lateral thinking as a description of a mental process leading to new insights. For him the twin aspects of lateral thinking are first the provocative use of information and second the challenge to accepted concepts. Lateral thinking involves viewing problems from a new perspective in order to create more innovative solutions and move away from conventional ideas. In contrast to logical or vertical thinking there are no paradigms to follow. Vertical thinking involves continuity, whereas one of the characteristic features of lateral thinking is discontinuity.

In general, people are predisposed to vertical thinking – therefore the transition towards illogical thought patterns does not come naturally. However, the skill can be developed and by looking at a problem from different perspectives, new ideas cam be generated rather than just variations on old ideas. The new ideas may well seem impractical in the first place but if explored further a viable solution can often be found.

Three major activities go into making up lateral thinking:

1 Awareness.
2 Alternatives.
3 Provocative methods.

AWARENESS

Here the concern is to redefine and clarify current ideas. It is argued that before old ideas can be discarded or new ones adopted, current ones must be fully appreciated in terms of their good points and limitations. Current ideas can be examined from five different perspectives (Figure 7.2)

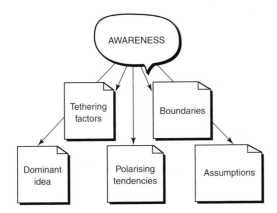

Figure 7.2 **Perspectives**

Dominant idea

Whether we like it or not we are likely to have predispositions or dominant thoughts and ideas about a problem when we first approach it. We have to take steps to recognise the dominant ideas in our mind so as not to limit the scope of the kind of solutions to the problem which we will entertain. This is in line with the suggestions of Rogers and Kelly as indicated in the opening paragraphs of Chapter 1. Knowing oneself and one's biases, attitudes, values and expectations is very important, for they influence one's perception of problems and the factors relating to them.

For instance, if we are looking at why the firm's products are not as profitable as they might be and the dominant idea in our mind is cost, then it is quite possible that we may overlook or pay insufficient attention to the other factors which influence profitability. Encouraging other people to give us their perspectives on a problem can be extremely helpful for they may see things as being important which we have marginalised in our own minds. The *dominant idea* bias is similar to *mind-set* explored in Chapter 2 and also to perceptual blocks which were discussed in the same chapter.

Example

Imagine for a moment that your male boss has sent around a message saying that he has noticed that people are coming in late from the lunch-break and that he assumes that it is because they are doing their personal shopping. How would you react? Depending upon whether you are male/female, married/single, old/young, have a family/have no family, may very well influence your immediate response to such a communication.

Tethering factors

Tethering factors are really assumptions; that is, factors that are assumed to be included in the problem situation and which are overlooked. If the fire alarm sounds from time to time and we come to learn that it is just a false alarm or simply random testing of the alarm then we come to believe that this is always the case. When a real emergency occurs we may not respond as quickly as we should to the alarm. We need to be very much aware of these tethering factors so that we are not caught out because of them.

Example

Workers have threatened to strike over a job demarcation issue. There has been no history of strikes in the factory so management acts in accordance with the principle that the workers are bluffing. This is a tethering factor for the workers may well come out on strike – we cannot assume that what has occurred in the past will as a matter of certainty continue into the future.

Polarising tendencies

This is reflected in an 'either/or' situation. Emotions may run high when a problem arises which involves the contrasting perspectives of individuals or groups of people. The emotions may lead to a polarising situation where neither party wants to step down from the way in which it views matters. Such a situation, of course, vastly reduces the number of possible solutions to such problems. Compromise is the order of the day.

Example

Trains are invariably held up for one reason or another. If passengers have to 'like it or lump it' they develop very unfavourable attitudes to the providers of the rail service and eventually may find alternative means of travel. This means lost custom as far as the railway company is concerned. By providing compensation to customers when trains are late or cancelled the railway company creates good will and although the customer may be disgruntled he or she will not be put off entirely from travelling with the railway company in future.

Boundaries

The boundaries one puts around a problem limit the amount of space that is available to solve it. Some problems may not be capable of solution unless we look beyond the currently defined boundaries. At the very best the solutions put forward may only be variations on old ideas and these may not function too well. If we think of the late nineteenth and early twentieth century writers such as H. G. Wells, while their ideas concerning space travel are now a reality, it was not something which could have been achieved with the technology at the time the works were written. It required the pushing back of the boundaries of science and technology for more than half a century before it was possible to do what H. G. Wells envisaged. Indeed, if we look at the work of more recent science fiction authors then we are still a long way from realising the fantasies that they propose.

De Bono suggests the technique of the *intermediate impossible* as a mechanism which can help us to go beyond the boundaries of a problem. This is discussed later in the chapter in the section on *provocative methods*.

ASSUMPTIONS

We have already given attention to assumptions under the heading of *tethering factors*. However, it is important to repeat it again here. All ideas relating to the solution of a problem make use of assumptions. We need to be aware of the assumptions we are making when we are looking for solutions to problems since the assumptions will limit the number of possible solutions that we can consider. If we assume, for example, that while wood will float on water, metals such as iron and steel will not float on water under any circumstances then we might naturally only think of building sea-going vessels out of wood and not out of metal. New insights into problems can often be made by challenging basic assumptions. There are several techniques that can help us to do this.

Assumption smashing

A useful technique for generating ideas is to list the assumptions of the problem, and then explore what happens as you drop each of these assumptions individually or in combination.

Example

When customers purchase software, they are encouraged to purchase support agreements for a cost of 15 per cent of the software value. The revenue from this maintenance funds the support personnel who answer telephones.

The assumptions of this situation are:

- customers purchase maintenance agreements;
- customers pay 15 per cent of the software's worth for support;
- support is a product and should therefore be sold;
- the software vendor provides helpful, timely support.

Now think about the situations as each attribute is dropped.

1 What happens if support is free? Maybe the software price should be increased and the support given away, creating the impression of free support.
2 Don't offer support. The vendor doesn't have to support it, so doesn't have to employ support staff.

3 If anyone rings for help, put the person off! This could lead to customers forming their own support groups (user groups) or turning to other areas such as the Internet, bulletin boards, newsletters, independent support specialists and so on.

CHALLENGING ASSUMPTIONS: WHAT CAN WE TAKE FOR GRANTED?

A well known international firm started losing money for the first time in many years. A new chief executive took over the running of the company and set about trying to remedy the situation. He had learned in the past that good control over costs could reverse the fortunes of an ailing firm. His main assumptions were:

1 If it seemed cheaper to buy in components than to produce them the firm should buy them in.
2 Making a resource work more is synonymous with more effective utilisation and hence should improve profitability.
3 Inventory should always be viewed as an asset.
4 Product cost is the main base for determining selling price.

His first job was get cost estimates for each one of the many thousands of parts made by the firm, along with the alternative cost of buying them in. Every part that cost more to produce than could be bought from outside was then outsourced. This was done and the result was that total costs increased. A further review of the situation showed that many more parts could now be bought from outside more cheaply than they could be produced. So the decision was then made to outsource all component parts and not to produce any parts at all.

The financial results still proved to be poor so the chief executive decided to look at the operation of the assembly plants. He found that plants were only operating five days a week and for two shifts. His next ploy was to get them to operate for seven days a week and for three shifts, thereby making full utilisation of capacity. The result was that the inventory of stocks built up and the firm seemed to be making a larger net profit. After 12 months in the job he seemed to have turned around the ailing firm. The directors of the company were pleased with his performance and he received a bonus. His very next step however was to resign his job and leave the company.

Questions

1 Can you explain why he left the company?
2 What do you think happened to the company's fortunes after he left the company?:
   (a) given a substantial increase in world-wide demand for the company's products?
   (b) given no change in the current world-wide level of demand for the company's product?
   (c) given an overall decrease in the world-wide demand for the company's product?
3 Can you identify inadequacies in any of the assumptions that the Chief Executive may have made during his short stay with the company?

See Appendix 3 for comments.

Assumption reversal

Not only can you drop or smash assumptions but you can also reverse them (Grossman, 1984). Where something involves a logical paradox this method may be appropriate. Doing more with less is a logical paradox. The method involves:

1 listing all the major assumptions about the problem, including the obvious;
2 reversing each assumption in any way you want – anything goes;
3 using the reversals as stimuli to generate new ideas.

Example

Suppose you are keeper of a museum containing a wide variety of everyday domestic and personal artefacts in use from the fifteenth century to the current day. One of the problems you encounter is having enough exhibits to show people and having enough variety to change the exhibits from time to time in order to get people to visit the museum more frequently. In addition, you have less money to spend on the acquisition of such artefacts than you had the previous year.

First you list all the major assumptions. One of these assumptions might be that museums buy artefacts for everyone to see. Reversing this assumption leads to the statement that museums don't buy artefacts for everyone to see. This statement then might be used as a stimulus to suggest a museum is a place to which people bring their own artefacts to be displayed free of charge and for a limited period – i.e. they are loaned for a fixed period of time and then subsequently a new set of loaned objects are displayed.

ALTERNATIVES

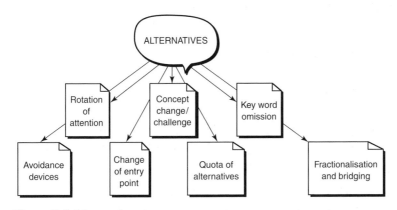

Figure 7.3 **Alternatives**

This is concerned with searching for as many different ways of looking at a problem as possible. Different perspectives provide different insights into the problem. There are a variety of approaches, as is indicated in Figure 7.3.

Avoidance devices

Avoidance devices consist of developing a frame of mind in which one tends to ignore old ideas and be open to new ways of looking at things. The essence of this approach is summarised in the well known saying 'prevention is better than cure'.

Rotation of attention

Rotation of attention involves moving away from the core of the problem and shifting focus to the surrounding factors. It is natural to focus attention on the core of a problem but this may not lead to creating new ideas. An example of rotation would be that if the core of the problem seemed to be reducing manufacturing costs then another aspect of such a problem might relate to staffing costs or administrative costs.

Change of entry point

The *change of entry point* is a method which entails identifying the starting point for viewing the problem. People think in sequence, therefore by changing the point at which that sequence is started, different outcomes can be achieved. For example the problem may concern improving the viewing figures for a television network. Initially the problem might be redefined in terms of there being insufficient funds invested in its programmes. Another starting point, however, would be to consider a more effective way of scheduling its programmes.

Quota of alternatives

Setting a *quota of alternatives* involves keeping only a few decidedly different options for consideration. This makes it easier to distinguish between ideas which may have too much in common and make it difficult to appreciate their fundamental differences.

Concept changing and challenging

Concept changing aims to prevent a problem being viewed from a fixed point. A barge, for example, might equally be considered as a mobile home or a holiday vehicle.

Concept challenge involves considering in depth any important statement usually taken for granted and challenging it in all ways possible. This assists with suspension of judgement and helps one to escape from habitual thinking patterns.

Example

The problem might be one of trying to find ways of reducing the need for telephone calls. The statement might be:

> 'Maintaining communication with business contacts without the aid of a telephone is impossible.'

The idea is to think of ways of communicating with business contacts without the aid of a telephone.

Challenging a concept usually taken for granted can lead to questions such as 'why does a product have to have certain properties or be made of a certain material, or be formed in a particular shape. For example, why do cars have to have doors on each side?' Another concept challenge might be 'why does a company need a marketing manager?'

Key word omission

Key word omission enables fresh ideas to be generated. In examining ways to improve productivity, wages and salaries may be dropped from a discussion and other terms may be used in their place – for example, payments to employees or work service payments. This may lead to ideas on how to increase job satisfaction and therefore get more productive work from employees for the same wage.

Fractionation and bridging divisions

Fractionation and *bridging divisions* are two opposite concepts. The former involves separating a problem into its parts without any regard to logical subdivisions, while the latter involves bringing the parts of a problem together. For example, a problem may be seen as how to increase attendance at meetings. The problem may have arisen because people often have other commitments and do not always feel that the content of the meetings are of particular value or interest to themselves. The problem may be subdivided into scheduling meetings so that they are convenient for people to attend and providing some motivation for people to attend. *Bridging divisions* causes the problem to be redefined as to how to schedule meetings so that they will be of interest to the most appropriate people.

PROVOCATIVE METHODS

In order to gain insights into a problem de Bono advocates the use of a number of ideation techniques. These, along with a number of associated techniques, are discussed below.

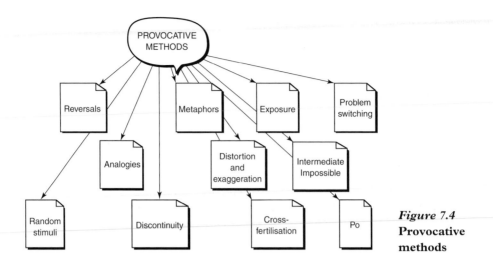

Figure 7.4
Provocative methods

Random stimulus

Random stimulus suggests that one should sample any rich set of random stimuli and seek a relationship between the object and the problem under consideration. De Bono argues that this restructures perceptions away from preferred patterns and enriches the content of the solution set.

Example

Imagine a position where two key members of the office are leaving at the same time and suddenly resources are very depleted. The random stimulus might be a 'ball'. How can we relate the concept of a 'ball' to the problem? Well, of course, the word 'ball' can be a ball as used in a game of cricket or football or it could conceivably be a gathering associated with a dance. The latter might lead onto the idea of having a 'party' to which lots of friends and acquaintances from other offices are invited. At such a gathering a temporary solution to the problem might well be found. There may well be suitably qualified and experienced people who can help out with the work for a while until suitable replacements can be found.

Random word interjection in problem solving brings about a *discontinuity*; that is, a change that does not arise as part of the natural development of the situation. The method involves trying to link a randomly generated word to the problem in some way. For example, the problem may be how to increase profits or sales and the random word chosen may be 'snooker'. Ideas may then be generated about aiming for pockets and achieving targets, not getting snookered into one position, scoring points with customers, taking the correct marketing angle, and so on.

Example

Assume that in a toy company there is absenteeism from the workplace. The problem is how to reduce it. The process starts by taking a random word. Suppose that this is the word 'butterfly'.

The properties of a butterfly are listed:

- starts as a caterpillar then blossoms;
- only lives for a short while;
- is very pretty to look at;
- is therapeutic to watch;
- has wings.

From these, a number of interpretations can be made:

- Starts as a caterpillar then blossoms:

This could show that the method implemented may commence slowly and that people may resist the changes. However, the company should persist with the plans as they will come together in the end.

- Only lives for a short while:

Can be compared to the staff interest level. How do we improve the interest levels of the staff so they do not get bored or lose interest?

- Very pretty:

We have to improve the working environment – people are more relaxed and comfortable in a pleasant working area. We need to make them feel that they are not actually going to work.

- Therapeutic:

How can we create a friendly fun atmosphere to avoid sickness due to stress or dullness. This might be done through group activities.

- Has wings:

Wings are flexible; adopt flexible working practices.

Or again the use of 'butterfly' with another problem: how to get people to attend meetings.

- short-lived;
- flutter around from place to place;
- caterpillar – chrysalis – butterfly.
- Short-lived:

Make meetings as short as possible.

- Flutter around from place to place:

Consider different venues for meetings.

- Caterpillar – chrysalis – butterfly:

Consider multi-level meetings – meetings at which all the same people need not attend.

Example

How to ensure people adopt a new system of working. Randomly selected object: videorecorder (the first column in the list below gives the 'property' of the videorecorder; the second, the implication of the property with regard to the solution of the problem).

Record: Establish a means of monitoring how well the new system is working.

Fast forward: Provide training in stages to allow some to progress at faster speeds than others.

Rewind: Additional training or refresher training for those who need it.

Timer: Automatic monitoring devices to identify additional training needs.

Change channels: Ensure that old and new systems run concurrently, initially to prevent total system collapse if the new one fails or has too many hiccups.

Remote control: Make sure that all concerned *are* involved in the training process and no one is considered to be too remote from the system for inclusion in the programme.

Intermediate impossible

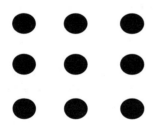

The nine dots problem (Figure 7.5) has much in common with the concept of the *intermediate impossible*. In the figure you have to connect all the dots with four straight lines – and without taking your pen off the paper (see Appendix 3 for one answer).

Intermediate impossible is associated with the idea expressed in lateral thinking that one should go beyond the traditional boundaries of a problem or situation if one is to find new insights into that problem. The technique involves thinking up an ideal but impossible solution to a problem and adapting it to make it a viable option. For example, the problem may be how to improve food in the canteen, the ideal solution to which may be to hire a top television chef; this may lead to the possible solution of sending the current chef on a training course.

Figure 7.5 **The nine dots problem**

The process is as follows:

1 The problem is clearly stated.
2 Absurd or impossible solutions are welcomed and all are recorded.
3 One of the wild ideas is taken forward and is then broken down so that more practical solutions can be found.
4 If no practical or suitable solutions can be found then another of the absurd solutions can be chosen.

Example

How to stop sales staff from making personal calls using the company's telephones.

Impossible solutions:

- Record all outgoing calls.
- Remove all telephones from the office.
- Anyone who is spotted making a personal call is sacked.
- Hire detectives to work under cover in the office.
- Make staff pay for all calls made and give them their money back for confirmed business calls.

The idea of using detectives was selected for further development.

- Use an electronic private eye to monitor telephone activities.
- As above, but employ members of staff to spy on each other.

The company chose to introduce a system whereby any sales member who observed another abusing the company's trust could tip off the managers in confidence. They were encouraged to do this with rewards and the culprit would be observed closely and further action taken.

Example

Returning to the 'reducing the need for telephone calls' problem we might suggest the impossible solution of shouting messages from the windows of the office instead of using the telephone.

This might lead to the idea of messages having to be delivered in person to people whose offices are not too far away, which in turn leads to the idea of messengers calling regularly on business clients who are based within a relatively small radius.

Example

How can we sell more televisions in slack periods of the year?
Give them away.

This may suggest a buy-now pay-later offer whereby the customer effectively gets the television free for a period of time before a payment is made.

Reversals

Reversals suggests that one should take a problem or a threat and seek various ways of refocusing so that the threat becomes an opportunity. The method:

- State the problem.
- Make the statement negative: for example, if you are dealing with Customer Service issues list all the ways you could make customer service bad.
- Doing what everybody else doesn't: for example, Apple Computers did what IBM didn't, Japan made small, fuel-efficient cars – something the Americans wouldn't consider at the time.

Example

Let us reconsider again the two members of staff who are leaving the office at the same time and leaving it somewhat depleted of resources. While this constitutes a threat to the smooth running of the office it also constitutes an opportunity to find other ways of dealing with the work-load of the office. For instance, perhaps it is not replacement staff that are required but additional labour saving devices in the form of office equipment.

REVERSAL

A large electronics distributor had 38 locations with about 1,300 employees, half of whom are sales people. The firm sold and packaged goods of over a hundred suppliers to meet the needs of over 30,000 customers. Until the early 1990s, it employed MBO-based compensation plans. It was very proud of its elaborate system of incentives for everyone in the firm. Then, the CEO and other senior managers in the company were exposed to the ideas of a creativity consultant who pointed out the disadvantages of MBO. They began to realise that the MBO system they were so proud of was actually a barrier to innovation as it discouraged full co-operation between business team members and increased suboptimisation.

Over a one-year period, the company eliminated all individual incentives, including sales commissions and all supplier-sponsored promotions. As a result it set up an environment which has created a doubling in sales and earnings, a reduction in employee turnover of over 50 per cent, and the achievement of an ISO 9002 certification in every warehouse and value-added operation in less than 6 months, without using outside consultants.

Distortion and exaggeration

This involves taking the problem to extremes. If there are many faulty goods being returned then rather than investigating what is causing the faults the method suggests that we should consider what we should do if all the good were faulty. The solution would then be to redesign the product. The technique produces fairly radical solutions to problems.

Exposure

This is a technique which makes use of the force fit method which we have encountered elsewhere in the book (see pp. 104–6). Laennec's idea for the stethoscope (see Chapter 1) and similarly obtained ideas fit in with the principle involved here. It is suggested that we should try to force fit together a stimulus which might be observed in the outside world to the problem with which we are concerned.

Cross-fertilisation

Here stimulation for an idea is provided by people working in different jobs or having different skills. One simply invites someone who is an expert in their field to say how they would approach a problem on which one is working – using the skill and knowledge they have achieved in their own field.

Recent developments in micro surgery have involved controlling the movement of instruments via movements simulation on a computer screen. In this case expert players at virtual reality computer games might be able to provide some assistance to surgeons regarding how to control movements on the computer screen with the aid of computer input devices such as joy sticks, keyboard, mice, etc.

Problem switching

Insights which we gain from working on one problem may well give rise to new insights into another. The method advocates switching from one problem to another – or even interspersing problem solving with other activities – in the belief that this will enable new insights to be obtained. Interestingly, the method and the theory behind it have something in common with Graham Wallas's ideas about incubation.

PROBLEM SWITCHING

One of my students told me of the following experience he had undergone while thinking about a particular problem. A puzzle set by a friend stated that a 200 lb man had to get across a long rope bridge with three bags of gold, each weighing 1 lb. However, the bridge was beginning to collapse and would only hold a total of 202 lbs. The man only just had time to cross the bridge once so how did he manage to get across the bridge with all the gold?

The student struggled with the problem for a while trying to think of ways to get the gold across. First, he thought the man could throw the gold across, but the bridge was too long. Then he thought that the man could remove his shoes and go across, but he could not be sure that this would lead to an overall weight of less than 202 lbs. Another idea was to go half way across the bridge with one of the bags, throw it the remainder of the way and then go back for the other bags. However, as stated, the man only just had time to get across once. Finally, accepting defeat, the student said that the man would just have to settle for taking 2 lbs of the gold across.

The student then said that he forgot about the problem and went back to reading his book. While reading the book, he suddenly realised, completely out of the blue, that the man could get across the bridge if he could juggle the bags of gold as he walked. Doing this would mean that the man would only ever have two bags of gold in his hands at any one time. As the student pointed out to me, it showed him that by taking someone away from the problem at hand and undertaking a seemingly unrelated task, it is possible to relax the mind and think in a more open manner.

Po

This is a symbol to indicate that the principles of lateral thinking should be applied. In the same way that *no* is used to reject an idea in the context of vertical thinking, *po* is used to indicate that a new patterning system is to be introduced through discontinuity. The symbol *po* is often used in conjunction with the intermediate impossible. It indicates that one should not reject or accept an intermediate idea which is unacceptable, but that judgement should be suspended for the time being.

METAPHORICAL THINKING

A metaphor is a thinking technique connecting two different universes of meaning. Examples: food chain, flow of time, fiscal watchdog. The key to metaphorical thinking is similarity. The human mind tends to look for similarities.

In making use of metaphors in creative problem solving, one starts by stating the problem, then selecting a metaphor and finally using the metaphor to generate new ideas.

Example

PROBLEM: How might employees be encouraged to work more effectively to increase productivity?

METAPHOR: The human body is composed of different organs. For the whole body to function properly each organ must operate individually and all the organs together must work harmoniously. Some organs are more important for the human organism than others (e.g. heart, brain) and if they cease functioning for a long period then the human body will die. Other inner-parts of the body have relative importance. Blood flows through inner parts of the human body.

INTERPRETATION: An organisation is made up of different departments. For an organisation to work effectively, each of the departments must operate properly and all of the departments must work together harmoniously. Some departments are more important for the correct functioning of the organisation than others (e.g. finance and marketing departments) and without their proper operation the survival of the business may be threatened. If something goes wrong in any of the departments the whole company will be adversely affected. All must function smoothly for the smooth operation of the whole enterprise.

Co-operation between employees within the departments and between the departments is essential for the efficient operation of the whole business. This may be achieved by holding meetings at which departmental representatives can discuss departmental and interdepartmental problems. Communication is the lifeblood of the organisation.

ANALOGY

The purpose of using analogies and metaphors is to raise sensitivity to a level which enables long term common sense to prevail. Domestic situations are ideal – such as comparing cashflow to a plumbing system and staff development to gardening (Rogers, 1993).

The analogy is a statement of similarity between two different things. An example of one would be: 'The noises produced were like those of a cat on a hot tin roof.' In many situations the use of analogies facilitates new problem perspectives without which the solutions to problems may never be found. They provide the problem owner with a possible escape from 'mental stuckness'. In practice analogous situations are examined and compared with the real problem to see if any new insights emerge. Suppose an organisation wants to improve its productivity and chooses as its analogy the building up of a successful football team:

Building a successful football team	*Increasing productivity*
Bringing in good players.	Recruiting experienced and well qualified staff.
Choosing the correct playing formation	Establishing efficient work groups.
Having enough players to cope with injury problems.	Having enough slack to cope with absenteeism. Train people to be multi-skilled.
Striking the right pay deal.	Performance related pay.
Creating team spirit and high morale.	Developing the social side of work.
A team that is well managed and couched, with a rigorous training system.	Having an effective operations system and ensuring its smooth running.

The football team analogy will be familiar to many people and each stage of its development has an organisational equivalent which may raise questions which might otherwise be overlooked.

TASK: HOW TO ACHIEVE A SUCCESSFUL PRODUCT LAUNCH

Analogy – booking a holiday

1 Stipulate criteria (e.g. hot weather, beach, water sports, scenic, quiet).
2 Consult brochures and travel shops.
3 Consider budget.
4 Check availability.
5 Book holiday.

Interpretations could include:

1 Stipulate target market (e.g. geographic, demographic, psychographic, behavioural, etc.).
2 Look at previous product launches or consult specialist agencies etc.
3 Consider the budget set aside for the product launch.
4 Check availability of media (e.g. air-time, poster space, print runs, etc.).
5 Commit to product launch, taking into account the above.

Forced analogy

Forced analogy is a very useful method of generating ideas. The idea is to compare the problem with something else that has little or nothing in common and gaining new insights as a result. You can force a relationship between almost anything, and get new insights – companies and whales, management systems and telephone networks, or a relationship and a pencil. Forcing relationships is one of the most powerful ways to develop new insights and new solutions. A useful way of developing the relationships is to have a selection of objects or cards with pictures to help you generate ideas. Choose an object or card at random and see what relationships you can force.

Example

Corporation as a matchbox:

Matchbox attributes	*Corporation*
Striking surface on two sides.	The protection an organisation needs against strikes.
Six sides	Six essential organisational divisions.
Sliding centre section.	The heart of the organisation should be 'slidable' or flexible.
Made of cardboard.	Inexpensive method of structure – disposable.

THE DISCONTINUITY PRINCIPLE

The more you are used to something, the less stimulating it is for thinking. When you disrupt your thought patterns, those ideas that create the greatest stimulus to your thinking do so because they force you to make new connections in order to comprehend the situation. Roger van Oech calls this a 'Whack on the Side of the Head', and Edward de Bono coined a new word, PO, which stands for 'Provocative Operation'. Programming interruptions into your day, changing working hours, getting to work a different way, listening to a different radio station, reading some magazines or books you wouldn't normally read, trying a different recipe, watching a TV programme or film you wouldn't normally watch, are all examples of this. Provocative ideas are often stepping stones that get us thinking about other ideas. Putting ideas next to each other, such that their friction creates new thought-paths, is a technique that flourishes in the East but causes discomfort in Western thinking.

QUESTIONS

1 Lateral thinking is more than a set of creative problem solving techniques. Discuss.

2 'Creative thinking is really analogical thinking.' To what extent would you agree or disagree with this statement? Explain.

3 Suggest how analogies might be used to help suggest ways of helping to improve time keeping.

4 What is lateral thinking? Illustrate how it might be useful to executives trying to find ways of introducing improvements in organisational procedures into their companies.

5 '*Lateral thinking* is not just a set of techniques but a way of thinking.' Critically evaluate this statement.

6 Illustrate how lateral thinking might help managers find ways of introducing improvements in staff motivation in their companies.

7 'There is nothing original in lateral thinking. It is simply a synthesis of the contributions of a few of the many writers on the subject of creative problem solving.' To what extent would you agree or disagree with this statement? Explain your viewpoint.

8 Suggest some problems to which the technique of assumption reversal might be usefully applied.

9 A firm is looking for ways of improving productivity on the shopfloor. Suggest how it might be done, using each of the following as an aid to creative thinking:
   (a) a metaphor;
   (b) an analogy;
   (c) a forced analogy.

10 Use the *intermediate impossible* technique to find ways of preventing shoplifting in a large department store.

11 Use the random word technique to find ways of improving interdepartmental communications.

12 Show how the 'keyword omission' method can help to find a possible solution to the problem of absenteeism in the workplace.

13 An airline wants to improve its profitability. How can *fractionalisation* and *bridging divisions* be used to good effect in helping to solve such a problem?

CASES

Hillchurch Council

Hillchurch Council are faced with the problem of how to cope with on-street parking problems and traffic congestion in the town centre. Originally, a by-pass was approved for the town but successive national governments have repeatedly delayed giving their support for the scheme and at the present time the prospect of a by-pass seems to have receded altogether.

Recent improvements to the town centre have included the opening of a large superstore and the develop of a high class shopping precinct. In addition, a new college of further education has opened up to serve the local community. All of these factors have led to an increased demand for parking space and this has only been achieved at the expense of on-street parking in neighbourhoods surrounding the town centre. Not only has this led to an increase in complaints from residents but it has also substantially increased the risk of accidents on the roads and increased congestion in the town. Indeed many of the streets which originally were available for parking have now had to be painted with double yellow lines to prevent parking and hence reduce the risk of serious accidents. There are no plans to build new car parks and there is no new space available for the building of car parks. At the present time there is one car park which can accommodate 50 vehicles and two which can accommodate 100 vehicles each. None of these sites are suitable for development as multi-storey car parks.

On market days (two days a week) and Saturdays the situation in the town is chaotic. Moreover, the situation is made much worse in the summer when travellers to a nearby seaside resort come through the town in their thousands to the seaside. Hillchurch is a veritable bottleneck straddling main north–south and east–west routes. Furthermore, only one major road runs north to south through the town and only one runs east to west through the town.

The town's sole traffic warden is hard pressed to keep up with the numerous complaints that are made daily but, despite requests made for additional wardens, the Council feels that providing more wardens will do little to alleviate the dreadful problems that exist.

The Leader of the Council feels that this is a problem which requires some creative insights and has approached a firm of management consultants to help with the problem. The consultants have indicated that they feel their expert on lateral thinking may be able to help with this particular problem and have assigned the task accordingly.

Question

Illustrate how the expert on lateral thinking would approach this problem. Use as many of the lateral thinking techniques as you like, to try to get some new insights into this difficult problem and come up with ideas which might be implemented.

Business books

Edwina Publishers were looking for ways of ensuring the successful launch of a new series of business books. 'What is required', said John, 'is a new approach. There are so many titles and series in the marketplace nowadays that readers, students and lecturers have too much choice and cannot easily make their minds up which books best suit their purposes. I think the choice process they must go through is a bit haphazard.'

Jane suggested that she thought it might be more to do with how the product was launched, and the kind of budgeting and marketing operations that went into launching a product. 'Look here,' she said, 'let us approach the problem from a creative problem solving perspective. A book I have recently looked at suggests that we might consider analogous situations when we are trying to get insights into a problem. It first suggests that we should define the problem. In this particular case I think that this is fairly obvious – i.e. how to achieve a successful product launch. It goes on to suggest that we next look for an analogy for the problem. In this particular case, one such analogy might be "booking a holiday". It then suggests that we consider what is involved in working with the analogous problem. This might mean such things as:

1 Stipulate requirements (e.g. good weather, good beach, water sports, scenic, quiet, etc.).
2 Consult brochures and travel shops.
3 Consider budget.
4 Check availability.
5 Book holiday.

'Interpretations could include:

1 Stipulate target market (e.g. geographic, demographic, psychographic, behavioural, etc.).
2 Look at previous product launches or consult specialist agencies, etc.
3 Consider the budget set aside for the product launch.

4 Check availability of media (e.g. leaflets, direct mail shots, print runs, etc.).

5 Commit to product launch, taking into account the above.'

'Well,' said John, 'I think we do those kind of things already. However, I like the idea of using an analogy. It might be worth spending some time exploring the approach in more detail.'

Question

How might John and Jane develop the analogy type approach in this instance? Provide illustrations. What do you see as the drawbacks, if any, to using this particular approach in this instance?

Finding out more about candidates for interview

'Another one having a nervous breakdown', said Jenny, closing the file and putting it in the pending tray.

'Yes, that's the third one this month', Arnold replied, hardly stopping from his task of keying data into the database. 'Something will have to be done about it.'

'I think the application forms and interview procedures need a shake up', said Sarah. 'Interviewers are making too many wrong assumptions when they read the application forms and conduct the interviews.'

'What do you mean?', asked Jenny.

'Well,' replied Sarah, 'do we really know whether application forms are filled in by the candidates themselves? Can we be sure that what the work experience candidates say they have is really true? Are references provided by referees really valid in the context of a candidate's application?'

'Some people are also better at selling themselves,' Arnold interjected, 'they just give the right impression.'

'Well,' said Sarah, 'perhaps we ought to write down all the assumptions we make about how people fill in application forms and all the assumptions we make when interviewing people.'

'What then?', Jenny asked.

Questions

List the various assumptions that short-listers might make about candidates for jobs when the latter are completing application forms. Do the same for assumptions made about interviewees by interviewers. How would you proceed to use this information to gain further insights into the problem. Illustrate your answer.

Rose

Using the random word technique to come up with ideas for getting customers to buy a new brand of perfume, the following list of associated words and phrases for a rose were obtained:

- petals
- perfume
- bright
- colourful
- stem
- fresh

- thorns
- needs room to grow
- needs good soil and plenty of sunshine and rain to grow
- attracts insects

Questions

1 Illustrate how the list of associations might be used to come up with insights into the problem.
2 Suggest other associations for 'rose' and interpret these into insights into the problem.
3 Take another word as the stimulus, list associations and generate insights into the problem.
4 Compare and contrast the various insights that have been generated.

Cash problems

A company had to generate a certain amount of cash in order to settle various loans by pre-specified dates. Unfortunately the business plan which provided the cashflow was too optimistic and the firm was in the unenviable position of being unable to generate the cash required to pay off the loans. Sales were unfortunately falling well short of expectations and, although profit was on target, insufficient cashflow would be generated.

Question

Illustrate how lateral thinking might help to suggest insights into this problem.

chapter eight

SYNECTICS

INTRODUCTION

The chapter looks at the subject of *synectics*. A method of using synectics is outlined and discussion given over to considering the various components that make up the synectics process.

SYNECTICS

Synectics is the most highly refined and universally applicable of all the creative problem solving techniques. Like brainstorming it is a complete problem solving process and is particularly useful for problem identification and idea development. The main aim is to use two operational mechanisms to *make the strange seem familiar* and to *make the familiar strange* in order to produce five psychological states which are necessary to achieve creative responses. These states are *involvement and detachment, deferment of premature solutions, speculation, autonomy of object* and *hedonic response*.

Synectics encourages the use of analogies to *make the familiar strange*; the personal, direct, symbolic and fantasy analogies. Synectics is perhaps the most difficult to perform of all the ideation techniques. Skill and experience need to be acquired before attempting to perform synectics. The origins of the technique are rooted in brainstorming. Synectics aims to open up a problem to new insights. It is the process of combining unrelated factors to allow problem solvers to view a problem from a different perspective.

Synectics was developed by William J. Gordon (see Gordon, 1961) as a result of research undertaken at the Arthur D. Little organisation into creative individuals and the creative process. He associated the creative process with certain psychological states, believing that if these could be induced then creative breakthroughs would increase their occurrence. He emphasised the need to make the familiar strange and vice versa.

> To make the familiar strange is to distort, or transpose the everyday ways of looking and responding . . . it is the conscious attempt to achieve a new look at the same old world, people, ideas, feelings, and things.
>
> (Gordon, 1961: 54)

This he anticipated would enable a problem to be viewed from different perspectives and thus support ideation based upon these various perspectives. Gordon encouraged the use of metaphors and analogies to aid the idea generation process. George Prince (who developed synectics, making it more efficient and productive – see Prince, 1970) joined William Gordon and together they established Synectics Incorporated in Cambridge, Massachusetts in the United States. In 1960, Gordon left the company and he and Prince each developed their own versions of the technique – the key factor differing between them is terminology.

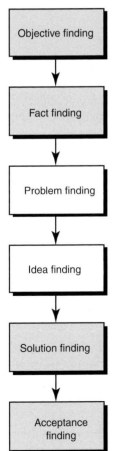

Synectics is a method for inventing new solutions to problems. No attempt is made to define the problem. The client's statement of the problem is taken as the starting point; he or she gives a brief explanation of the background, as he or she sees it, and the group and client proceed to restate or paraphrase the problem in a language of 'how to' statements. These can be as speculative, unrealistic, wishful or challenging as the group feels inclined to produce. Their purpose is to open up the whole problem area and give the client an opportunity to get away from conventional ways of looking at the problem.

The synectics slogan – 'stay loose 'till rigour counts' – expresses a basic feature of the process. Rigour, precision, accuracy, and realism are necessary and valuable in their place, but they are not the material of which creativity is made. We have to make a conscious effort to suspend normal acceptable intellectual standards if we are to give free rein to speculation, imagination and originality.

Conventional treatment of ideas makes two assumptions about the nature of ideas: first that they are monolithic entities and second that their value is binary – good or bad. Our experience is that both

Figure 8.1 **Position of this chapter within the CPS process**

these assumptions are incorrect and destructive. An idea is not monolithic, it has many facets. There is always something good about an idea.

A synectics group is made up of 6–8 people, plus a leader, and all the people in the group need to be trained in the use of the technique. Ideally, the group members should not be acquainted with the problem situation. No attempt is made by the problem owner to define the situation; however, 'initial solutions' held by the group members should be offered up in order that those that have not already been tried can be recorded as viewpoints. During the next stage, group members paraphrase the problem using 'how to', wishful thinking and fantasy statements. Having completed this, analogies and metaphors are used to take the group on an excursion. Ideas generated on an excursion, or if necessary in series of them, are next related to the original problem in the hope of converting them to a practical application. Often expert guidance will be required to transform these ideas into final solutions.

There are various types of excursion which can be used, depending upon which the leader deems to be most suitable: personal analogy, direct analogy, symbolic analogy and fantasy analogy.

Personal analogy

Personal analogy is the use of emotions and feelings to identify an individual with the subject of a problem.

The problem may be how to vary a food product such a fish finger. It may feel pain, be boring and may have a fishy odour which may not appeal to people. This may lead to some new element such as a tomato sauce filling being added to the product to negate the undesirable characteristics.

Personal analogy can involve:

(a) describing the object by listing its basic characteristics and relating these to the problem;
(b) describing the emotions the object might have in a given situation;
(c) describing how someone feels when using the object;
(d) describing what it feels like to be the given object.

Based upon such an approach it might then be possible to develop solutions to the problem.

Example

Imagine that the problem is 'how to market a bottle of wine'. The personal analogy could be to imagine what it feels like to be 'the bottle of wine'. Some suggested feelings might be:

- 'I feel wanted'
- 'I feel important'

Alternatively, of course, we could consider the characteristics of the wine – clear, fruity, etc.; the emotions that the wine might have in given situations,

- **Characterisitics**
- clear
- fruity
- **Emotions**
- happy at dinner
- freindly at parties
- **Feeling when using**
- sophisticated
- tired
- **Object feelings**
- wanted
- important

Figure 8.2
**Personal analogy –
a glass of wine**

etc. – happy at dinner, friendly at parties; or what one might feel like when using the wine – sophisticated, tired, etc.

We might then look at ways of how we could try to incorporate these feelings into the promotion of the product (or, where negative, compensate for them in our promotional messages!). It is through such a technique that we are able to release ourselves from looking at a problem in terms of its previously analysed elements.

Direct analogy

The *direct analogy* compares the problem with homogeneous facts, information or technology.

A heating system might be compared with a volcano and from this new ideas may arise.

A direct analogy is a mechanism by which we try to make comparisons with analogous facts, information or technology. In making use of this device we have to search our experiences and knowledge to collect together phenomena that seem to exhibit familiar relationships to those in the problem in hand. It is often fruitful to compare animate systems with inanimate systems, or to make comparisons between biological, ecological and other natural science systems and social systems.

Example

Decision making can be likened to finding one's way across paths over a marsh. There are many pitfalls and wrong turnings along the way. The various paths have different pay-offs so we need to estimate the value of the various pay-offs. Will they enable us to reach our destination or objective?

The idea is to describe a clear, straightforward relationship between the problem and some object, thing or idea with the expectation of being able to transfer insights back to the problem in hand.

- What are seemingly paths across the marshes often lead you the wrong way.
- Unfamiliar and potentially hazardous options need careful prior analysis when making decisions in order to ensure that good choices are made.

Figure 8.3
Direct analogy – paths across marshes and decision making

Symbolic analogy

Symbolic analogy is the use of objective and personal images.

If the problem is to fit 50 people into a small conference room it may be likened to cramming sardines into a can or the London Underground.

Symbolic analogy involves making use of objective and personal images to describe a problem (e.g. like an Indian rope trick, like a thief in the night, like a pirate).

Example

It may be difficult to get hold of the boss because the boss is nearly always out of the office. Finding the boss may be likened to finding the elusive Scarlet Pimpernel. It might well be that in trying to suggest ways of finding the elusive flower (or fictional character of Baroness Orczy, who shares the same name) we may get some further insights into how to keep tabs on the whereabouts of the boss.

Figure 8.4
Symbolic analogy – the Scarlet Pimpernel

- Getting hold of the boss is like finding the Scarlet Pimpernel. "We seek her here, we seek her there, we seek her everywhere!"

Fantasy analogy

This is based on Freud's notion that creative thinking and wish fulfilment are strongly related. It is usually prefaced by the words 'How do we in our wildest fantasy . . . ' For example, when considering a problem dealing with managing difficult staff at work we might pose the question:

'How do we in our wildest (IOWF) fantasy manage difficult staff without undue acrimony in the workplace?'

This may well take us into the realm of considering conflict avoidance or conflict mollification management strategies.

Fantasy analogies take the most desirable solutions, which may be impossible to implement but which may lead to some further practical ideas. This is similar to the intermediate impossible technique advocated in lateral thinking.

- How do we IOWF want to manage the office?
- So that peace reigns all the time
- Solution: adopt style of management based on conflict avoidance

Figure 8.5
Fantasy analogy – peaceful management

CONDUCTING SYNECTICS SESSIONS

The management of synectics sessions is crucial to their success. If the session is not well carried out then the psychological states which are required by users of the technique will not be achieved.

Gordon laid down quite specific criteria for group membership and composition. He suggested that group members should be frequent users of analogies and metaphors, have an attitude of assistance, well co-ordinated bodily movements and the capacity to generalise. They should possess personality traits such as emotional maturity, 'constructive childishness' and 'risk taking' and be non-status oriented. They needed to show a commitment to the group and its purpose and be 25 to 40 years of age. Gordon's suggestion, however, should not be seen as an absolute guideline as far as age is concerned!

The group should not have too many experts. The problem owner will invariably be the problem content expert. It is easier on the leader if all are of equal status. It is also useful to have a couple of people who are good at coming up with wild ideas. These people may set the cultural norm of the group which otherwise might be unwilling to try wild ideas. It is also advantageous to have some members who have been trained in the use of synectics.

The problem owner

He or she should be warned of what to expect, so that he or she is not alarmed when the proceedings appear to be running off in a seemingly irrelevant direction. It is also useful for the problem owner to understand the synectics process.

The group leader

The role is that of a process leader who guides only the problem solving process. The leader should not get involved with the problem content in any way. Leaders should direct the process, not contribute ideas, suggestions or possible solutions, let alone the best way of resolving the problem. The group leader should determine the success of the process by observing, and asking for, the client's reactions to what is going on.

The synectics session leader needs to be seen as serving the needs of the group in order to gain commitment, enthusiasm and the best ideas. The group leader is also responsible for ensuring that the group members obey the rules; for encouraging speculation; for recording all the ideas; for checking with the problem owner that the group is on the right track; and for managing the time.

The group

Since the group may generate ideas faster than the leader can write them down on the flip charts, group members should be encouraged to jot ideas down on notepads until required. Half formed and wild ideas should be recorded and group members should support each other's efforts by complimenting them where appropriate.

Process

The problem owner first describes the problem. The next stage in the process is 'goal orientation'. Here one tries to view the problem situation in a variety of ways, so that one looks for a solution on the most appropriate direction. 'Goal wishing' stresses that speculation/wishing is permitted and desired. We are seeking different angles or restatements of the problem. This is a time when the group members must not evaluate their own ideas. Way out ideas often trigger other ideas in group members. The problem owner should offer directions as to which of the ideas appear to offer the best way forward and so direct the group members. 'How to' or 'I wish' statements are quite useful. The latter encourages speculation, while the former conveys positive direction.

Selection

The problem owner needs a chance to reflect on the restatements made in order to select two or three that best describe the problem situation. He or she should be warned against selecting only those that appear obviously practical, and be advised to choose those that are intriguing, novel and interesting. The problem owner is asked to say what led him or her to choose the selected 'springboards'.

If no specific action is indicated by a 'springboard', the next step is to generate ideas as to how the circumstances it describes might be brought about – possibly by using an excursion.

Excursion

Various types of excursion are used in the synectics process. The choice of excursion depends on the degree of novelty required in a solution, the element of risk the leader is prepared to take and the type of material which is being worked upon. Hicks (1991) distinguishes between 'imaging or fantasy excursion' and 'example excursion'. The imaging excursion is possibly the most unorthodox form of excursion and can be a potential disaster with a conservative-minded group – though it often works dramatically well when it is least expected and produces the most innovative ideas.

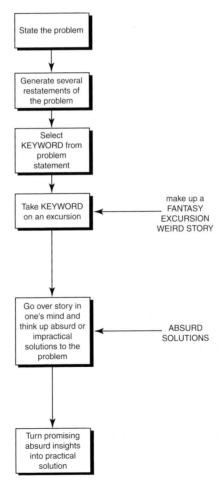

Figure 8.6 **The synectics process: fantasy excursion method**

Fantasy excursion

For a fantasy or image excursion the group is asked to describe a mental picture/story inspired by the last item in a word association preliminary exercise, starting with a word taken from the 'springboard'. One person will lead off and then every other person in the group has to add to the story. They should be invited to jump in whenever they like and told that the more colourful, outlandish, weird or exotic the story the better. It is usually better to keep the story in the same location, if possible, as this makes for better imagery. Everyone should try to add about a minute to the story and then someone else takes over. The changeover may be left to the discretion of the leader.

If the story tends to stagnate on some minute detail of one particular image the leader can ask someone to make something surprising happen. Conversely, if images are insufficiently developed because storytellers move too quickly to other images the leader can pin people to one scenario by asking for more detail. People may be anxious about producing mental images in public and about their ability to contribute to the story. It is, however, the violent changing of direction and having to build another mental image after the destruction of the first that makes the story rich in speculation and evocative images.

Absurd solutions

When every group member has had at least one chance to contribute to the story the leader stops the imaging and asks the group to replay the story in their minds and try to think up some really absurd or impractical solutions to the problem. The absurd solutions are written up on the flip chart.

Having moved so far from the problem with the fantasy excursion it usually becomes desirable to return to the real world and the problem in several stages, the first of which is this drawing up of *absurd* solutions. If a group member immediately comes up with a sensible and novel solution one should obviously not reject it.

The leader needs to check with the problem owner to see if any of the absurd solutions intrigue, fascinate or appeal to them. There should be no problem with picking too practical a solution as there should not be any. After the problem owner makes his selection the leader asks the group to examine the chosen absurd solutions and to try to find ways of changing them into something more practical and closer to reality, while retaining as much of the original idea as possible. It is better not to attempt to do this in one step but to spend some time modifying them because there is a tendency to lose the novel feature contained in the absurd solution by jumping back to reality to quickly.

Example excursion (includes the use of analogies)

The *example* excursion is perhaps most commonly applied and easiest to interpret, though it is thought to be less generally applicable. It is introduced in the same general way as the fantasy excursion. When moving into the excursion we ask the group for examples of a keyword chosen from the problem restatements in a different 'world'. The choice of appropriate world is a matter of past experience and knowledge of those that seem to have worked well in the past. Almost any 'world' can be used – e.g. sport, fashion, warfare, Nature, physics, astrophysics, engineering and so on. Examples, of course, are only one form of analogy and one can also ask for other forms of direct, personal, fantasy or symbolic analogy – see the examples of synectics in action in the next section. One often combines examples with some other form of analogy. All ideas are of course written up and eventually explored to see how they can provide insights into the problem under study.

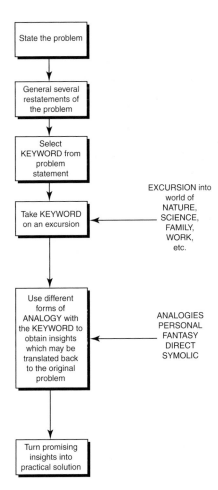

Figure 8.7 **The synectics process: example excursion method**

A typical session might involve:

1 State and restate the problem.
2 Choose a keyword.
3 Take the keyword on an excursion into a different world – e.g. Nature – asking for examples of the keyword in that world.
4 Ask what it feels like to be that example in the different world – *personal analogy*.
5 See if any of the material listed so far gives insights into the problem.
6 If required, continue with more excursions.

SYNECTICS IN ACTION

Fantasy excursion

A firm was looking for capital to invest in some risky ventures.

Problem statement: how to finance risky ventures.

Word selected: ventures.

Word association preliminary: ventures, adventure, excitement, journey, aspiration, jungle, desert, joy.

Weird story: 'Joy sat entrenched in the bob-sleigh. The ice seemed to seep up through the runners as it began to move. The speed gathered. The sun glinted on the mountains overlooking the course. The first corner came. All was safe. The angle steepened and the speed increased. Joy's helmet touched the ice wall. A reverberation rang through her ears. Everything went out of focus, except the track. It was white, fast and steep. A big corner. Almost turned over. The finish in sight. Would she stop? Yes. Hugs and kisses. All over.'

Absurd solutions

1 Win the money on the races.
2 Give potential backers a ride on a bob-sleigh and charge them exorbitant fares for the ride.
3 Put on very risky bob-sleigh tournaments and charge spectators for the privilege of watching.
4 Produce all kinds of spectacular events which will have great entertainment value and will attract sponsorship and TV rights.

Practical solution

Make the ventures look very attractive propositions, stressing that what appears to be a risky venture will in fact be quite safe and have substantial pay-offs.

Example excursions

Two groups, on separate days, but under the direction of the same synectics leader, were assigned the task of finding insights into the problem of how to reduce stress in the work situation. The following episodes occurred:

Group 1. Problem definition/redefinition:

- How to reduce stress in the work situation.
- How to work in a positive way.
- How to improve morale and reduce absenteeism.
- How to improve relations between staff.

The word *reduce* was chosen by the leader and the group suggested the world of *forestry* for an excursion. The group was then asked to think of examples of using *reduce* in the world of *forestry*.

- putting fires out;
- reducing tree disease;
- cutting the undergrowth;
- removal of weeds;
- cutting paths through the forest;
- deforestation;
- stop illegal hunting of animals in the forest.

The leader then focused on *animals being hunted in the forest* and asked the group to imagine what it would be like to be *an animal being hunted in the forest*:

- browned off;
- scared;
- premature death;
- looking for relatives that have been killed;
- running all the time;
- trying to find somewhere to hide;
- feeling it never stops (relentless pursuit);
- thinks it is a game;
- unfairness;
- pain, misery, suffering;
- survival of the fittest;
- revenge;
- victimised.

Group 2. Problem definition/redefinition:

- How to reduce stress in the workplace.
- How to make work pleasurable.
- How to work in a more peaceful company.
- How to reward good performance.

The word *pleasurable* was taken and the suggested excursion was the *family*. Examples of *pleasurable* things in the context of the *family* generated by the group were:

- home cooking;
- support;
- cosiness;
- birthdays;
- family outings;
- holidays;
- gatherings;
- family intimacy;
- quarrelling;
- story telling at bedtime;
- sports (doing it together);
- having meals together.

The word *gatherings* was then chosen for a further excursion and the group was asked to give examples of the kind of *emotions* that might be encountered at a family gathering:

- happiness;
- sadness;
- satisfaction;
- proud;
- frustration;
- protection;
- love;
- anger;
- togetherness;
- belonging;
- boredom;
- tension.

Now you consider how the data might be used to give insights into the original problem:

PROBLEM : 'HOW TO MAKE OUR ADVERTISING MORE EFFECTIVE'

Restated as 'How to give our advertising more punch'.

Key word taken 'punch'.

Ideas about 'punch' from the world of boxing: jab, hook, knock-out, body, head, ribs, rabbit, clinch . . .

What does it feel like to be a 'knock-out':

1 Significant.
2 Penetrating.
3 Finishing touch.
4 Strong.
5 Rampant.
6 Explosive.

All of the above seem applicable to the advertising problem. For example it suggests content – the advertising must contain highly significant messages and images which will awaken interest in the target audience. Moreover, in the presence of all the 'noise' created by competitive advertising, the advertisement must be able to penetrate through to the reader. There must be something very attention-getting about it. Perhaps it should contain strong, rampant and explosive messages and images. The finishing touches to the advertisement are also important – its timing, media slot, etc.

Itemised response

We should not reject ideas which are not perfectly formed. Indeed the suggestion is to work on and develop the ideas into more practical solutions. Synectics has developed this simple technique (IR) that allows a possible solution to be developed from any idea, using gentle evaluation that encourages the ironing out of minor concerns rather than dismissal of the idea. It starts from the assumption that all ideas have value, and thus before any flaws or imperfections in the idea are pointed out, first some of the good points (say 3–5) are listed. This reinforces the value of the idea, and justifies the additional time that will be spent overcoming concerns about it.

The problem owner is asked to identify practical, helpful or attractive aspects of an idea, giving reasons wherever possible. It may be helpful to let the group contribute to this also, since they may see the benefits not immediately apparent to the problem owner. The leader asks for the problem owner's major concern with the idea, expressing this as a 'How to/I wish' in order to give the group a direction for further development of the idea in order to overcome this concern. The leader then gathers ideas from the group and writes them on the flip charts while asking the problem owner to paraphrase the suggestions to ensure understanding. If the group comes up with a suggestion that only partially overcomes the concern, the IR process is repeated with this latest suggestion. As the idea develops in this way it becomes more difficult to get three 'new' good points each time, but the time spent trying is usually worth while.

Having resolved the major concern, the group tackles other concerns the problem owner may have with respect to the original idea, always taking them one at a time. The process continues, gradually homing in on a possible solution, a course of action which the problem owner can implement without further help from the group. The leader then writes up the possible solution.

THE SYNECTIC TRIGGER MECHANISMS

- Synectic trigger mechanisms catalyse new thoughts, ideas and inventions.
- Synectic theory is based on disruptive thinking – similar to the Po operation of Edward de Bono.

THE SYNECTIC WAYS OF WORKING

- Synectics is based on the fusion of opposites.
- Synectics is based on analogical thinking.
- Synectics is synergistic. Its action produces a result which is greater than the sum of its parts.

QUESTIONS

1 A firm is having problems in recruiting new managers to join its ranks. Discuss how the use of synectics might lead to ideas on how to get to grips with this problem.

2 What is synectics. Illustrate its application to a problem of your own choice.

3 When might synectics be most appropriately used in creative problem solving?

4 Illustrate the different forms of analogy that might be used in a synectics session (i.e. personal, direct, symbolic and fantasy analogy).

5 What is the purpose of an excursion? Suggest 'excursions' and an example of the following italicised keywords, in the excursions in each of the cases below:
   (a) How to *ignite* enthusiasm for a project.
   (b) How to *liquidate* assets to solve a financial problem.
   (c) How to *purify* the air in departmental meetings

6 Work through a synectics session to gain insights into each of the following problems:

(a) How to improve communications between management and workers.

(b) How to prevent industrial espionage.

(c) How to minimise the number of industrial accidents.

(d) How to do more management work with less resources.

CASES

Jo Soap

Helena is deputy head of department and is in charge of the office when the boss is away. Her usual duties involve preparing departmental budgets and reports for the company's directors and handling complaints and other difficult problems both by letter and over the telephone. She is tactful, efficient and co-operative.

Jo Soap is in charge of the secretaries and manages a group of five female employees. She has to ensure that clerical work is progressed when it is passed on by the department head, Helena or any of the administrative assistants in the department. Unfortunately, Jo tends to have an authoritarian attitude which is resented both by the women who work under her direction and other people in the department. She has demonstrated her rigidity to Helena on many occasions in the past, insinuating that Helena has not been reasonable in expecting work to be done by a particular time because reasonable advanced notice has not been given. There is little truth in these allegations, though on occasion expectations might have been regarded as ambitious by some people.

A short while ago an official complaint was lodged with the head of department by the secretaries about Jo Soap's approach to managing their work. The women even cited Jo's inappropriate behaviour towards Helena as confirmatory evidence to support their complaint. The head of department had approached Helena concerning the matter, but the latter thought she was well equipped to handle her personal difficulties on her own account – a response which seemed to please the boss who did not really want to get involved in hassles of this type.

In the last few weeks, Jo's attitude towards Helena has become more hostile. Finally, just before Easter, when the head of department was away for a few days, Jo told the secretaries that they need not come in the two days before the start of the holidays. She also said that she would not be in either. This was something that had not been the custom and practice in the past and secretarial support was always available up until the start of the holiday period. Helena did not know about the planned additional holidays until the day before the women were about to take the time off. Furthermore, Jo had been taken ill and was not available for consultation purposes. The result was that there were pressing jobs which required doing and no one to do them. However, following a persuasive talk with Helena a couple of the women agreed to make themselves available to cover any necessary work that was required to be done.

After the break, Jo complained bitterly to Helena about interfering in her work. She was extremely rude to Helena, despite Helena's explanation that at the time Jo had been ill and she had therefore to intervene herself as there were urgent jobs to be done.

Helena recognises that Jo is very efficient in her job but is rightly concerned that matters could get out of hand, and she dreads having to interact with Jo at all. Something will have to be done about the problem but she is unsure what action to take.

Question

How would you advise Helena? Use synectics to gain some insights into the problem.

Consultants who don't like meetings

Creative Marketing Consultants offers a wide range of expert marketing consultancy services to its clients. The firm employs ten consultants and is based in the West End of London in exclusive offices not far from Hyde Park Corner. Unfortunately, although the team the chief executive has got together are very good individual thinkers they hate having to attend internal meetings and prefer to work outside of the office with clients. Internal meetings are poorly attended and a variety of plausible excuses are usually offered for being absent. The chief executive feels that in order to foster a creative spirit in the staff it is essential to encourage an atmosphere in which people are free to come and go as they please and to have as much flexibility as possible in terms of their working arrangements.

The chief executive called in a creativity consultant to help deal with the problem. A one day seminar was presented to the staff in which, ostensibly, a range of creative thinking and problem solving techniques were presented and discussed. In one of the afternoon sessions a synectics session was held during which the problem of getting staff to attend meetings was discussed. Six of the consultants attended the synectics session, which proceeded along the following lines:

First the problem was stated: how to encourage staff to attend meetings.

The word *meetings* was selected as the keyword for an excursion and the world in which the word was taken on an excursion was the *family*.

Examples of meetings suggested included:

- weddings
- funerals
- birthdays
- parties
- Christmas dinners
- golden weddings
- christenings

'Weddings' was selected for further exploration and the group was asked to suggest what it felt like to be a bride or bridegroom. Answers included:

- late
- hassled
- nervous
- anxious
- over-dressed
- putting on a show

- happy
- well organised
- showered with confetti
- watched
- religious experience
- expensive on someone's pocket

The leader felt that the above ideas represented food for thought with respect to the original problem that was posed, but that the line of reasoning was not as productive as he would like. He decided therefore to select another word from the list of meetings for the family. 'Funerals' was taken and the group was asked what it feels like to be at a funeral. Answers included:

- depressed
- intoxicated

- boxed in
- missing a friend

The leader then selected the word 'depressed' and asked what it would take to make someone who was depressed at a funeral not 'depressed'. Answers included:

- someone friendly to talk to
- free drinks
- entertainment

- party atmosphere
- being a beneficiary under a will

Question

Suggest how the session might have continued and concluded.

Busy lines

'What are we going to do about these phone bills,' Sam asked, exasperated by the rising costs. 'Not only are expenses from this source rising out of all proportion but it is becoming increasingly difficult to cope with the number of incoming calls because of the time customers are spending on the phone to us.'

'But is this the real problem', Sally asked. 'Perhaps we ought to think more about it?'

The two of them decided that they ought first to try to define the problem and then to try and think up some ideas. This produced some interesting results. Redefinitions such as:

'How to ensure people have the right knowledge.'
'How to reduce customer calls, or stop them all together.'

However, when conventional brainstorming was used to try and dream up ideas to solve the problem – both as given and as re-defined – no really good answers seemed to be forthcoming.

'What we really need to do is try one of the more adventurous techniques, such as synectics', Sally suggested.

Sam agreed, and the two of them decided to get together a team of people in the offices to generate some ideas.

'Which definition should we take?', Sam asked.

'How about: 'How to reduce customer calls, or stop them all together', Sally suggested.

'OK', said Sam. 'Let's take "reduce" or "reduction" as our keyword and take it for an excursion.'

Questions

1 How might the synectics session continue from the point arrived at in the case.
2 How else might it have developed if a different problem definition had been taken? Illustrate your answer.
3 Compare the kind of solutions you obtain with the two approaches.

Finding a new advertising platform

There is so much clutter surrounding advertising. If you want to get your message across to the target market you would do better to stand on the roof-top of your office in Central London and shout it out to all who pass by. Such is the frustration that many firms now feel about advertising. People just ignore it, look the other way, switch it off (if it is on TV) or hum songs in the car if it is on the radio, yet firms still spend millions of pounds, dollars, euros and rupees to get messages about their products and services in to the media.

Advertising, on the face of it, is wasteful and arguably much of the money spent on it could be put to better use. That, however, is a rather negative way of looking at matters. Advertising messages have to be marketed in the same way that products and services are marketed. Successful products have unique selling features and this is exactly what advertising messages should strive to have as well.

An advertising agency was keen to put the above ideas into practice and was working on a particular campaign for a particular client. The agency decided to use synectics to come up with some insightful ideas. The problem was stated as:

How can the product be advertised in a unique and different way?

The keyword chosen was the word *unique* and an analogy was sought in the world of Nature. The group sought first to think of things which were unique in the world of Nature. Ideas included:

- patterns on butterflies;
- patterns on the bark of trees;
- snowflakes;
- rain streaming down the window pane.

Using the idea of patterns on butterflies the group next sought to use a personal metaphor. They were asked what it would be like to be patterns on butterflies. The following ideas were generated:

- stationary
- multi-coloured
- bright and distinctive
- vivid
- floating on air

Question

Illustrate how the session might continue and conclude.

Coping with stress

'Every time I have to make a presentation I get stressed out', Joanna complained, shaking her ringlets as if to signify that she was throwing off the effects of stress. 'What shall I do?'

'Well let's have a *synectics* session to see if that will produce any ideas', Jan smiled. Jan always smiled, no problem was too difficult for him to consider and solve.

'How do we do that?', Joanna asked.

'Well, first we have to state the problem and then take a word from the problem statement on an excursion.'

'The problem is me and stress', Joanna sighed.

'What about "how to deal with stress when delivering presentations".'

'I think "how to stop feeling sick every time I am under pressure", is better.'

'OK! Let's take the word "pressure" on an excursion. Let's go into the world of cooking. Give me some examples of pressure in the world of cooking.'

'Pressure cooker, getting meals ready for you, crushing garlic, grinding nuts or coffee, making a purée, making bread, squeezing the icing onto a cake, rolling pastry, getting the juice out of apples and oranges, mashing potatoes and parsnips . . .'

'Stop, stop. That's great – now we are getting somewhere. Just let me finish writing all this down', Jan interrupted.

Question

Suggest how the session might continue. Try to gain some useful insights which might help Joanna with her problem.

Fantasies about competition

'Competition is the root of all evil', sighed Wendy.

'Competition is good for business', John retorted. 'That just shows how much you know about business.'

'Well, somehow we have just got to meet the new menace.' Wendy smiled. 'If we don't then it will soon put us out of business.'

'Exactly. So we are going to have to respond to their price cutting strategy somehow', John said seriously.

'Synectics, that is the answer', Wendy grinned. 'Let us have a synectics session. I suggest that we get the team together and have a go at a fantasy excursion.'

'Well, it might work', John said quietly. 'I know, let's take the word competition . . . '

'And find a word associated with it', Wendy interrupted.

'Football, cricket, cup, cigarettes, lighter, fuel', Ben cried out, rising from obscurity in the recesses of the open plan office.

'Right', said John. 'Let's have a weird story about fuel.'

Question

Illustrate how the session might continue. See if you can find any general strategies as a result which might help counter the competition's moves.

chapter
nine

MISCELLANEOUS
IDEATION

INTRODUCTION

There are many ideational techniques and you can of course make up your own. I have just included a few that are not covered elsewhere in the book. These are divided into non-graphical and graphical methods. This chapter considers the non-graphical methods of _scenario writing, scenario day-dreaming, free association, clichés, proverbs and maxims, suggestion boxes, exhibits and competitions, storyboarding_ and _story writing_. Graphical methods described, illustrated and discussed include _vision building, symbolic representation, mind maps, fishbone diagram_ and _Lotus Blossom_.

SUGGESTION BOX, EXHIBITS AND COMPETITIONS

Suggestion box

Suggestion box systems are usually slow in generating ideas but give everyone in the organisation a chance to contribute. Employees provide suggestions using either a special form or simply by writing ideas on pieces of paper and putting them into the box. One disadvantage of the method is that suggestion approval is subject to rather arbitrary decisions by managers who may not understand anything about the problem the idea is supposed to deal with. The biggest difficulty with suggestion boxes is not the concept, but how the concept is managed. The power of a suggestion box is enhanced by a quick and objective response.

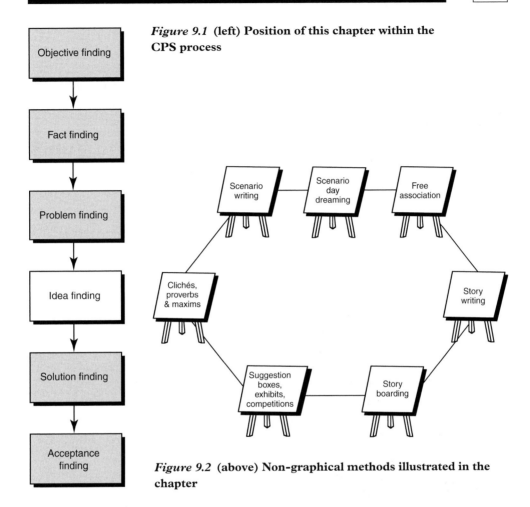

Figure 9.1 (left) Position of this chapter within the CPS process

Figure 9.2 (above) Non-graphical methods illustrated in the chapter

Suggestion exhibits

This is a process whereby people can bring their suggestions, ideas and new inventions for all to see. The organisation provides a display area and provides time for this purpose. It is most suited to a manufacturing or technical oriented company, but other kinds of business and organisations might be able to use the system to advantage.

Suggestion competitions

Management asks departments or other organisational sub-units to make suggestions. Each unit reports the number of suggestions they make and posts them each week or month on a wall chart in a public area. What is reported is the number of ideas. Names are not used. Variations include rewarding the best idea each month or week, or an award may be given to the group of people having 100 per cent participation.

CLICHÉS, PROVERBS AND MAXIMS

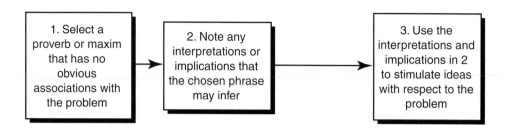

Figure 9.3 **Clichés, proverbs and maxims**

1 Select a proverb or maxim that has no obvious associations with the problem.
2 Note any interpretations or implications that the chosen phrase may infer.
3 Use the interpretations and implications in 2 to stimulate ideas with respect to the problem.

Suppose the problem concerns getting employees to be more positive in their attitude to adopting new working practices.

First proverb/maxim: *If the shoe fits wear it.*

Implications

1 Try a shoe before you buy it.
2 You buy a new shoe when your old ones are no longer fashionable or are worn out.
3 Buy a shoe which is of quality regardless of its price or label.
4 If a shoe does not fit then throw it away.

Interpretations

1 Make sure people will respond to the company's needs by testing their suitability first.
2 Point out to people that they need to adapt to the changing needs of the times and that it is in their own best interest to do so.
3 Make sure that people adopt the new practices and then be prepared to pay the price whatever it costs to do so.
4 Fire people that are not co-operating and hire new personnel.

The key seems to be to recruit the right people who find new methods challenging and interesting.

Example

PROBLEM: how to familiarise the company's staff with computers and make them more productive.

STIMULUS: when the cat's away the mouse will play.

Interpretations

- mice are afraid of the cat;
- why are the mice afraid of the cat?;
- the mice play often;
- how far away does the cat go before the mice start to play?;
- the mice take advantage of the fact that the cat is away.

Implications for the problem

- Employees are afraid of computers.
- How can we reduce fear in the employees?
- When the boss is away the employees will play around and not try to familiarise themselves with the computers.
- Managers must encourage the employees to work with the computers.

Ideas

Provide games etc. to enable the employees to play with their computers and gain familiarity with them. This should dispel the fear.

STORYBOARDING

Walt Disney and his staff developed a storyboard system in 1928 to help with cartoon animation. Disney wanted to achieve full animation, and for this he needed to produce an enormous number of drawings. Managing the thousands of drawings and the progress of a project was nearly impossible, so Disney had his artists pin up their drawings on the studio walls. This way, progress could be checked, and scenes added and discarded with ease.

Storyboarding is like taking your thoughts along with the thoughts of others and spreading them out on a wall as you work on a project or solve a problem. When you put ideas up on storyboards, you begin to see interconnections, how one idea relates to another, and how all the pieces come together. Once the ideas start flowing people 'hitch-hike' onto other ideas. Software programs are now available such as Corkboard (Macintosh).

One starts with a topic card, and placed under the topic card are header cards containing general points, categories, considerations, etc. that will come up. Under the header cards one puts sub-heading cards containing the ideas that fall under each header; they're the details/ideas generated in the creative thinking session, ideas that develop or support the headers.

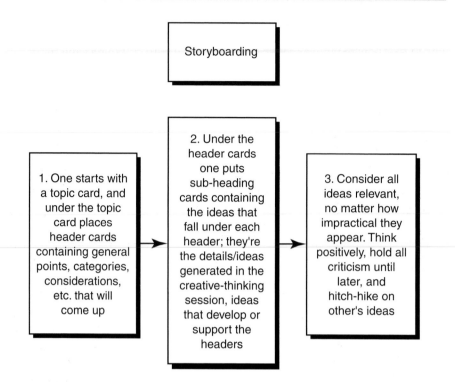

Figure 9.4 **Storyboarding**

Storyboarding works well in group sessions. There are four major types: Planning, Ideas, Communication and Organisation storyboards. During a storyboarding session, consider all ideas relevant, no matter how impractical they appear. Think positively, hold all criticism until later, and hitch-hike on other's ideas.

SCENARIO WRITING

This is a tool developed and used originally in long term planning and technological forecasting. It is a particularly useful method for speculating on the likelihood of new paradigm shifts.

Scenario writing is a method of looking ahead and forces an organisation to be receptive to the need for change and creative thinking. It is an experience which involves considering new possibilities and opening up one's mind to consider what might happen.

The method involves all members of a team of co-workers and requires a leader or facilitator who introduces and co-ordinates sessions and who has the responsibility for producing a final report. Members of the team are referred to as scenario writers and each member is usually an expert in his or her own field. One needs to make sure that there are experts in the group whose expertise is relevant to the problem under study.

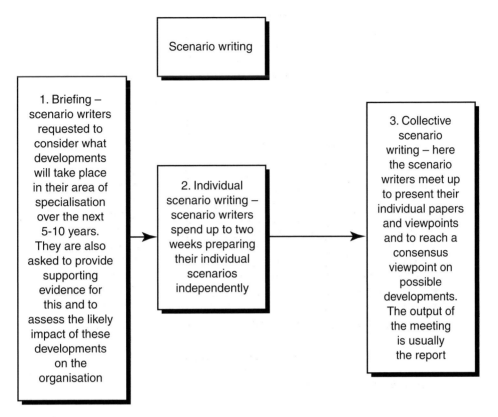

Figure 9.5 **Scenario writing**

At the start of the exercise the scenario writers are briefed with the task of considering the developments in their area of expertise over the next 5–10 years. When they have done this individually they are brought together under the guidance of a leader to examine the situation collectively. Participants need to be reminded that they should be tolerant of the views of others because a consensus of informed opinion has to be reached.

The procedure adopted is as follows:

1 Briefing – here the scenario writers are requested to consider what developments will take place in their area of specialisation over the next 5–10 years. They are also asked to provide supporting evidence for this and to assess the likely impact of these developments on the organisation (see the cross-impact matrix on p. 182).
2 Individual scenario writing – scenario writers spend up to two weeks preparing their individual scenarios independently.
3 Collective scenario writing – here the scenario writers meet up to present their individual papers and viewpoints and to reach a consensus viewpoint on possible developments. The output of the meeting is usually the report.

Scenario writing can be extremely useful and productive where the situation under review is a very complex one; it is, however, extremely time consuming.

CROSS-IMPACT MATRIX

	Existing	Product Planned	Possible	Total
Environment	6	12	14	32
Technology	–2	3	2	3
Regulation	1	2	3	6
Economic	2	2	3	7
Cultural	2	2	3	7
Demographic	3	3	3	9
Market	6	2	–2	6
Europe	3	3	–2	4
Far East	3	–1	0	2
Competitor	2	0	–8	–6
Alpha	1	0	–4	–3
Beta	1	0	–4	–3
Customer	–5	6	6	7
Wholesalers	–3	3	3	3
Large Retailers	–2	3	3	4
Total	9	20	10	39

CROSS-IMPACT ANALYSIS

One of the first things one has to do in strategy formulation at any level in an establishment is to examine how the organisation relates to the environments around it. In particular one must focus on the impact that these environments can have on the enterprise's future prosperity.

Cross-impact analysis is a technique that helps in examining the impact that a mixture of external threats and opportunities can have on the undertakings of an organisation. In implementing the technique one has to obtain data from a range of sources, including customers, competitors, the market and the environment. The procedure involves assessing the impact that changes or trends in these factors are likely to have on present, proposed or potential activities of the organisation. Anything that threatens the prosperity of the organisation is viewed as having a negative effect on the establishment, while opportunities are reasoned to have positive effects.

One records the various impacts on a grid and on a scale ranging from +4 to –4, where 0 specifies a lack of impact. The sum of various extraneous threats and opportunities on each one of the identified business/organisational activities is then noted. In addition the total scores of opportunities and threats facing each activity of the organisation are recorded. All ratings are a matter of the subjective opinions of executives.

Although scenario writing is a formal procedure it is still speculative in nature since it aims to predict the future of an organisation, thus aiding the strategic planning process. The exercise can be conducted over a fairly lengthy time period (say two weeks) for its participants have to prepare a written report explaining their view of the future. The participants will be experts on the various functions of the organisation. The benefits of bringing together experts from various functions enable an integrated vision of the future to be examined with documentary evidence to support each argument. An awareness of the future environment (internal and external) and the change which may take place in it will provoke more creative responses to current situations.

SCENARIO DAY-DREAMING

Like scenario writing this method also looks into the future and tries to assess the impact that trend will have on the organisation. It is, however, less formal in its approach and it is not the custom and practice to produce a report. It is usual for the entire process to take up only a couple of days and is an ideal activity for an 'away day' venue, provided there are at least two away days available.

Scenario day-dreamers are not expected to substantiate their contributions. The purpose is to stimulate people's imaginations to think in the broader context and to consider more unusual ideas. A good group size is 8–10 people, but of course much depends on the size of the organisation and the complexity of its business.

Again there is a leader or facilitator whose role it is to plan the sessions in detail, advise on the selection of participants, brief the participants about the sessions, lead the sessions and help summarise the conclusions which are reached. Minutes of the session also need to be taken by someone. The procedure for the session is summarised below.

Preparation

The nature of the proceedings are explained.

The scenario day-dreaming session described:

1 The session has to be divided into a beginning, a middle and an end.
2 It is helpful to have a warm-up session prior to the main session.
3 The first step is to identify the various factors that are likely to affect the future of the organisation. These factors usually reflect aspects of the environment such as economic trends, cost of commodities, political and governmental policies, changes in demography, technology, social structure, consumer requirements and competitive activity.
4 The main factors should be summarised on a flip chart and possibly entered into a cross-impact matrix to indicate their importance.
5 Those present are then split into groups and each group is given several of the factors to consider in depth and arrive at a future scenario for each

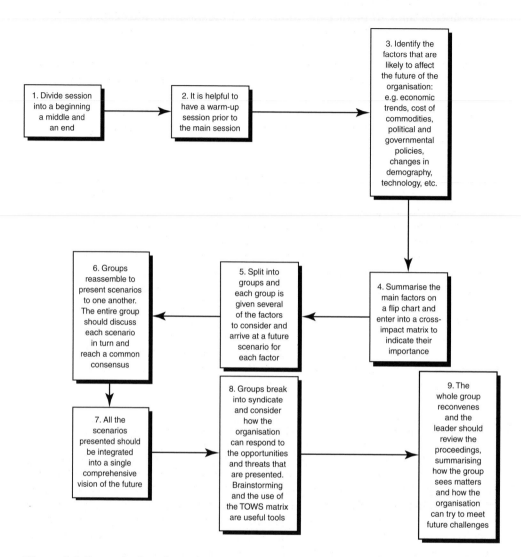

Figure 9.6 **Scenario day-dreaming**

of them. Group members should have the expertise to be able to scenario day-dream effectively for the factors they have been allocated. Roughly half an hour per scenario should be taken.

6 Groups should then reassemble to present their scenarios to one another. The entire group should discuss each scenario in turn and reach a common consensus.

7 All the scenarios presented should be integrated into a single comprehensive vision of the future.

8 Groups break into syndicate again and consider how the organisation

Table 9.1 **The TOWS matrix**

	Strengths	*Weaknesses*
Opportunities	Maximise on strengths and opportunities	Maximise on opportunities, minimise on weaknesses
Threats	Maximise on strengths, minimise on threats	Minimise on weaknesses, minimise on threats

can respond to the opportunities and threats that are presented. Brainstorming and the use of the TOWS matrix (see Table 9.1) are useful tools to use at this point.

The TOWS matrix presents a mechanism for facilitating the linkages between company strengths/weaknesses and threats and opportunities in the environment. It also provides a framework for identifying and formulating strategies. Opportunities, threats, strengths and weaknesses have to be identified and listed in the matrix. Next, various combinations of opportunities and strengths, opportunities and weaknesses, threats and strengths, and weaknesses and threats are examined in order to generate possible strategies. It should be observed that in generating strategies one seeks to maximise on strengths and opportunities and minimise on weaknesses and threats. Brainstorming may be used effectively in helping to identify factors and generate strategies.

SWOT ANALYSIS AND THE TOWS MATRIX

SWOT analysis is a technique specifically designed to help with the identification of suitable business strategies for an organisation to follow. It involves specifying and relating organisational strengths and weaknesses and environmental opportunities and threats. In practice this is often an activity that is not carried out well. It is all too easy, having identified all the important points, not to know what to do with the data generated. Although intended as a mechanism to explain strategy rather than to facilitate its generation, the TOWS matrix (Weihrich, 1982) presents a mechanism for facilitating linkages and presents a framework for identifying and formulating strategies. Implementing the TOWS matrix requires that the following steps are followed:

1 Pin-point and assess the impact of environmental factors – economic, political, demographic, products and technology, market and competition – on the organisation.
2 Make a prognosis about the future.
3 Undertake an assessment of 'strengths and weaknesses' in terms of management and organisation, operations, finance and marketing.
4 Develop strategy options.

Working systematically through this process enables internal and external factors to be entered on a grid and different combinations to be studied. For example, the entry to one cell of the grid could involve maximising opportunities and maximising strengths. This would amount to putting together at least one strength and one opportunity to produce a strategy that capitalises upon this combination.

THE TOWS MATRIX

Product: Plastic Bags

	Strengths	Weaknesses
	1 Brand name 2 Distribution 3 Low costs	1 Exports 2 Sales force
Opportunities 1 Need for robust rubbish disposal bags 2 European markets 3 Scented bin-liners	Use existing distribution and brand name to market scented bin-liners (S1, S2, O3)	Strengthen sales force and export skills. Look to European markets (W1, W2, O3)
Threats 1 Substitute materials 2 Imports	Capitalize on brand name, distribution, and low costs to meet competition from imports (S1, S2, S3, T2)	Develop capability in substitute materials particularly for products that can be sold to export markets (T1, W1)

Any kind of organisational unit can benefit from this type of analysis as well as any situation that involves strategic decision making. Originally, Weihrich (1982) illustrated a conceptual application of the TOWS matrix to the strategic dilemma facing Volkswagen in the USA during the 1970s. His account demonstrated how the TOWS matrix could be used as a structuring device for analysing strategic problems. For the writer, this raised the interesting question of whether the use of the TOWS matrix could lead to the identification of appropriate strategies for an organisation. In pursuing this question the writer has examined over fifty cases in which the TOWS matrix has been employed in commercial organisations. In all of these cases the users of the technique have felt that the method has enabled them to gain a deeper insight into the process of strategy formulation, has helped to structure their thinking, and has often enabled them to come up with good new strategic ideas.

9 The whole group reconvenes and the leader should review the proceedings, summarising how the group sees matters and how the organisation can try to meet future challenges.

BIONICS

This is a special application of analogies and involves looking for stimulation in similar objects, products and processes. The search is usually restricted to examining biological and botanical systems using the argument that Nature provides clues with regard to how to solve problems because it has itself solved many such problems.

Examples of where the method has resulted in useful applications include the Sidewinder heat-seeking missile (based on the temperature-sensing organs of a rattlesnake) and Velcro (based on the idea of burdock seeds which tend to cling to one clothes if blown into contact with them – see pp. 53–4). The latter have minute hooks attached to them and this is why they tend to cling to clothes. Velcro uses this same principle and provides a very effective fastening mechanism to supplement or even replace a zip or other fastener on clothing.

Nature, of course, does not always provide the right kind of guidance, so care has to be exercised in using bionics. Many years were spent in trying to mimic the wing flapping movements of birds before flight was eventually achieved using the principle of the fixed wing.

TWO WORDS

The two words technique employs forced relationships and related problem stimuli to generate ideas. The stimuli are obtained from examining different combinations of alternative descriptions of two keywords in the problem statement. The rationale behind this approach is that the phrasing of the initial problem statement may be limited in terms of its ability to provoke certain types of ideas. By restating the problem using alternative meanings the technique will provide new perspectives that will give rise to new ideas. As suggested by Olson (1980), this involves the following steps:

1 Select two words (a verb and a noun) from the problem statement.
2 List alternative meanings for each of the keywords.
3 Select the first word from the first list and combine it with the first word from the second list.
4 Using this combination as a stimulus write down any ideas suggested.
5 Combine the first word from the first list with the second word from the second list and record any ideas suggested by this combination.
6 Continue combining words in the above manner until all possible combinations have been exhausted.

Finally, different two-word combinations are examined for possible idea stimulation.

Example

How to ensure a high level of customer service:

1   ensure and service

2

ensure	*service*
assure	aid
clinch	assistance
confirm	help
guarantee	effort
guard	labour
protect	benefit
safeguard	utility
secure	wear

3

assure	aid
assure	assistance
assure	help
etc.	

4–6   *assure assistance*: assure customers that the firm is always available to help with problems

assure effort: inform customers that the utmost effort will always be expended to ensure customer satisfaction, etc.

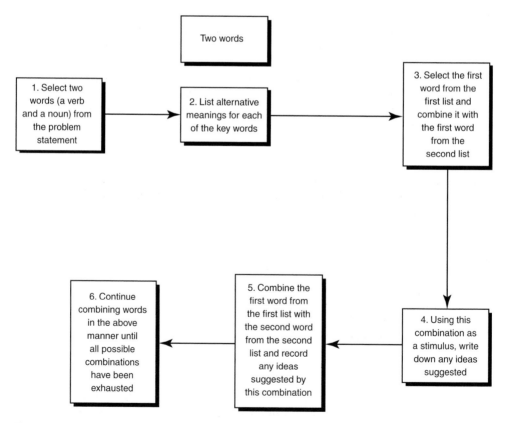

Figure 9.7 **Two words**

The major strength of the two-word technique is that it provides a variety of new problem perspectives – any one of which might prompt a high quality solution. It is also very easy to use and takes up very little time.

FREE ASSOCIATION

Of all the idea generating techniques this is one of the simplest. One idea is used to generate another, which is then used to produce a third, and so on. There are two forms of free association:

- *Unstructured free association*

Here ideas are listed as they naturally occur and where one idea then leads to another. It is very similar to classical brainstorming.

- *Structured free association*

Here the procedure adopted attempts to increase the relevance of ideas to a problem. The procedure adopted is as follows:

1 A symbol – word, number, object, condition – that is directly related to the problem is drawn or otherwise recorded.
2 Whatever is suggested by the first step, whether or not it seems relevant to the problem, is recorded.
3 Step 2 is repeated until all possible associations have been listed.
4 Associations that seem most relevant to the problem are selected from the list.
5 The associations selected at stage 4 are used to develop and produce ideas that appear capable of solving the problem. If the first effort does not produce useful insights then it is repeated using another symbol as the starting point – i.e. one recommences at stage 1.

Example

A hotel wants to improve the facilities and services it offers to holidaying guests and is looking for ideas. It uses structured free association in the following way to gain new insights.

1   Stimulus word: history

2–3 Thoughts recorded:
     visits to local museums and art galleries
     tours of local historical sites
     films and videos about local history
     library of books and documents on history round about
     antiques and collectors fairs
     displays

4   Antiques/collectors fairs and displays

5   Hold weekly antique/collectors' fairs for the benefit of the paying guests and outsiders. Also mount permanent displays of antique/collectors' items which might be of interest to visitors.

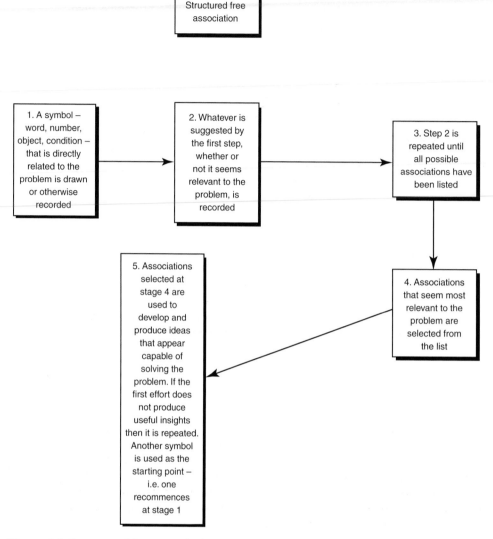

Figure 9.8 **Structured free association**

STORY WRITING

The technique, as the name suggests, involves writing a highly imaginative fictional story of, say, a few hundred words, and then relating it to the problem in hand. The story is then examined closely and major principles, themes, expressions, thoughts, objects, etc. are listed separately. A long story can of course take considerable time to analyse for its relevance to a problem. On the other hand, of course, a very short story may not be rich enough in ideas to stimulate thought with respect to the problem under consideration.

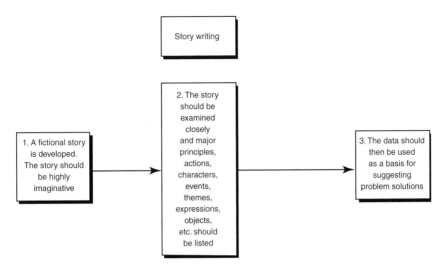

Figure 9.9 **Story writing**

The routine may be carried out in various ways. One such approach is the round robin story and involves a group of people. Each member of the group contributes a line in the story writing process. An alternative might be for one person to write the story, with the remainder of the group then working on its analysis and interpretation.

Example

PROBLEM

The firm in question produces alcoholic beverages and its position in the market has been threatened by changes in consumer tastes and a change in the taxation system, both of which have encouraged the entry of imported drinks. The firm produces traditional local drinks which are similar to whisky and brandy. The problem is that the firm feels that it has lost its competitive advantage and wants to regain its former position. It is not sure, however, what strategy it would be best to adopt.

THE STORY

Shading his eyes with his right hand, the Colonel surveyed the distant mountains. He could just about pick out the unfamiliar, narrow valleys seeming like tiny scars on the distant landscape. He observed his demoralised troops going about their routine chores drenched in sweat under the blistering sun. The town seemed quite close, glinting white through the haze, and as he watched he perceived an enemy soldier waving a white flag drawing near. He was a messenger from the town's mayor asking to meet with the Colonel because, as he said, they were tired of the siege. Before nightfall the Colonel met with the town's mayor and all was settled. Later, the Colonel slept soundly. The plan of the battle lay on the table and by its side a bunch of flowers. The Colonel had put his gun point next to the flowers as a sign of peace. He felt good when he awoke.

SOME POINTS

1 demoralised troops;	5 tired of the siege;
2 unfamiliar narrow valleys;	6 bunch of flowers at the gun point;
3 a message from the mayor;	7 plan of the battle.
4 asking to meet;	

INTERPRETATIONS FOR IDEA GENERATION

1 demotivated sales force and other staff – need to find some way of motivating them;
2 need to explore new segments of the market which have neglected until now;
3 should look out for those competitors who are in the same boat and who have been in the business for a long time;
4 need has arisen to make business alliance with competitors identified in 4, above;
5 find an appropriate opportunity to move ahead in the market when others have started to make mistakes;
6 long term interests are the priority;
7 establish superiority in quality and special features of your products.

The firm eventually merged with a competitor which had good access to some of the market segments. Together they worked in marketing new brands, making an issue of the quality of the product and focusing on the purity of the water and special ingredients that were used to give it its own special flavour.

What other ideas might have come from the story?

MIND MAP

Mind maps can be drawn by hand and this is the quickest way to perform the task. However, there are advantages in using mind mapping software. Some of the better software includes Inspiration, Mind Maps Plus, Mind Mapper and Mindman (see Chapter 12).

Mind mapping is a graphical means of taking or making notes. Graphical noting has been used since the dawn of humankind – early cave paintings and Egyptian hieroglyphics being obvious examples. In more modern times, process engineers and concept-oriented people have used flow charts and process diagrams to develop and explain their trains of thought and procedural flow (Figure 9.12).

The structure of the Mind Map allows for making intuitive associations, and capturing them within the 'notes' structure. Mind maps use a central image to connote the overall theme, keywords, colours, codes and symbols. Buzan (1994), who synthesised graphic noting techniques and evolved them into modern mind mapping, writes:

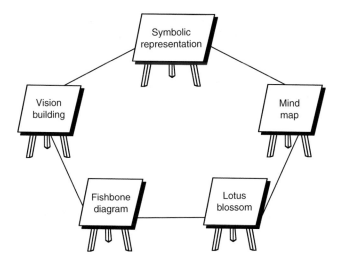

Figure 9.10 **Overview of graphical methods illustrated in the chapter**

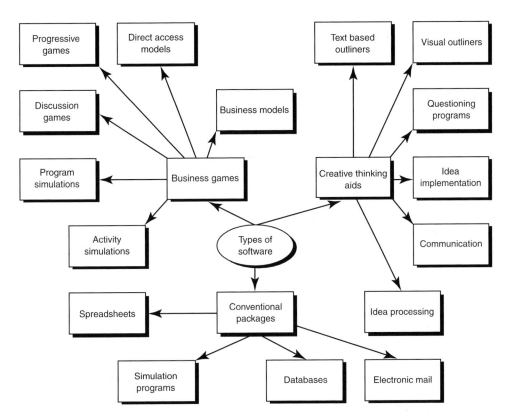

Figure 9.11 **Mind map showing the type of computer software that can be used in creative problem solving**

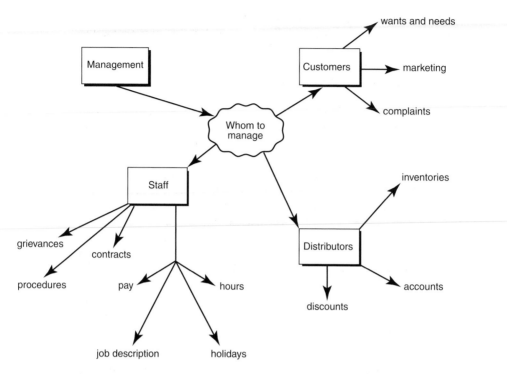

Figure 9.12 **Mind map of whom to manage**

The Mind Map can be applied to every aspect of life where improved learning and clearer thinking will enhance human performance. The Mind Map has four essential characteristics:

(a) The subject of attention is crystallized in a central image.
(b) The main themes of the subject radiate from the central image as branches.
(c) Branches comprise a key image or keyword printed on an associated line. Topics of lesser importance are also represented as branches attached to higher level branches.
(d) The branches form a connected nodal structure.

(Buzan, 1994: 59)

Gelb (1988) offers seven guidelines to effective mind mapping:

1 Start the map by drawing a picture of the topic in the centre of the paper.
2 Use keywords.
3 Connect the words with lines radiating out from the central image.
4 Print the keywords.
5 Print one keyword per line.
6 Use colours, pictures and codes for emphasis.
7 Free-associate, then organise.

To appreciate why the mind mapping process works as well as it does, one has to go back to how the brain functions. The left side of the brain has been shown to process information in a linear/sequential fashion – analysing the various parts that make up the whole. The right side of the brain, on the other hand, processes concepts, patterns, and relationships. The right side synthesises while the left side analyses.

Mind mapping uses both sides of the brain. It allows the mapper to build out ideas by expanding the branches. Entering new ideas is as easy as adding another branch to either the central theme or to one of the other main branches. Information presented later in the discussion or book can easily be related to a concept that was developed early in the programme by extending the branch. Once completed the mind map presents the concepts and relationships, along with the keywords that will trigger memory.

One of the central concepts of mind mapping is the use of keywords. Keywords are the seeds of intuitive association. They are easy to create and much easier to remember and recall than full sentences. The use of keywords also forces our creative brain to add the context (the rest of the story) to the keyword – in its own words or pictures. The emphasis must be on concepts and not on isolated facts. The use of keywords can help us to conceptualise. Keywords tend to be strong nouns or verbs. They are words that evoke strong images that can trigger our contextual recall.

Buzan (1991) writes:

> Every word is 'multi-ordinate', which simply means that each word is like a little center on which there are many, many little hooks. Each hook can attach to other words to give both words in the new pair slightly different meanings. For example the word 'run' can be hooked quite differently in 'run like hell' and 'her stocking has a run in it'.

LOTUS BLOSSOM TECHNIQUE

This method starts with a central theme or problem and works outward, using ever-widening circles or 'petals' (shown as stars in Figure 9.13). Central themes lead to ideas that themselves become central themes, and so on. The unfolding themes trigger new ideas and new themes.

1 Copy the diagram shown in Figure 9.13.
2 Write your central theme or problem in the diagram's centre.
3 Think of related ideas or applications and write them in the surrounding stars. For instance, one company's central theme was 'establishing a creative climate'. They surrounded this statement in the central box with: 'offer idea contests', 'create a stimulating environment', 'have creative-thinking meetings', 'generate ways to "get out of the mould"', 'create a positive attitude', 'establish a creative-idea committee', 'make work fun', and 'expand the meaning of work'.
4 Use the ideas written in each of the eight surrounding stars as the central themes for another eight ideas. (New layer of stars not shown in Figure 9.13.)

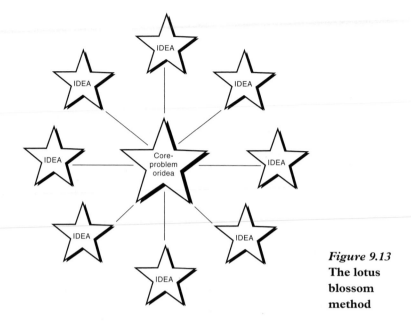

Figure 9.13
The lotus blossom method

5 Try to think of eight new ideas involving the new central theme, and write them in the stars surrounding it. Use the idea stimulators to help you generate ideas. Fill out as many stars as you can.
6 Continue the process until you've completed as much of the diagram as you can.
7 Evaluate the ideas.

FISHBONE DIAGRAM

The fishbone diagram was proposed by Professor Ishikawa of Tokyo University (Majaro, 1991). The diagram depicts all possible causes contributing to a problem, or can be used as shown in the illustration to depict all factors relating to a problem or concept. The shape of the diagram resembles that of a fishbone structure – hence its name.

To draw the diagram one first places the problem under consideration (or the topic of interest) at the 'head' end. All possible causes of the problem or principal features of the concept are inserted at the end of the bones and at 45 degrees to the backbone. Further breakdowns of the causes or features are listed on additional branches running off those already inserted at 45 degrees to the backbone.

Having completed the diagram the group uses it as a discussion vehicle and it is customary to consider the points that are raised in ascending order of complexity, starting with the simplest relationships.

In the example diagram (Figure 9.14) we see that the concept under study is the design for a new car. The diagram picks out the main features of the car and indicates the specifications for each feature. Of course, in

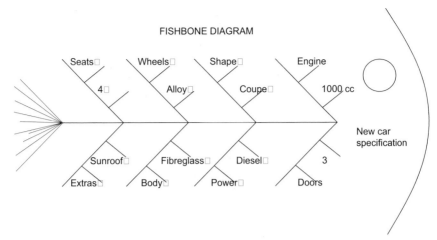

Figure 9.14 **Fishbone diagram**

practice such a diagram would be much larger and contain many more features and their corresponding specifications.

The fishbone diagram encourages one to look at every aspect of a problem or a topic of interest and to highlight the various relationships along with the relative importance of its various parts. It also helps to establish a logical sequence for handling various parts of a problem in a systematic way and enables one to visualise the parts within the whole.

VISION BUILDING

Visions play an important part in how we conduct our life. A vision is a wish of what we want to happen. In some cultures it is believed that by making a wish that wish will come true, and day-dreaming is an excellent form of visionalising. Vision building has become an effective means for individuals and organisations to set and achieve goals. The vision is believed to reinforce and reorient efforts to create and achieve organisational goals (see Parker, 1990; Saxberg, 1993). Forsth and Nordvik (1995) describe a method for building visions in organisations. An important aspect of this method is that communication is achieved through visual pictures. They suggest that one needs to build up a 'picture language' comprising not less than 50 and not more than 200 pictures. The pictures should evoke pleasant feelings rather than unpleasant ones. Roughly 25 per cent of the pictures used in a session should relate directly to the kind of vision being built. Examples include people working or playing together, or animals/flowers (these symbolise the organisation). Another 25 per cent might represent emotional states which are relevant to the vision – pictures symbolising happiness, stability, change, etc. Yet another 25 per cent of the pictures should be highly stimulating – pictures using strange colours, unusual forms or even amusing pictures. The final quarter should comprise a mixed bag of pictures of all kinds. Photographs and artwork may be used.

In essence a group of individuals from an organisation are invited to browse the pictures and see if they can relate the symbolism of whichever pictures take their fancy to their own organisations. Through subsequent group discussion in which they share their own experiences of the pictures, they are able to create a group vision for the company.

SYMBOLIC REPRESENTATION

One constructs a diagram or picture of a problem or situation with the use of symbols (see Van Gundy, [1981] 1988; Hicks, 1991). It may be useful to generate a set of symbols which can be used on a regular basis by those involved in the creative problem solving sessions. Users of this method will then quickly learn the meaning of the symbols, be able to develop the list of easily understood and recognised symbols and quickly build up complex pictures of the problem situation.

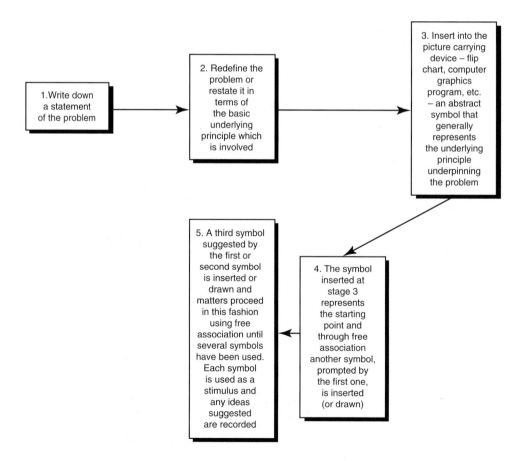

Figure 9.15 **Symbolic representation**

Figure 9.16 **Symbols that can be used in pictures**

Figure 9.17 **A problem in symbols**

The steps are as follows:
1 Write down a statement of the problem.
2 Redefine the problem or restate it in terms of the basic underlying principle which is involved.
3 Insert into the picture carrying device – flip chart, computer graphics program, etc. – an abstract symbol that generally represents the underlying principle underpinning the problem.
4 The symbol inserted at stage 3 represents the starting point and through free association another symbol, prompted by the first one, is inserted (or drawn).
5 A third symbol suggested by the first or second symbol is inserted or drawn and matters proceed in this fashion using free association until several symbols have been used. Each symbol is used as a stimulus and any ideas suggested are recorded.

In the problem depicted in the symbols shown in Figure 9.17, the alarm bells are sounding at the factory because there is a problem. The key seems to be to cut out as much of the paperwork at the factory as possible so that people can get on with the job of making things.

QUESTIONS

1 Use the story writing technique to come up with ideas on how to deal with a difficult person at work.

2 Using any problem of your own choice, illustrate how you might try to solve this problem with the help of *either* a mind map *or* the story-writing technique.

3 Imagine you have the task of managing the production of one of Gilbert and Sullivan's operettas. Use the technique of storyboarding to record your ideas on planning, organising and communicating your ideas on the production to all parties who will be associated with the project (i.e. participants, sponsors and potential audiences).

4 Use the Lotus Blossom method on a problem of your own choice.

5 Evaluate the usefulness of bionics as a means of generating insights. Provide some illustrations of how it might be applied on different kinds of problems.

6 Illustrate the use of the two-word technique on a problem of your own choosing.

7 What is free association? Illustrate how it might be used in helping to come up with solving water shortage problems during the summer or dry season.

8 Construct a fishbone diagram to sketch out the relevant factors impinging on a problem of your own choice.

9 Evaluate the usefulness of suggestion boxes, exhibits and competitions.

10 Show how you would apply the technique of clichés, proverbs and maxims in coming up with insights concerning the following problems:

(a) How to improve efficiency in the warehouse.
(b) How to reduce lost time through accidents in the office.
(c) How to make the most of the time available in meetings.
(d) How to reduce the impact of organisational politics on decision making.
(e) How to avoid making major errors when setting down policy.

11 Indicate how you would use vision building as a technique in solving different types of business problems. Are there any limitations? Explain.

12 When might an organisation use scenario writing? What are its major limitations?

13 How would you use scenario day-dreaming to come up with ideas about the strategic direction a company should be taking?

14 Use the TOWS matrix to identify SWOT for a business with which you are familiar. What kind of strategies might you formulate for each cell in the TOWS matrix. Be specific by giving example strategies.

15 Apply the cross-impact matrix to a situation of your own choice. How does it help identify which factors are likely to be important in influencing future operations of the organisation?

16 Develop a mind map to help you plan a forthcoming seminar on the 'future of work'.

17 Employ the Lotus Blossom method to find ways of making yourself more efficient at work.

18 Use the fishbone diagram to examine a problem of your own choice.

19 Suggest how vision building might be employed in helping to sort out the strategic mission of an organisation.

20 How might symbolic representation be used in a manufacturing company that wants to improve its efficiency in distributing its products to wholesalers and other distributors in the electrical white goods industry?

CASES

Strategy formulation with mind maps

The team was exploring what seemed to be the best overall marketing strategy to adopt. As part of its strategy-making the firm decided to record in a mind map, all statements that it could think of that were relevant to the problem in hand (Figure 9.18). Each person wrote down an account of the

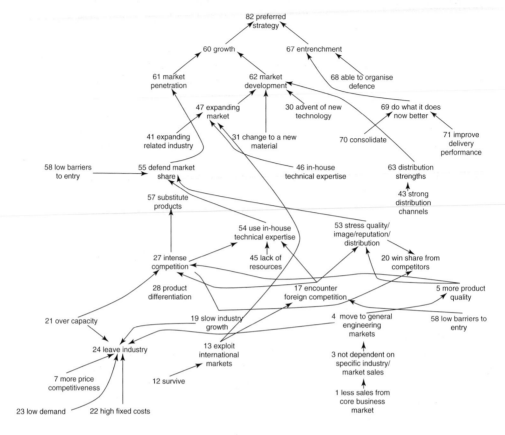

Figure 9.18 **Cognitive map**

situation and factors affecting the situation. The accounts were then analysed for statements thought to have some bearing on the outcome – i.e. choosing a strategy. Just over eighty such statements were collected and were entered into the mind-map *concepts*. When all the data had been entered the various relationships that existed in the map were examined. In particular the *consequences* of a statement and the *explanation* for a statement were examined.

The selected strategy option in this case was a combination of growth and entrenchment.

Question

Can you suggest why the executives might have reached this decision?

The conference

John is organising a creativity and innovation conference to be held in Brussels. It is very important that he records all the things that he has to do, but, inevitably, when he draws up lists of things to do he leaves important things out. He is expecting over 500 delegates to the conference, which he plans to hold at one of the city-centre hotels. In addition to the actual conference itself there is the matter of guest speakers to sort out, plus their transport from different parts of the world – not to mention their accommodation. Many of the guest speakers require special equipment, such as large screen TVs , video-player, computer and projection panel, as well as the basic things like flip charts, markers, overhead projector, etc. Then there are the meals, the paperwork, the bound copies of the proceedings, and of course the helpers who are going to make the conference run smoothly.

John does not know where to start, but someone has told him that mind maps can be very useful in such an instance.

Question

Produce a mind map of the kind that you think would be helpful to John in this instance.

Problem solving with symbols

'Everything is in a mess. Orders are not sent out on time. There are too many accounts receivable overdue. We haven't enough secretaries in the typing pool. There is grumbling in the warehouse about overtime payments. Sales are declining and we have cash-flow problems. All this and now we have a product liability case on our hands.' The MD raised his hands in exasperation at his regular meeting with the Chairman and the other directors.

'I heard Rumbles is entering the market with a new product. I bet it passed every standard there is', the Chairman sneered.

'Well I feel that my time has come to resign', the MD spoke solemnly. 'We probably can get out of this product liability mess by hiring a good lawyer, but I feel that I am not getting all the backing I need from my colleagues on the board and in the middle management ranks to enable me to keep the company on an even keel. It's true Rumbles are going to get a leg up with their new product. I can't see any way in which this company can match it. I have been saying for years that we need specialist marketers in the organisation, as well as good R&D people. We certainly can create opportunities for ourselves, but we cannot market ourselves or our products and so exploit those opportunities to the full. Our distributors are just fed up with the poor level of service we offer them. They expect us to advertise and pull the product through to their customers – but is that really our job? I've been grappling with this problem for years and still we haven't got anywhere. Somewhere along the line there has been a loss of rapport with the middlemen.'

'I thought it was the MD's job to market the product!', the Chairman exclaimed. 'It is certainly not a job for any of us. We don't have any sales experience.'

'Marketing isn't selling. How many times do I have to spell it out to you. We need marketers not sales people. We are in an industry where the customer is king and we have to serve the customers' interests. This is precisely what we are not doing at the moment. The R&D team think all they have to do is dream up some new ideas for improving products and everything else will take care of itself. As long as you put a rein on the expenses we can incur for staffing I cannot obtain a good marketing team.'

'You have a budget. You can spend the money how you like!', the Chairman retorted.

'But I can't', the MD replied. 'Most of the budget is spent on fire-fighting the problems created by the inadequacies of the previous budget. I am never in the position where I can actually say "now I can plan".'

'Stuff and nonsense', growled the Chairman. 'You have always had a free rein.'

Question

Construct a rich picture to illustrate the problems, threats, opportunities, etc. that appear to exist in the company and the time of the reported conversation.

A tall story

'If you are all sitting comfortably then I will begin.' Andrea drew her breath.

'There was a gnome who lived not far from a railway bridge. The bridge was a dark and damp place and people said that a troll named Zeino lived under the bridge. The gnome was a happy go lucky fellow and every day he would go to market on the other side of the railway line. He would not pass under the bridge, however, because he was afraid of the troll. People said that the troll was a horrible creature who used to eat all his victims alive and spit their bones at passing railway trains.

'One sunny morning the gnome set off for the market. He took a road through the woods which led him to a level crossing over the railway. In that way he avoided the need to pass under the bridge. As he walked along the gnome whistled a happy tune and thought about all the nice things he would see at the market. Just as he was about to reach the end of the clearing he heard the sound of running feet behind him. Turning round he saw the most beautiful young woman that can ever have lived. She had fair hair and blue eyes and cried out to him to stop.

'"I am a fairy princess", she cried. "Please help me find my way home from this dark wood." The gnome stopped and said to the young woman: "Well that is really very easy, all you have to do is follow me for I am going to the market."

'At that moment, Zeino the troll appeared from behind a tree. He bared his teeth and chuckled: "Ah, ah! A gnome for dinner and a princess for supper. What a lucky troll am I!" But the fairy princess waved her wand,

and behold it became a fire-breathing dragon. With one deep breath the dragon burned the troll to a cinder and the princess and the gnome lived happily ever after.'

Question

Explore the extent to which the above short story can help in getting insights into a range of different management problems.

chapter
<u>*ten*</u>

EVALUATION

INTRODUCTION

Methods of evaluation range from simple checklists to complex weighted scoring systems. First, however, we look at sorting methods and then we go on to look at evaluation methods. Many of the ideation methods we have examined in the previous chapters produce a large quantity of ideas. Before we can evaluate these ideas we need to sort them into categories or themes. This facilitates the process of making comparisons and evaluations.

SORTING

An individual was asked to brainstorm ideas for the use of aluminium foil. These were first written down on a sheet of paper. Ideas were then examined for those that looked interesting (*highlighting*) and the remainder were discarded. The remaining ideas were then grouped according to different *hotspots* or *themes*. An idea could be appended to more than one *hotspot* or *theme* (indicated by the entries in brackets).

1 *Cooking*
1.1   covering roast chicken
1.2   wrapping baked potato
1.3   covering food for storage
1.4   milk bottle tops
1.5   wrapping food for storage w/o fridge
1.6   keeping food warm
1.7   lining a grill pan

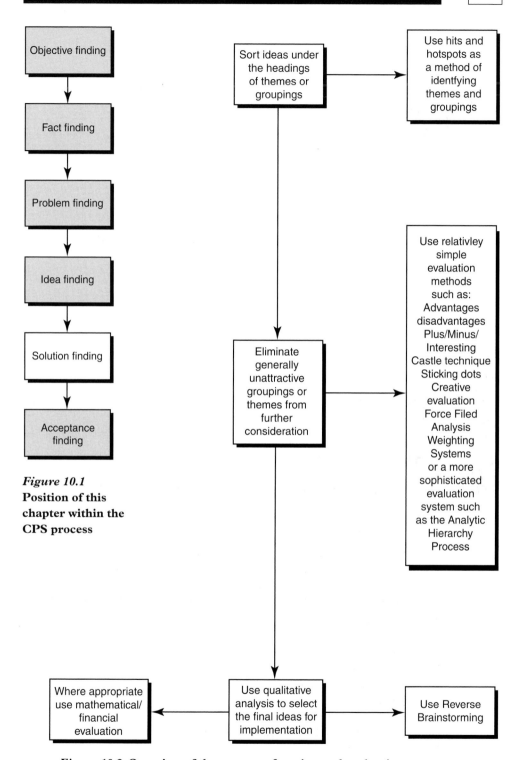

Figure 10.1
**Position of this
chapter within the
CPS process**

Figure 10.2 **Overview of the process of sorting and evaluation**

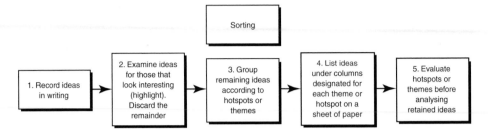

Figure 10.3 Sorting

    1.8   wrapping sandwiches to keep fresh
    1.9   lining cake storage tins
    1.10 (cooking food on campfire)
    1.11 reflecting heat source
    1.12 keep food cold

2 *Fun*
    2.1   baby's rattle
    2.2   screw up to make ball
    2.3   making a cat's toy
    2.4   stepping stones
    2.5   flapping fish game
    2.6   (water in Brownie pool)
    2.7   (making children's jewellery)

3 *Practical*
    3.1   making a cup
    3.2   making a plate
    3.3   smooth to make a mirror
    3.4   lining wall behind radiator
    3.5   glue/paint dish
    3.6   temporary curtains
    3.7   (wrapping button hole stem)
    3.8   (cutting strip to make bookmark)
    3.9   (make milk bottle tops)

4 *Camping/out of doors*
    4.1   reflecting sunlight for SOS
    4.2   lining under sleeping bag
    4.3   wrapping food on campfire
    4.4   keeping matches dry
    4.5   (keep food warm)

5 *Decorative*
    5.1   wrapping button hole stem
    5.2   Christmas decorations

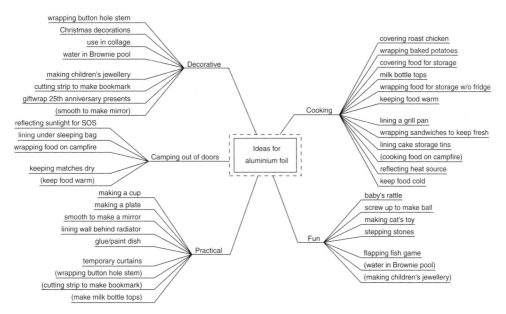

Figure 10.4 **Mind map of ideas on the uses of aluminium foil**

5.3   use in collage
5.4   water in Brownie pool
5.5   making children's jewellery
5.6   cutting strip to make bookmark
5.7   gift-wrap 25th anniversary presents
5.8   (smooth to make mirror)

To help group the ideas five columns were drawn up on a piece of paper and each column was headed with the title of the *theme*. Ideas were then listed as appropriate under each column heading, thus:

Cooking	Fun	Practical	Camping/ out of doors	Decorative
ideas	ideas	ideas	ideas	ideas

The next stage involved evaluating the hotspots or themes before analysing retained ideas (one or other of the methods described below can be used to evaluate themes or hotspots). Interesting hotspots are retained so that the ideas within the hotspots can be individually evaluated.

EVALUATION METHODS

The following methods may be used to evaluate all the ideas that have been generated along a particular theme or grouping, or to evaluate/eliminate particular themes or groupings.

ADVANTAGE–DISADVANTAGE TABLES

Perhaps the simplest method of evaluating ideas makes use of tables which permit the comparison of the advantages and disadvantages of various ideas. For example, suppose there are two ideas about how we should reorganise the office – method A and method B. First we list the criteria against which we want to compare and evaluate the ideas. The same criteria are used for both of the options and space is left to indicate whether the idea was rated as having predominantly advantages or disadvantages when considered against that criteria.

The technique is useful as a rough evaluation tool and in the example in Table 10.1 it will be noted that method B seems to have the better rating. However, except for possible use as a preliminary screening device this approach has too many limitations. Its main weakness is of course that it assumes that all the criteria carry equal weight and that it is the overall score that is important (it overlooks the fact that some of the criteria may be critical – i.e. they must be satisfied).

Table 10.1 **An advantage–disadvantage table**

	Options			
	Method A		Method B	
Criteria	Advantage	Disadvantage	Advantage	Disadvantage
Efficiency	x		x	
Cost		x	x	
Employee satisfaction	x		x	
Score	2	1	3	0

More elaborate screening methods have been suggested by Hamilton (1974). The methods involve 'culling' ideas which fail to satisfy key criteria, and rating and scoring ideas against desirable criteria.

PMI: PLUS/MINUS/INTERESTING

PMI stands for 'Plus/Minus/Interesting'. It is a development (by Edward de Bono) of the 'pros and cons' technique used for centuries.

One simply draws up a table headed 'Plus', 'Minus', and 'Interesting'. In the column underneath the 'Plus' heading one writes down all the positive points of taking the action. Underneath the 'Minus' heading one writes down all the negative effects. In the 'Interesting' column one writes down the extended implications of taking the action, whether positive or negative.

Scoring the PMI table

One may be able to make an evaluation just from looking at the table. Alternatively, each of the points written down can be considered and assigned a positive or negative score. The scores assigned can be entirely subjective. Once done the score is added up. A strongly positive score is a favourable evaluation while a strongly negative score suggests the idea is a poor one.

Example

Should I move from my house to a flat (see Table 10.2)?

Table 10.2

Plus		Minus		Interesting	
More luxurious	(+5)	More expensive	(−6)	Easier to get to work?	(+1)
Close to city centre	(+5)	Less space	(−7)	Meet more people?	(+1)
		More noise	(−4)		
		No garden terrace	(−5)	Easier to get to places?	(+1)
Totals	10		−22		3

Overall total = −9: I'm happier living where I am!

CASTLE TECHNIQUE

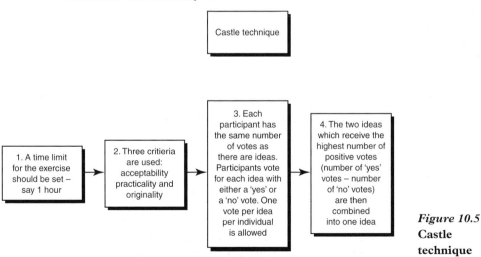

Figure 10.5 **Castle technique**

The Castle technique is useful for evaluating a large number of ideas and is made up of four steps:

1 A time limit for the exercise should be set – say 1 hour.
2 Three criteria are used to evaluate each idea: *acceptability* (the extent to which it leads to a satisfactory solution), *practicality* (the extent to which it satisfies financial and time constraints), and *originality* (the extent to which it makes a significant improvement on the *status quo*).
3 Each participant in the evaluation exercise has the same number of votes as there are ideas. Participants are instructed to vote for each idea with either a 'yes' or a 'no' vote. One vote per idea per individual is allowed.
4 The two ideas which receive the highest number of positive votes (number of 'yes' votes minus number of 'no' votes) are then combined into one idea.

STICKING DOTS

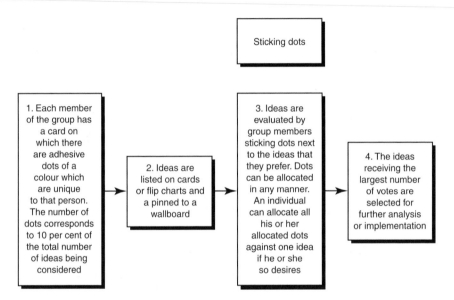

Figure 10.6 **Sticking dots method**

This is a useful method for a small group of individuals to employ when trying to make an evaluation (see Geschka, 1979). Each group member has a fixed number of votes (usually these are physically represented in the form of self-adhesive, coloured dots). Group members can then vote in any way they wish. The procedure is as follows:

1 Each member of the group has a card on which there are adhesive dots of a colour unique to that person. The number of dots corresponds to 10 per cent of the total number of ideas being considered.
2 Ideas are listed on cards or flip charts and pinned to a wallboard.
3 Ideas are evaluated by group members sticking dots next to the ideas that they prefer. Dots can be allocated in any manner. An individual can allocate all his or her allocated dots against one idea if he or she so desires.

4 The ideas receiving the largest number of votes are selected for further analysis or implementation.

Figure 10.7 **Sticking dots method: an example**
What type of show should the theatre offer next? The sticking dots indicate a preference for a musical

IDEA					
three act play	●	●	●		
musical	●	●	●	●	●	●
musical concert	●	●	●	●	
variety show	●	●	●	●	●

CREATIVE EVALUATION

This also is a method which is useful for dealing with a large number of ideas. It attempts to present ideas in a format that will reduce the amount of time required for evaluation. All ideas are evaluated in terms of time and financial requirements. The procedure is as follows:

1 List the ideas.
2 Categorise the ideas into *simple*, *hard* and *difficult*. Note that simple ideas are those which can be put into action with a minimum of expenditure of time and money. Hard ideas require more expenditure, while difficult ideas require the most expenditure.

Like the advantages–disadvantages method, this approach is most suitable for a cursory examination of a large number of ideas.

FORCE FIELD ANALYSIS

This is a method used to get a whole view of all the forces for or against a plan so that a decision can be made which takes into account all interests. In effect this is a specialised method of weighing pros and cons. Where a plan has been decided on, force field analysis allows you to look at all the forces for or against the plan. It helps you to plan or reduce the impact of the opposing forces, and strengthen and reinforce the supporting forces. To carry out a force field analysis, follow the following steps:

• List all forces for change in one column, and all forces against change in another column.
• Assign a score to each force, from 1 (weak) to 5 (strong).
• Draw a diagram showing the forces for and against, and the size of the forces (see Figure 10.8).

Once you have carried out an analysis, you can decide on the viability of the project. Where you have decided to carry out a project, it can help you to analyse how you can push through a project that may be in difficulty. Here you have two choices:

- to reduce the strength of the forces opposing a project;
- to increase the forces pushing a project.

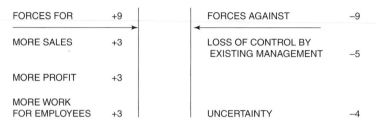

Figure 10.8 Force field analysis

Often the most elegant solution is the first: just trying to force change through may cause its own problems (e.g. staff can be annoyed into active opposition to a plan instead of merely not welcoming it).

If you were faced with the task of pushing through the project in the example above, the analysis might suggest a number of points:

- By looking for a strategic alliance loss of management control could be reduced (reduce loss of management control by 2).
- Coping with uncertainty is necessary for business survival (new force in favour, +2).
- More work will mean a more productive workforce (new force, +1).
- More sales will increase morale of sales force (new force, +1).
- More profit will increase satisfaction of shareholders (new force, +1).

These changes swing the balance from 9:9 (neither for nor against the plan), to 14:7 (in favour of the plan).

Force field analysis is an effective method of getting a picture of all the forces for and against a plan. It helps you to weigh the importance of these factors and to assess whether a plan is worth pursuing. Where you have decided to proceed with a plan, carrying out a force field analysis helps you identify changes that might be made to improve the plan.

WEIGHTING SYSTEMS

The first step is to generate evaluative criteria. Next, one assigns different weighting for each criterion reflecting its importance with respect to the problem under consideration. Next, each idea is rated on the degree to which it satisfies each criterion. The lower the number, the less the criterion is satisfied. Finally, one multiplies the criteria importance rating one has assigned to obtain the rated score. Weighted scores are then summed to obtain an overall weighted score for each idea or theme. An example of a weighted decision matrix is shown in Table 10.3, in which case weights

Table 10.3

Criteria	Criteria importance	Idea 1		Idea 2	
		Score	Subtotal	Score	Subtotal
1 a	5	2	10	3	15
2 b	5	1	5	2	10
3 c	4	2	8	3	12
4 d	4	3	12	5	20
5 e	3	3	9	5	15
Totals			44		72

and scores are out of a maximum of 5 where 5 is considered very important or high scoring and 1 is relatively unimportant or low scoring.

Generally, ideas with the highest overall scores are considered the best. However, one must take account of the fact that there may be some critical criteria that have to be satisfied, and even if an idea has the best score of those available it may still not be considered adoptable simply because it has failed to satisfy the requirements of particular criteria. In addition one might specify that an idea must obtain a certain overall score before it can be considered adoptable. If the best idea available does not satisfy this criteria then it may not be adopted.

THE PROCESS OF CHOOSING

As can be seen from the foregoing, when exercising choice it is usual to have a set of alternatives and a set of evaluation criteria. Evaluating a list of alternatives involves measuring, trading off or scoring them in terms of the specified criteria and determining the relative importance of the criteria. This may involve several complexities:

- multiple criteria and multiple alternatives;
- a large number of criteria and sub-criteria;
- criteria which are not all equally important to the decision maker;
- some criteria may be qualitative while other criteria are quantitative.

Some of the typical suggestions for analysing such data involve:

- discussing the pros and cons of each alternative;
- analysing the costs and benefits, or weaknesses and strengths, of each alternative;
- ensuring the effective utilisation of financial and other quantitative information in evaluating alternatives;
- sifting back through evidence provided in situation analysis to help reach a conclusion;
- assessing whether a chosen alternative solves a problem without creating new problems;

- justifying why an alternative has been selected *and* outlining why others may have been rejected.

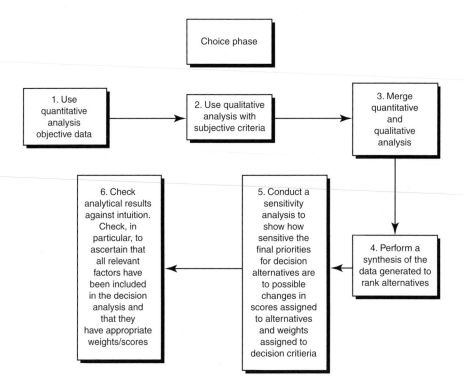

Figure 10.9 **The choice phase**

The general approach to adopt at the choice phase is as follows:

1 Use quantitative analysis on objective data:
   (a) acquire data on the anticipated outcomes of each alternative with respect to each criterion;
   (b) perform descriptive or experimental research to measure each alternative's performance on the criteria;
   (c) consider whether quantitative tools such as simulation and optimisation methods might be usefully applied;
   (d) conduct a sensitivity analysis with the quantitative data.
2 Use qualitative analysis with subjective criteria.
   (a) conduct a pro/con analysis;
   (b) make use of expert judgement in dealing with the evaluation of alternatives with respect to the qualitative criteria.
3 Merge quantitative and qualitative analysis.
4 Perform a synthesis of the data generated to rank alternatives.
5 Conduct a sensitivity analysis to show how sensitive the final priorities

for decision alternatives are to possible changes in scores assigned to alternatives and weights assigned to decision criteria.

6 Check analytical results against intuition. If they agree you can be more assured that the decision is a good one. If they do not agree find out why this is the case. Check, in particular, to ascertain that all relevant factors have been included in the decision analysis and that they have appropriate scores or weights.

The merging and evaluating of quantitative and qualitative data presents considerable choices. Moreover synthesis and sensitivity analysis of such data presents a daunting task for all but relatively simple decision situations. One sophisticated tool that can be used to get to grips with this process is the analytic hierarchy process (Saaty, 1980).

The analytic hierarchy process (AHP) enables the decision makers to set priorities and make choices on the basis of their objectives and knowledge and experience in a way that is consistent with their intuitive thought process. It has substantial theoretical and empirical support, overcomes problems associated with pro/con analysis and the weights and scores technique by using a hierarchical structure of the decision problem, pair-wise relative comparison of the elements in the hierarchy and a series of redundant judgements. The approach reduces error and encourages consistency in judgements. The use of redundancy allows accurate priorities to be derived from qualitative judgements, even though the wording may not be very precise. This means that words can be used to compare qualitative factors and derive ratio scale priorities that can be combined with quantitative factors.

Expert Choice helps a decision maker examine and resolve problems involving multiple evaluation criteria. The software uses the AHP methodology to model a decision problem and evaluate the relative desirability of alternatives.

QUALITATIVE EVALUATION: REVERSE BRAINSTORMING

The technique was developed at the Hotpoint company (Whiting, 1958) as a group method for discussing all possible weaknesses of an idea, or what might go wrong with an idea when it is implemented. It is almost identical to classical brainstorming except that criticisms rather than ideas are generated.

Imagine the problem being how to counteract declining sales and that the following potential ideas for solutions were generated by classical brainstorming or some other ideation method:

- new advertising strategy
- offer discounts
- door to door sales
- change or improve packaging
- find new markets

The first step in reverse brainstorming is to suggest criticisms for the first of these ideas – new advertising strategy. Criticisms developed might be:

- too expensive;
- unable to target the specific areas required.

After exhausting criticisms for the first idea the group begins criticising the second idea and the process continues until all the ideas have been criticised.

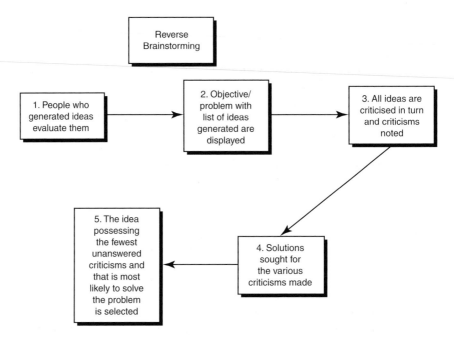

Figure 10.10 **Reverse brainstorming**

Using classical brainstorming the group then re-examines the ideas to generate possible solutions for each weakness that has been identified. For example, in the case of the second idea 'offer discounts' the criticisms might be that people might perceive the quality of the product not to be good as a result of offering discounts. In the case of 'door to door selling' it might be the fact that unacceptable training and added costs will be incurred because of the need to employ more sales staff. Other criticisms will no doubt be found for the other ideas. As far as solutions to these criticisms are concerned, it may not be felt that there are any in, say, the case of 'a new advertising strategy'; however, in the case of 'door to door selling' it may be felt possible to employ part-time workers in order to lower the cost.

The idea that possesses the fewest number of weaknesses and that will be most likely to solve the problem is usually selected for implementation. Of course, one does also have to bear in mind the comparative seriousness of any unresolved criticisms.

Example

PROBLEM: getting people to have a positive attitude towards adopting new ways of working.

IDEAS:

1 Rewards associated with adopting new methods.
2 Firing those who do not co-operate and hiring new staff.
3 Training people and giving them the right kind of skills to do the new tasks.

CRITICISMS:

1 (a) May be too costly.
   (b) May not believe they will receive rewards, or seen as further manipulation by management.
2 (a) Will cause even more hostility and resentment.
   (b) Difficult to identify best method of recruitment – may still hire inappropriate people.
   (c) Effort and time need to be spent on recruitment and interviews.
3 (a) Training requires additional time and cost.
   (b) Not possible to provide training for every situation.

SOLUTIONS TO WEAKNESSES:

1 (a) Link the new methods with productivity increases.
   (b) Provide written agreements to show commitment.
2 (a) No solution.
   (b) Agree that all new appointees be on probation for a fixed period.
   (c) Hire recruitment consultants.
3 (a) Provide training on the job.
   (b) As (a), plus make sure first line managers can provide proper guidance and support to workers.

Although both ideas 1 and 3 seem to have resolved all the difficulties associated with them, 3 might well be the preferable alternative. This is because the problem at the core of the matter lies in a decrease in productivity which is incurred as each new method is adopted.

FINANCIAL/MATHEMATICAL EVALUATIONS

Mathematics can be used effectively to aid/evaluate possible solutions. In essence one is interested in assessing the potential pay-off of problem solutions. One way to achieve this is to consider the probabilities of certain pay-offs in the light of previous experience. Of course, this method can only be used where there is enough experience to calculate the odds with some degree of accuracy and, of course, probabilities of this kind are of no use in a case where it has never been necessary to consider a similar instance before.

CREATIVE EVALUATION METHOD

Here the approach involves evaluating the ideas in terms of their time and money requirements (Moore, 1962). Ideas are categorised into three groups: simple, hard and difficult. Simple ideas are those which can be put into action with the minimum of expenditure of both time and money. Hard ideas require more expenditure of time and money, while difficult ideas require substantial expenditure of time and money.

The method can often lead to further ideas or insights.

PAY-OFF TABLES

Alternative solutions to a problem can be laid out in a pay-off table (Table 10.4). Three probabilities are shown with respect to both costs and benefits associated with the ideas (.25, .50 and .25). Thus for option A, for example, it is estimated that there is a 25 per cent chance the costs will be £2,500, a 50 per cent chance it will be £3,000 and a further 25 per cent chance that it will be £4,000. Benefits are calculated in a similar way.

Table 10.4 **Example of pay-off table**

	Cost (£)			Expected cost (£) (EC)	Benefit (£)			Expected benefit (£) (EB)	Expected pay-off (£) (EB – EC)
Probability	.25	.50	.25		.25	.50	.25		
Option A	2,500	3,000	4,000	3,125	5,200	6,000	7,600	6,200	3,075
Option B	1,500	2,000	3,000	2,125	3,600	4,800	5,600	4,700	2,575
Option C	2,000	2,500	3,000	2,500	4,200	5,700	6,000	5,400	2,900

Using the expected pay-off concept we can see that option A appears to have the best expected pay-off.

DECISION TREES

While pay-off tables are adequate for most purposes, decision trees enable one to see what effect one decision made at a particular moment will have on the options to be faced in the future.

For example, suppose that a firm is operating at full capacity and demand for its products is rising. A 20 per cent rise in demand is expected and this can be met by either adopting one of two new methods of working (A and B). The net cash-flow in the case of a 20 per cent rise in demand will be $460,000 if new method A is used, or $440,000 if the extra production is obtained by method B. However, there is a body of opinion in the firm that sales will not rise and that they will in actual fact decline by 5 per cent even though the rise is more likely. There is general agreement that there is a 60 per cent probability of a rise in sales of 20 per cent and a 40 per cent probability of a 5 per cent drop in sales.

If there were a 5 per cent sales drop then the cash flow would be $340,000 if the company were to use method A and $380,000 if it were to opt for method B. The alternatives are presented in the decision tree (Figure 10.11).

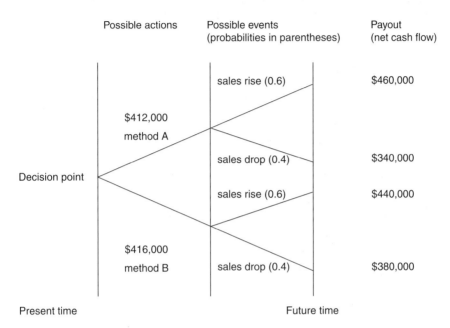

Figure 10.11 **Decision tree**

In order to take account of the probabilities, one has to make the following calculations:

Method A: $460,000 × 0.6 + $340,000 × 0.4 = $412,000
Method B: $440,000 × 0.6 + $380,000 × 0.4 = $416,000

The method B alternative seems preferable. However, one does have to take account of future years' sales and assuming predictions can be made for a further couple of years this would introduce another two decision points and extend the branches of the decision tree. Care, however, has to be exercised in terms of extending a decision tree into the future as uncertainty increases the further ahead one looks.

QUESTIONS

1 Describe *two* different techniques which can be used to assist in the evaluation of ideas.

2 'Ideation techniques only generate insights into a problem and not solutions to a problem.' To what extent would you agree or disagree with this statement? How does this influence how we might set about the process of evaluating the output of an ideation process?

3 A manager has a number of proposals for improving communications in the office. How might he or she set about evaluating the different proposals?

4 When might one use reverse brainstorming? Describe the process.

5 What are the advantages of using reverse brainstorming compared with other methods of evaluation? What are its limitations? Illustrate its application to a situation of your own choice.

6 What is the purpose of reverse brainstorming? Illustrate its use through an example of your own choice.

7 A canning company is considering vertical integration as a means of obviating supply and distribution chain problems that have become apparent in the past few months. Discuss how force field analysis might be used to good effect in helping to analyse such a situation.

8 A company is considering three alternative ways of improving productivity. The expected costs, expected pay-offs and associated probabilities of events occurring are show below. Using expected pay-off tables calculate the value of the best option.

Option 1:   expected costs   £450,000, probability   .35
                ditto   £290,000, probability   .25
                ditto   £300,000, probability   .40

          expected benefits   £750,000, probability   .40
                ditto   £490,000, probability   .35
                ditto −£200,000, probability   .25

Option 2:   expected costs   £440,000, probability   .30
                ditto   £250,000, probability   .45
                ditto   £380,000, probability   .25

          expected benefits   £650,000, probability   .35
                ditto   £390,000, probability   .25
                ditto   £200,000, probability   .40

Option 3:   expected costs   £430,000, probability   .15
                ditto   £390,000, probability   .55
                ditto   £320,000, probability   .30

          expected benefits   £850,000, probability   .35
                ditto   £190,000, probability   .35
                ditto −£250,000, probability   .30

9 Given the following information construct a decision tree and assess the best course of action.

A firm is operating at full capacity and demand for its products is falling. A further decline is expected and this can be met by either adopting one of two new methods of working (A and B). The net cash-flow in the case of a decline in demand will be £150,000 if new method A is used or £140,000 if method B is adopted. However, there is a body of opinion in the firm that sales will not fall and that they will in actual fact rise, even though the fall is more likely. There is general agreement that there is a 55 per cent probability of a fall in sales and a 45 per cent probability of a rise in sales. If sales rise then method A would yield a net cash flow of £148,000 and method B £142,000.

CASES

Liverpool and Manchester Railway Company

Hits, hotspots and reverse brainstorming

The Manchester and Liverpool Railway Company is looking for ways to improve the quality of the service it offers to passengers making use of all its short distance journeys – that is, journeys between Liverpool and Manchester and within a radius of thirty miles of each of these two cities. As a starting point the company decided to have a brainstorming session and at the session a list of over fifty ideas was generated. Ideas that appeared interesting were then noted and the following hits extracted:

1 Have trains in which all passengers can be seated.
2 Use wide gauge railtrack to ensure stability of trains.
3 Use tilting trains so that greater speed can be achieved around bends.
4 Have powerful engines so that acceleration and deceleration can be improved.
5 Use lightweight carriages.
6 Use lightweight motors and aluminium wheels.
7 Use monorail system where train floats on cushion of air.
8 Give the trains a streamlined appearance.
9 Have a buffet service on all the trains.
10 Have open carriages and a bar/lounge where people can be served drinks and snacks.
11 Have TV and radio facilities which can be accessed from all seats.
12 Have a much wider range of prices reflecting time of day or week at which people travel.
13 Price according to seating and other facilities offered.

These were then listed under a number of different hotspots:

Comfort 1   Food and drink 9, 10
Prices 12, 13   Entertainment 11
Speed 2, 3, 4, 5, 6, 7, 8

Each hotspot was then examined carefully and one additional ideas was produced:

Comfort: have full adjustable reclining seats.

All fourteen ideas were then taking on to the stage of reverse brainstorming so that they could be fully evaluated.

The following criticisms were produced for each of the ideas:

Comfort:

1 All passengers to be seated
    (a) inadequate capacity at peak periods.
14 Fully adjustable and reclining seats
    (a) journeys too short for passengers to get any real benefits from these.

Speed:

2 Wide gauge trains
    (a) too costly – Railtrack would not provide.
3 Tilting trains
    (b) could not really get the benefits of high speed on short journeys.
4 Powerful engines
    (a) maintenance problems.
5 Lightweight carriages
    (a) maintenance problems.
6 Lightweight motors and aluminium wheels
    (a) maintenance problems.
8 Streamlined trains
    (a) coupling and shunting difficulties;
    (b) maintenance problems.

Food and drink:

9 Buffet service
    (a) staffing difficulties;
    (b) difficult to serve everyone on short journeys.
10 Bar facilities
    (a) staffing difficulties;
    (b) difficult to serve everyone on short journeys.

Entertainment:

11 TV and radio accessible from seats
    (a) passengers not able to watch feature length programmes;
    (b) headsets soon damaged and need expensive regular replacement;
    (c) if no headsets used then disturbance for other passengers created.

Prices:

12 Wider range of prices relating to time of travel
    (a) confusing for the customer;
    (b) need extensive periodic revisions.

13 Price according to services provided
    (a) need to provide a wide range of services, but this could be effectively offered.

Ways of getting round the problems raised about each idea were then sought. However, it was not felt that any of the problems identified could be satisfactorily resolved. It was decided to evaluate the ideas, taking account of their existing inadequacies.

Based on this analysis it was felt that only the ideas based on providing food and drink facilities could be implemented with the least difficulties. However, given the nature of the criticisms expressed it was decided first that a survey of passengers on different routes should be undertaken to establish whether there was any unmet need or want for this service and, if so, what might be the best type of service to offer.

Question

Work through the above steps yourself (even include as an extra the redefinition of the problem) and see if you can come up with any different ideas or suggestions to those arrived at by the railway company. Evaluate the ideas you produce using reverse brainstorming.

Leaking yoghurt cartons

JOHN: 15 per cent of yoghurt cartons in the supermarkets are leaking.

BILL: Perhaps stronger cartons are required.

JOHN: But that could increase the price of the yoghurts and make them too expensive.

SALLY: Perhaps it may be possible to obtain cheaper material with which to have the cartons made up?

LEN: I've heard there is a cheap source of cartons in Poland.

SALLY: Could be import and supply problems there.

JOHN: What about lower grade materials for the cartons?

LEN: They leak now – surely that would simply weaken the cartons and make them more likely to leak!

SALLY: But it might be possible to redesign the cartons using the new materials so that they are actually stronger.

JOHN: It is possible, but we would need to have that explored in some depth and get expert advice.

BILL: What about new materials?

SALLY: Perhaps we could ask the help of professional carton designers or some other experts?

JOHN: Maybe.

BILL: Could be that we should be looking at *when* the damage occurs.

SALLY: I gather it is mainly during transportation.

JOHN: Perhaps those handling the goods should receive some additional training.

SALLY: Or better handling equipment at each end. It may be the handling equipment that is unsatisfactory.

LEN: I gather no use is made of fork-lift trucks at all.

BILL: Yes, but not all supermarkets have that sort of equipment.

SALLY: Perhaps we should have some sort of publicity campaign to make everyone concerned with the handling of the product aware of the potential problems of rough handling?

LEN: Punishments and rewards for careless and careful handling?

JOHN: Does it really matter to the customer if some of the cartons leak?

SALLY: Too many health hazards and scares associated with food products. We cannot afford risking adverse press!

JOHN: I'm not sure. Shouldn't we perhaps investigate it?

LEN: This transportation idea – maybe it's because of the distance the yoghurts have to travel before they reach the supermarket shelves. Perhaps if we could find some way of shortening the distance to be travelled.

SALLY: Maybe we could deliver the yoghurt in bulk and pack it on the premises of the supermarket?

BILL: Would the sales volume warrant it? Could we do that and maintain our profitability?

SALLY: We could use supermarket staff and pay the supermarkets.

JOHN: I don't know. It seems that it might be too expensive to do that.

SALLY: We could supply in bulk to the large supermarket's group central distribution and warehousing points and have it packed there.

BILL: It could still get damaged in transport.

LEN: Perhaps we could supply the yoghurts in bottles?

JOHN: There would be breakages and leakages too.

LEN: But perhaps nothing like as much.

BILL: What about bulk delivery – either to individual supermarkets or central distribution points, coupled with an emphasis on private brands?

JOHN: Yes, I suppose we could explore that possibility.

Question

Assume that the above has been generated by on-line discussions between a team of people wanting to find a solution to the identified problem of leaking yoghurt containers. Use highlighting and reverse brainstorming to evaluate the ideas. Add ideas and criticisms of your own to facilitate the analysis and insights into the problem that can be generated.

The Go-Ahead garage

The proprietor of the Go-Ahead garage is looking for ways of improving its image with its customers and, through word of mouth communication is hoping to persuade more car-owners to make use of its services. A brainstorming session came up with the following ideas:

1 Get rid of all excess grease and dirt on all cars serviced or repaired.
2 Ensure prices charged are very much in line with those of competitors.
3 Double check all repairs involving tightening of screws.
4 Inform the customer of the exact nature of all guarantees regarding repairs.
5 Always consult customer before carrying out any repairs.
6 Make sure that the estimate corresponds well with the actually price charged.
7 Ensure cars always ready for collection by a pre-specified time arranged with the customer in advance.
8 Make sure that the mechanics are neat and tidy before they talk to customers.
9 Have a comfortable reception area for customers.
10 Ensure that staff understand the importance of being courteous to customers.
11 Provide a while-you-wait service for small jobs.
12 Offer do-it-yourself facilities.
13 Provide free advice regarding repairs or problems reported by customers.
14 Provide written estimates for all jobs.
15 Offer a 24-hour service.
16 Offer a free car loan service while undertaking repairs or service.
17 Better petrol pump dispensers which do not damage car paintwork around the filler orifice or allow petrol to drip onto the bodywork.
18 Readily visible price list for standard servicing charges in the reception area.
19 Provide details of mechanics' experience and qualifications in a 'hall of fame' board in the reception area – and make sure that it is up to date.
20 Have an experienced member of staff inspect all repair jobs prior to vehicle release to customers and make sure that customers know who the inspector is.
21 Attract well-qualified staff.
22 Make sure all equipment and tools are regularly inspected and replaced at regular intervals.
23 Get AA and RAC approval.
24 Ensure adequate stocks are kept of common parts to avoid delays and reduce costs which are normally passed on to the customer.
25 Ensure the service management personnel who interact with the staff are well trained in customer interaction.
26 Better advertising.
27 Lower prices for regular customers.
28 More detailed reports for the customer of work carried out on the car.

Recently the garage had commissioned a market research survey to ascertain customer satisfaction with its services. The following had been ascertained using a ten-point scale:

Satisfaction with:	Importance (mean value)	Garage rating (mean value)
Reliability of repairs	10.0	7.3
Prices for repairs	6.5	6.5
Prices for service	5.3	7.2
Guarantees	7.5	5.5
Time taken for repairs	6.2	4.6
Time taken for service	5.4	3.9
Appearance of staff	3.2	6.5
Availability of spares	4.1	2.6
Help given to DIY	3.0	2.2
Helpfulness of staff	6.5	4.1
Opening hours	8.0	7.5
Forecourt petrol facilities	5.5	6.0
Staff expertise	9.0	4.2
Staff courteousness	7.1	3.5
Realism of estimates	8.0	3.1

How would you suggest the garage sets about evaluating its ideas. Can you improve on the ideas suggested, evaluate all the ideas and make some positive recommendations?

Customer loyalty campaign

A petrol station is looking for ways of attracting customers and has come up with the notion of a customer loyalty scheme where free gifts are given to customers after they have collected a given number of tokens. Ideas suggested for free gifts include:

sweets	jigsaw puzzles	hammers
chewing gum	packs of playing cards	letter openers
adhesive tape	calculators	dusters
glue	silver pendants	potato peelers
model kits	music tapes	manicure set
car shampoo	music CDs	after-shave lotion
maps	torches	hand-held TV
key rings	writing pads	pocket radio
sachets of tea	sandwich boxes	cheap camera
sachets of coffee	spanners	cheap quartz watch

Questions

1 Add to and expand the list of possibilities.
2 Use evaluation highlighting to sort ideas and gain more insights.
3 Use reverse brainstorming to pick out the best ideas.
4 How many tokens should be collected to redeem each of the items you finally suggest should be included in the loyalty scheme?

chapter eleven

IMPLEMENTING IDEAS

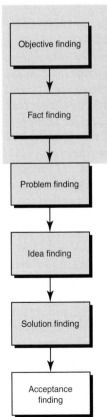

INTRODUCTION

In this chapter we examine some of the problems of implementing ideas. First we consider the various sources of resistance to change. Next we look at the role of communication in overcoming resistance to change. This is followed by an examination of how ideas might be put into action. Lastly we look at how we might foster a climate for change in an organisation.

The successful introduction of new ideas helps maintain an effective organisation and sustain a competitive advantage in the marketplace. New ideas are not accepted automatically – they are often resisted. Knowing what resistance there will be is the first step in introducing change. Getting people to accept the need for new ideas through good communication is a key element in the process of effecting change. Various communication models are considered, along with identifying within an organisation, spheres of influence needed to implement ideas and change. The chapter considers how various computer application packages –

Figure 11.1 **Position of this chapter within the CPS process**

such as COPE/Decision Explorer, PERT and computer simulation can help the implementation and acceptance of new ideas. Contingency plans are necessary when implementing ideas. One needs to anticipate the problems that will arise and the objections that will be raised. The importance of 'potential problem analysis' as a technique that can be used to good effect in this latter context is considered in the chapter.

IDEAS ARE NOT READILY IMPLEMENTED

THE PROBLEMS OF INTRODUCING NEW IDEAS

In *The Prince*, chapter 5, Machiavelli wrote: 'there is nothing more difficult to take in hand, more powerless to conduct or more uncertain in its success than to take the lead in the introduction of a new order of things because the innovators have for enemies all those who would have done well under the old conditions and lukewarm defenders in those who may do well'.

Getting new ideas off the ground can meet considerable opposition and it is important to recognise this before embarking on introducing change into an organisation. Some insights into the reasons for this can be obtained by looking back into the past, even before the times of Machiavelli.

We may wonder why the ancient Greeks, who produced so many great philosophers, artists and writers, did so little in the sphere of applied science. The reasons were both sociological and psychological. It was generally accepted in those times that the normal condition of a large part of mankind was that they must toil for the few. A shortage of labour or energy was never a problem. When a job had to be done the slaves had to do it and they were whipped until it was done (Larsen, 1961).

It is easy to imagine that throughout history the ideas of original inventors were sufficient to start off some new development. However, it is obvious on deeper reflection that the inventions themselves, as well as those who produced them, would be bound to fail if there was no need, necessity, demand or social basis for the ideas. As a consequence it is not surprising that many so-called inventions have been produced several times until eventually the time for their introduction has been appropriate. At the same time, developments in people's ways of life, new social orders influencing production and demand, have stimulated inventors to work along certain lines. It may not therefore have been pure chance that the rail and steam-engine reached maturity both at about the same time, and that they were brought together for the first time in England, the country, at the time, where social and economic developments were more rapid than anywhere else in the world. 'The locomotive is not the invention of one man', said Robert Stephenson, 'but of a nation of mechanical engineers' (Larsen, 1961: 125).

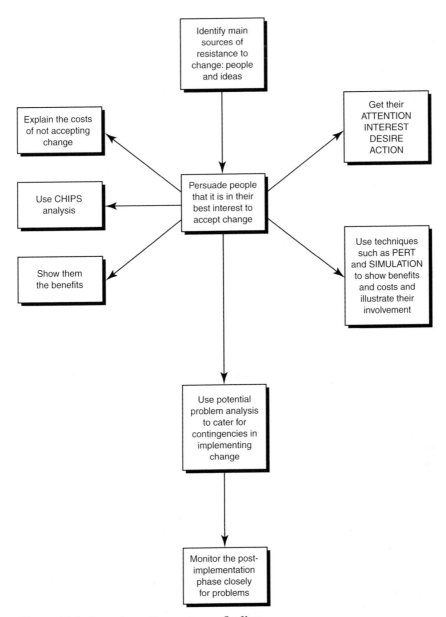

Figure 11.2 **Overview of acceptance finding**

SOURCES OF RESISTANCE TO CHANGE

People are often afraid of new ideas. They may feel threatened by new ideas and fear that they will not be able to cope with a change in working patterns that is demanded of them or that they will not understand how to use a new technology.

There many sources of resistance to change. Perhaps the most significant is that many people are afraid of new ideas. They may feel threatened by new ideas and fear that they will not be able to cope with a change in working patterns that is demanded of them or that they will not understand how to use a new technology. Even today there are many older people who are afraid of the desktop computer! Another point is that people may have a vested interest in not accepting change. Why change when you are doing very nicely with things as they are?

Resistance to change has many sources (see for example Lawrence and Greiner, 1970). Fear of the unknown, lack of information, threats to status, fear of failure, and lack of perceived benefits are examples of such sources. However, one of the most important sources is that people resist being treated as pawns in an organisational reshuffle. People like to feel that they are in control of what is happening to them and the more that change is imposed from the outside by others the more they will see it as something to feel threatened about and the more they will resist it. People resort to using their last remaining power base – their will to co-operate.

> **People like to feel that they are in control of what is happening to them and the more that change is imposed from the outside by others the more they will see it as something to feel threatened about and the more they will resist it.**

Human and technological factors produce implementation blocks. While some of the blocks are intentional and are designed as checks to ensure that an organisation always functions smoothly, other blocks are unintentional and may arise from how the organisation has developed historically – Levitt (1988), for example, argues that organisations tend to stagnate as they age. A third type of block may arise from an outside source – a change in market demand, for example, can act as a barrier to idea implementation.

Blocks to implementing ideas and change reflect such things as a lack of adequate resources to implement ideas, a lack of commitment and motivation in those required to implement ideas, resistance to change, procedural obstacles, perceived risk associated with implementing ideas, political undercurrents, lack of co-operation in the organisation and so on. The important thing is to uncover what resistance is likely to arise and what the reasons for the resistance are likely to be. With this information one can look for ways of implementing ideas so that the resistance encountered can be reduced.

ROLE OF COMMUNICATION IN OVERCOMING RESISTANCE TO CHANGE

> **The key to effecting change is to involve people in the process early, to consult with them and to get them to take ownership for themselves, of the new ideas that are to be introduced.**

The key to effecting change is to involve people in the process early, to consult with them and to get them to take ownership for themselves, of the new ideas that are to be introduced (see for example Coch and French, 1948). To sustain a programme of change it is essential to understand the culture of the organisation in which new ideas are to be introduced. New ideas that run counter to the traditional values of an organisation are the ones that are most difficult to introduce. Organisational culture is the pattern of shared values and norms that distinguishes it from all others (Higgins, 1994; Kotter, 1997). Before one should think about implementing change one needs to create a readiness for change within an organisation. One needs to think of the organisation as an internal market for change initiatives where ideas have to be marketed. This means that opinions and attitudes have to be assessed and potential sources of resistance have to be identified. Commitment to change can be instigated by helping people to develop a shared diagnosis of what is wrong in an organisation and what can and must be improved (see Kotter, 1997).

Communication is the spearhead of ensuring that successful change can take place (see for example Higgins, 1994). It helps to overcome ambiguity and uncertainty and provides information and power to those who are the subject of change. It enables them to have control over their destiny, to understand why change is necessary and provides the suppressant to fear. Through open communication channels people can express their doubts about the effectiveness of proposed changes and can understand the necessity for new ideas. Relying on an attempt to implement ideas only from the top is likely to meet with difficulties. Grassroots change is the only way to ensure that process becomes firmly embedded. It is natural for people to resist change and by anticipating, identifying and welcoming resistance we convert resistance into a perceived need for change.

PUTTING IDEAS INTO PRACTICE

There are a variety of tools and techniques which can be used to good advantage in helping to introduce new ideas in a systematic and planned way into an organisation. 'Consensus mapping', recommended by Hart *et al.* (1985), is one such tool. It helps those involved in the process of implementation to visualise, analyse and organise ideas that are sequence dependent. In applying the technique a graphic map is produced which portrays implementation steps and ideas in relationship to one another and shows how they are related to one another. *COPE* or *The Decision Explorer* is a computer package which can be used to achieve a similar goal (see pp. 238–9). *PERT* networks and research planning diagrams may also be used to good effect in facilitating the implementation of new ideas. Similarly, computer simulation methods can provide a basis for showing the impact new ideas will have on people and processes as well as on costs and efficiency. Another useful method, put forward by Kepner and Tregoe (1976), is 'potential problem analysis'. This method places an emphasis on a systematic approach to anticipating problems that are likely to stand in the way of the successful implementation of a project, changes or ideas. Some of these methods are discussed in this chapter.

> **Ideas may have to be sold to people who can authorise their implementation. This may make it easier to arouse subsequent motivation to implement ideas among those who have to do the job and make the chance of a successful implementation more likely.**

Besides the use of tools to systematise the introduction of new ideas there is also the task of persuading people who are going to make use of those ideas that they are worth using. Ideas may have to be sold to people who can authorise their implementation. This may make it easier to arouse subsequent motivation to implement ideas among those who have to do the job and make the chance of a successful implementation more likely. Putting ideas into practice usually requires:

1 an ability to get people to accept ideas;
2 an ability to cope with difficult obstacles;
3 an ability to plan and manage time in an effective manner;
4 an ability to create the enthusiasm and motivation to follow through ideas.

Persuading people to view new ideas in a favourable light when they are not readily disposed to do so essentially involves influencing and changing attitudes. To do this it is first necessary to convince people that they need to be dissatisfied with the *status quo*. It is important to note that people may not readily recognise that they are dissatisfied with the current situation. One cannot assume that people will readily accept that a problem exists, even when it is blatantly obvious to an outside person. It may be necessary to:

1 Create an awareness of problems that exist and make people recognise that there is a need for change and a need to adopt the idea that is being put forward.
2 Point out to people the potential hazards and pitfalls of not accepting the need for change.
3 Stress the benefits of change to the individuals involved since they will only be motivated to accept and to adopt new ideas when they perceive and acknowledge that it is in their own best interest to do so.

Spheres of influence

We have to recognise that people are part of a group situation in the organisation. Getting people to change means getting the group to change and involves understanding the nature of group dynamics. Identifying opinion leaders, action initiators, people with status and influence in the group, and those most affected in carrying out the changes required, is therefore very important. It is also important to have the backing of someone who has the authority and the resources to enable an idea to get off the ground. Knowing how to communicate with the target audiences is therefore an important skill when trying to implement new ideas and effect change.

Communication models

Communication theories offer several different descriptive models of the process by which it is thought that people adopt ideas as a result of receiving information about them. The models can also be used prescriptively as aids to producing communications that are intended to bring about action. One of the earliest models used was the AIDA model (origin uncertain). The model comprised four stages:

- attracting ATTENTION;
- maintaining INTEREST;
- arousing DESIRE;
- getting ACTION.

The early 1960s saw considerable interest in advertising models. Lavidge and Steiner (1961) developed the 'hierarchy of effects' model. This model was directly related to understanding how marketing communications worked. The model implied a six-stage process where the customer moves through stages from awareness to purchase:

AWARENESS → KNOWLEDGE → LIKING → PREFERENCE → CONVICTION → PURCHASE

Different persuasive activities were considered fitting to move customers through the various stages. To develop AWARENESS teaser campaigns, sky writing, jingles, slogans and classified advertisements are considered suitable. In order to convey KNOWLEDGE, announcements and descriptive copy were recommended. Image advertising and status or glamour appeals are envisaged to be ways of producing a LIKING, while competitive advertisements and argumentative copy are more relevant to generating a PREFERENCE. Finally, price appeals and testimonials may produce CONVICTION, while deals, last chance offers and point of purchase retail store advertisements are seen as ways of encouraging actual PURCHASE.

Contemporary with Lavidge and Steiner, Colley (1961) produced a model called DAGMAR, which stands for defining advertising goals, measuring advertising results. It was argued that a communication must carry a prospect through four levels of understanding:

AWARENESS → COMPREHENSION → CONVICTION → ACTION

Shortly after, Rogers (1962) suggested the 'Innovation Adoption' model. In this case the theory was not directed specifically at the relationship between marketing communications and sales but rather on the adoption of a new idea. Several stages were suggested in the model:

AWARENESS → INTEREST → EVALUATION → TRIAL → ADOPTION

All of these models seem to fit in well with the more general communications model of:

EXPOSURE → RECEPTION → COGNITIVE RESPONSE → ATTITUDE →
    INTENTION → BEHAVIOUR

The point about all the above models is that attitude change and subsequent action are seen as a gradual step-by-step process. The models will be appropriate for different circumstances depending upon exactly what is required concerning the idea that is being implemented. Moreover, different ways of communicating, and even different communication media, may be more appropriate for moving people from one stage to the next.

Effective communications need to appeal to the needs and wants of the recipients. They should give the recipient a motive or incentive to act.

Effective communications need to appeal to the needs and wants of the recipients. They should give the recipient a motive or incentive to act. They also need to generate involvement with the message on the part of the recipient by asking questions which leave the message incomplete. In addition they should also explain exactly what course of action it is expected the recipient will follow.

Getting people to consider adopting an idea or changing behaviour can be achieved through appealing to their cognitive processes (see Burnett, 1993). One needs to arouse desire, indicate a need, or offer a logical reason why they should co-operate. In so doing the message becomes implanted in the recipient's memory and can be triggered by future needs, motives and associations. However, one does have to remember that the rational approach may not be so effective for some recipients or in situations where there is likely to be less involvement in the action required. In these cases emotional appeals may be used. The appeal, theme, idea or unique selling proposition is what the communicator has to get over to the target audience to produce the desired response. Benefit, identification, motivation are all concepts that can be built into the message. Messages can be built around rational, emotional or moral appeals, themes, ideas or unique selling propositions. Economy, value and performance are used in messages with a rational content. Emotional appeals make use of both positive and negative aspects. On the negative side this involves fear, guilt and shame (Janis and Feshback, 1953), while on the positive side it comprises humour (Beggs, 1989), love, pride and joy. Too much fear in a message may cause the audience to reject it. The use of humour may generate 'noise' and interfere with the message. Moral appeals appeal to people's sense of what is right and just.

REDUCING RESISTANCE TO CHANGE

> **A good way to counter resistance to change is to pre-empt the possibility of it occurring. As is mentioned above, getting people involved in the idea development process in the first place anticipates resistance to change. Resistance is reduced because people feel that they have had the opportunity to participate and express their view.**

Getting people to change their attitudes is fundamental to reducing resistance to new ideas. While creating dissatisfaction with the *status quo* is one method of effecting attitude change and getting ideas implemented there are other ways of achieving the same objective. A good way to counter resistance to change is to pre-empt the possibility of it occurring. As is mentioned above, getting people involved in the idea development process in the first place anticipates resistance to change. Resistance is reduced because people feel that they have had the opportunity to participate and express their view.

In the same way that attitude change is seen as a gradual process, the implementation process should follow a similar pattern. New ideas that involve substantial change need to be implemented gradually, smoothly and systematically. Resistance to change can be softened by making the changes tentative rather than definite or permanent. It is a good strategy to get people to try out ideas initially for a short period. In addition people should be encouraged to give comments whether they think an idea is working. If a new idea fails it does not cause its originator as much loss of face under such circumstances.

Encouraging people to recognise that change is a normal facet of life is important. If they come to accept this viewpoint they will not see change as being out of the ordinary when it is applied to them. It can help them to become less emotionally attached to the *status quo*.

In introducing a new idea one has to be reasonably sure that it is worth while. There is a cost associated with change for it causes disruption to those who are concerned. However, provided that the required change is accompanied by demonstrable benefits, which more than offset the costs of disruption, the new idea is more likely to meet with little resistance. In addition it will pave the way for the introduction of future new ideas in that it is more likely to be seen as in the interests of the organisation.

Cognitive mapping devices

Cognitive mapping is a modelling technique which portrays ideas, beliefs, values and attitudes and their relationship to one another in a manner which facilitates examination and analysis. Such data is collected through focus group interviews or in-depth personal interviews. Cognitive mapping is a practical development of the implications of Personal Construct Theory, which in turn purports to reflect how people construe their world (Kelly, 1955). A cognitive map is a network of ideas and is illustrated as nodes linked by arrows, representing goals and actions. SODA (Strategic Option Development Analysis) is such a methodology and uses a computer model called *COPE* to help in the analysis. A facilitator interviews individuals involved with a problem and draws up their cognitive maps of the factors relating to and influencing the situation subsumed in the problem. A single person might suggest tens of factors relating to particular problem. The facilitator constructs a *COPE* model to reflect a person's view. The group as a whole can express thousands of views and *COPE* is designed to accumulate and compress this diversity of ideas.

COPE has been deployed to help identify resistance in implementing ideas (see Bessant and Buckingham, 1989). By showing groups their own and others' perspectives on an issue it is often possible to ease problems encountered in implementation.

COPE is primarily designed to produce such cognitive maps, and recent versions facilitate this through a graphic user interface. Since it also has the facility to trace paths throughout the very complex network structures that can be constructed, it can also help to establish cause–effect relationships and hence build causal models. Simpler devices such as mind maps and research planning diagrams can also be used to good effect. While they lack the sophistication of such programs as *The Decision Explorer* (*COPE*) they do enable one to graphically record the relationship between events and people's attitudes as they impinge on the implementation of new ideas. Such tools facilitate consensus mapping and their visual impact can be helpful when trying to get the co-operation of those who are needed to ensure the success of a project.

PERT

Planning, scheduling and control in the introduction of new ideas and the implementation of organisational changes can be greatly enhanced with the aid of *PERT* (project evaluation and review technique). The tool helps to monitor and organise resources to enable a project to be completed on time and within budget limits. It is customary to model projects and planning activities as networks to capture the nature of the interrelationships and sequencing of their various component parts.

PERT/CPM is basically a three-part technique:

1 *Planning* – this incorporates an in-depth analysis of the project or planning task and construction of the network to describe it.
2 *Scheduling* – this involves the analysis of the project or exercise to determine completion time, critical activities and start and finish times for each activity.

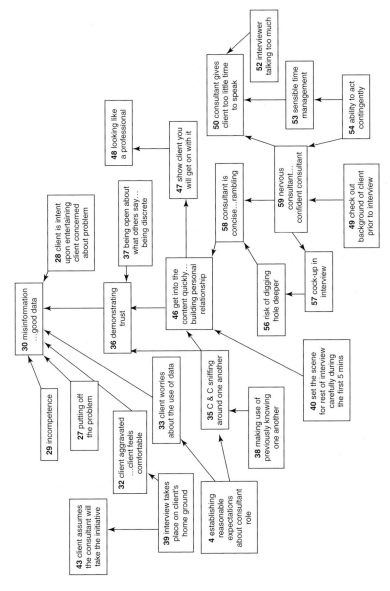

Figure 11.3 **An illustration of the use of the *Decision Explorer* (*COPE*)**

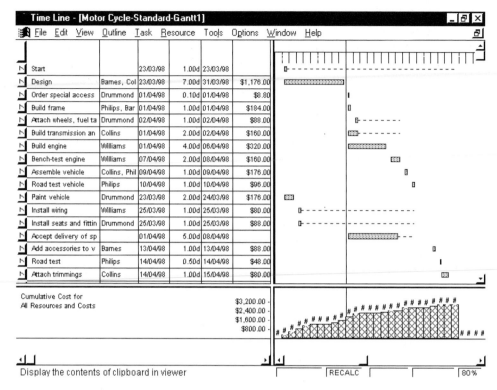

Figure 11.4 **PERT** network chart using *Time Line for Windows*™

3 *Controlling* – this includes using the network and schedule to keep track
of progress and to make any revisions necessary to keep the project on
schedule and within budget.

Seeing a whole project in perspective helps those involved to understand
what is happening or about to happen and can help to dispel people's
uncertainties. PERT provides a framework and time-scale within which
new ideas are to be implemented.

In the example shown in Figure 11.4, a firm wants to get a new racing
motor-cycle off the ground ready for the Isle of Man TT races. While the
firm normally plans things long in advance it has suddenly been presented
with a totally new idea. The major problem is one of getting the idea into a
tangible form for the start of the races and it means getting the team of
workers to produce the bike within a tight time schedule. The CEO wants
to know exactly what the labour costs will be and each of the five-man team
wants to know what will be required in the way of his services.

Computer simulation

Computer simulation models enable one to study how a system reacts to
conditions that are not readily or safely put into practice in a real situation.

With the aid of a computer simulation model the user can study how the behaviour of an entire system can be altered by changing individual parts of the system. A computer simulation model is usually defined in mathematical terms within a computer program. The functional relationships among elements within a system are represented by mathematical equations, and when the program is executed the mathematical dynamics become analogous to the dynamics of the real system.

The illustration in Figure 11.5 is taken from a simulation conducted by the writer to look for ways of managing scarce resources more effectively in the context of the health service. Better planning and scheduling of work considering anticipated demand for services held the promise of providing a more cost-effective service both to users (patients) and those providing the financial funding to make the services available. Through simulation one could demonstrate the advantages of changing working arrangements.

Computer simulation brings life to planned changes and helps people to appreciate what will be the result of making such changes. The dynamic and visual nature of this way of showing the effect of change actually can help people to visualise for themselves the effect of accepting new ideas and change.

Potential problem analysis

Kepner and Tregoe (1976) developed potential problem analysis (PPA) to alleviate the risk of new problems occurring during the implementation of new ideas and processes. Eight steps were involved in PPA:

1 Determine exactly what should take place if the task is to be done successfully.
2 Employ *reverse brainstorming* to identify everything that can go wrong during implementation.
3 Detail highlighted problems.
4 Assess and evaluate the impact of each identified potential problem on the implementation of the whole project.
5 Look for causes of the identified new problems.
6 Assess the probability of occurrence of each one of the potential problems.
7 Determine ways of minimising the effect of the potential problems.
8 Develop contingency plans for the most serious potential problems.

PPA provides a systematic framework to help implementers of ideas avoid the occurrence of the events of Murphy's Law (Bloch, 1990). Murphy's Law states that if anything can go wrong it will. PPA also helps to get to grips with many of the possible corollaries to Murphy's Law. For example,

1 Nothing is as easy at it looks.
2 Everything takes longer than you think.
3 If there is a possibility of several things going wrong, the one that will cause the most damage will be the one to go wrong.
4 Left to themselves, things tend to go from bad to worse.

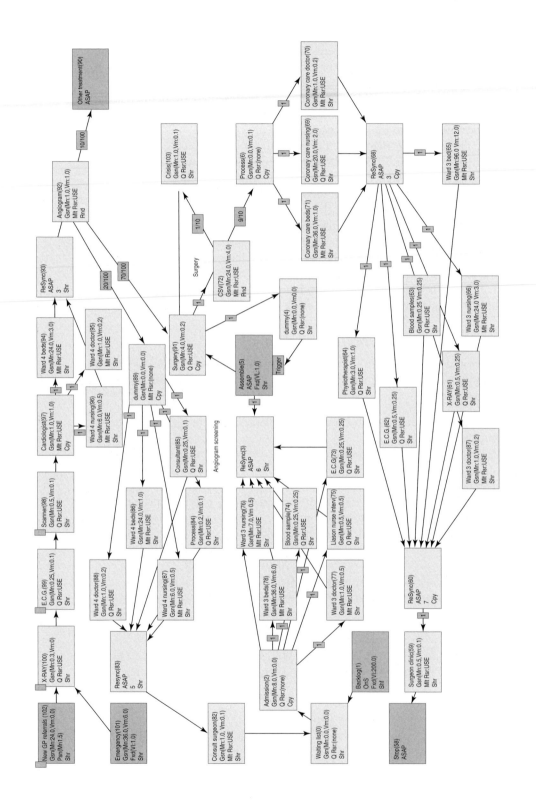

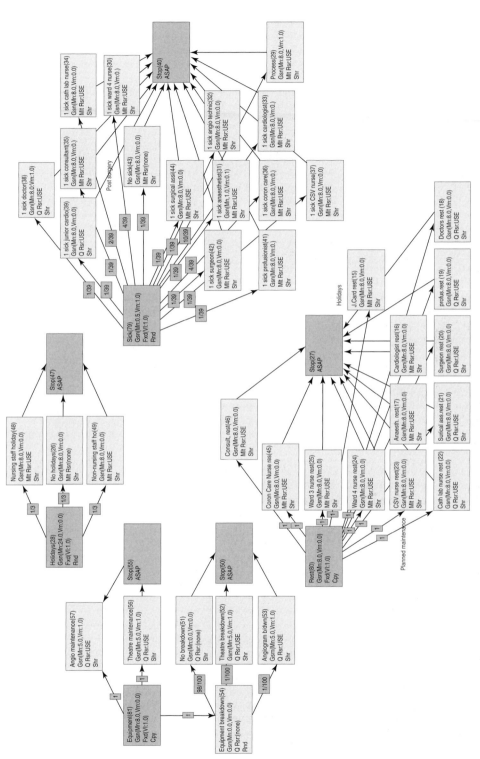

Figure 11.5 Simulation of the coronary artery deficiency treatment process in a UK hospital using Dynametrics

5 Whenever you set out to do something, something else must be done first.
6 Every solution breeds new problems.

Post-implementation

One has to make sure that what has been implemented actually works for more than just a couple of days and does not fall down because of something which has not been foreseen. That is not to say that there will not be complaints about what has been implemented. It is quite likely that the change agents or idea implementers will be inundated with messages, both from people who supported the new idea and people who opposed it saying that things do not seem to be working properly.

Feedback messages about new ideas that have been implemented may take the form of:

(a) *Grousing* – this usually does not require action and simply reflects people's resistance to change. People may complain because they are required to do things in a different way.
(b) *Errors of detail* – aspects of detail may have been overlooked. When the detail is not critical it is usually possible to remedy the situation fairly easily. Elements that are critical to the functioning of the whole, however, are more problematic and may require thorough analysis and reflection. In some cases they may even temporarily hold up matters until they can be resolved.
(c) *Apparently major errors* – these can be either real or supposed. In the latter case it is simply a matter of reassuring all concerned that it is only supposition. Where the problem is real then the implementation of the whole project may be at risk.

Ideas and changes must be workable and reliable. Thinking through and testing out ideas before they are finally implemented is highlighted as a critical stage of the process.

CLIMATE FOR CHANGE

Any organisation wanting to become more creative needs to be aware of the necessary conditions for creativity to thrive. Majaro (1992) suggested three prerequisites. These are:

1 The right climate.
2 An effective system of communicating ideas.
3 Procedures for managing innovation.

A firm in which the climate is either hostile or indifferent to ideas is unlikely to be creative. But what is the right climate? Firstly the organisation must be prepared to finance creative ideas. It is also very important that top management should encourage creativity at all times. Negativity has to be avoided at all costs. If those at the top do not take creativity seriously they send out messages to others in the organisation who will also tend to accept the same perspective. In an organisation without good communications good ideas can be lost simply because people do not know whom to inform about their ideas.

Old behaviour and attitudes are often deeply imbedded in the (comfortable) relationships which have been built up over the years. Any significant change generally suggests an upset or reshuffling of these relationships, and a change of one's relative position to others in the workplace. It appears that new thinking and new behaviour patterns are most readily and firmly established when they are conditions of regular membership in a new group, for group members exercise the most powerful tool for shaping behaviour.

MANAGING CHANGE SUCCESSFULLY

To get change in an organisation introduced successfully it is suggested that one should:

- React quickly to change – you need to think in a creative and innovative way.
- Accept that dealing with a continually changing situation is a normal part of your job. Don't bury your head in the sand when new or different problems arrive.
- Maintain a well-informed knowledge of developments in your industry or profession.
- Monitor the environment for signals, trends and developments in the attitudes and behaviour of competitors, customers and the market.
- Stimulate a positive attitude to change by regularly discussing new ideas and issues with colleagues.
- Encourage your staff to raise issues affecting their work.
- Discuss future plans and issues with your staff, both individually and as a group, on a regular basis.
- Communicate internal changes to your staff unless there is good reason not to do so in the short term.
- Be experimental and flexible in your approach to people's ideas.
- Try out new techniques and ideas whenever appropriate.
- Mobilise staff quickly and boldly, but in a co-ordinated fashion.

Create a working atmosphere in which ideas and issues do not fall between bureaucratic cracks.

QUESTIONS

1 A firm is trying to get its employees to participate in a new job enlargement scheme. Indicate the difficulties that might be encountered when trying to implement such a scheme. Outline the mechanisms that can be used to help deal effectively with such problems.

2 An organisation is experiencing problems in implementing a new computer based information system in its finance department. Illustrate how a cognitive mapping device such as *COPE* might be used to help gain insights into this problem.

3 Discuss the problems encountered in implementing ideas and indicate the various ploys which can be used to help get around these problems.

4 Machiavelli wrote: 'there is nothing more difficult to take in hand, more powerless to conduct or more uncertain in its success than to take the lead in the introduction of a new order of things because the innovators have for enemies all those who would have done well under the old conditions and lukewarm defenders in those who may do well (Machiavelli, chapter 5).

Discuss the implications of Machiavelli's thinking for the implementation of ideas. What steps can be taken to try to circumvent some of the difficulties that might arise in the way that Machiavelli suggested?

5 A firm is trying to get its employees to change their operating procedures to improve efficiency in the workplace. What kind of difficulties might be encountered when trying to implement such a scheme? Indicate what you would do in order to deal effectively with such difficulties.

6 Getting good ideas adopted by management can often pose problems. Indicate the nature of the problems and outline the mechanisms that can be applied to overcome the difficulties presented by the problems.

7 A firm is trying to get its employees to join a new pay scheme. Indicate the difficulties that might be encountered when trying to implement such a scheme. Outline the mechanisms that can be used to help deal effectively with such problems.

CASES

The Northern Bank

The CEO of the Northern Bank is concerned about the ability of the bank to give the type and quality of services that its customers require. He feels that the branch managers and their staff are coming under too much pressure to enable them to do their jobs properly. The branches have to be involved in all aspects of banking and operate at the sharp end of the business. Many of the jobs and operations that are performed at branch level are becoming increasingly expensive to operate, difficult to perform and need to be looked at in detail. The processing of routine activity takes up a good deal of the work and costs, and less than 30 per cent of time and money is put into improving customer relations and the marketing of services. Moreover, the nature of the marketing task has become increasingly complex. Not only does the organisation have to market itself to its customers but the management of the organisation has to engage in extensive internal marketing to gain the commitment and co-operation of staff in providing the kind customer service which the bank thinks desirable. Moreover, the CEO feels that the requirements of personal customers are now too wide and too costly to be fully met by every branch.

In essence the CEO believes that the bank must be able to deliver to its customers the kinds of services and products that they want if they are to stay in business and return satisfactory profits. Furthermore he does not believe that the onus of this task should be the sole responsibility of the senior management or the bank's marketing staff. Achieving the required profile demands the support of the whole of the bank's staff.

Questions

1 How would you define the problem in this case?
2 What ideas can you think of that may lead to a solution to the problem?
3 Evaluate the ideas that you develop.
4 What problems would you expect to encounter in implementing these ideas? How would you try to overcome these problems?

Re-siting the sorting office

Green Star parcels operates a parcels delivery service from its base in West Bromwich. Opened in 1993, during the first three years of operation the firm grew rapidly from employing ten people on sorting to over fifty by late 1996. During the first three years of operation labour relations were good, but during the past three years they have somewhat soured due to a number of wildcat strikes, mainly on issues regarding pay and conditions of work. Ninety-five per cent of those engaged in sorting are members of a trade union.

The company operates a three shift, seven days per week operation and guarantees next day delivery on 90 per cent of its business. Because of the wildcat strikes, however, its delivery reputation has become somewhat tarnished of late.

Late in 1998, largely because of the continuing troubles (but not actually giving this as the reason for change), the company decided to re-site its operations at three new depots in the West Midlands and close the existing one. The new depots were close enough to where existing workers lived to enable most of them to retain their jobs and be employed at one or other of the depots. The company felt that it could take on additional workers since the actual demand for its services was far outstripping its capacity, despite the recent adverse publicity it had been receiving. It felt that by splitting up the workforce, those with a tendency to create trouble would be less in number on any one of the sites.

Question

Draw up a plan of action to implement this project. What do you consider to be the most important aspects that management should bear in mind?

chapter twelve

COMPUTER ASSISTED CREATIVE PROBLEM SOLVING

INTRODUCTION

In general, so far, computers themselves have not been specifically harnessed to produce creative ideas and insights by themselves. Rather it has been through the interaction of people and computers that ideas have been produced. However, Simon (1985) discussed a computer program called *BACON*, which he had developed with co-workers. He argued that if a computer program was able to make discoveries which, if made by a human, could be considered creative, then the processes it used should provide useful information about the creative process. The *BACON* program received raw observational or experimental data and produced, when successful, scientific laws. Simon wanted to show that scientific discovery is an understandable phenomenon which can be explained in terms of all the same kinds of basic information processing mechanisms that account for other forms of human problem solving and thinking. Simon's efforts were directed at getting a computer to undertake creative problem solving by itself.

Computer aided creative thinking and problem solving mechanisms began to appear in the late 1970s, reflecting some of the ideas of Rogers

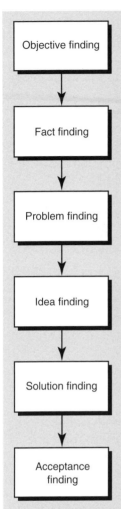

Objective finding

Fact finding

Problem finding

Idea finding

Solution finding

Acceptance finding

Figure 12.1 **The stages in CPS covered by this chapter**

(1954), Maslow (1954) and Kelly (1955). Rogers and Maslow had argued that self-discovery might lead to creative insights, while Kelly had suggested that the loosening of constructs produced the same results.

Rokeach (1979) put together a computer program which enabled individuals to examine their own value systems and clarify their knowledge. *Planet* (designed by Shaw, 1982) was a later program which helped the user to uncover the themes and variations with respect to their problems. A central component of this latter program was the Repertory Grid discussed by Kelly, and it is this which helped comprehension of the classifications people construct around their experiences and, if required, to reconstruct views on a problem. *COPE* was devised by Colin Eden (Eden *et al.*, 1983) and was designed to help map the relationship between ideas connecting interrelated sets of problems.

A growth in interest in the development of computer programs to aid creative thinking problem solving took place in the 1980s. *Brainstorm* was typical of a number of programs designed to help people be more systematic in their thinking. Essentially, it was an idea processor working rather like a word processor and a database combined. It permitted the user to type in ideas, or the outline of a plan or schedule, as they came to mind. Subsequently, it allowed the user to reorganise ideas or points entered under any number of headings or sub-headings so that the structure of a document, and the user's thoughts too, could be meaningfully organised.

While the above programs assisted in making the users more aware of their own thought processes, none facilitated the restructuring of the user's thinking in order to provide a basis for creative thought. The fact that people understand their thought processes and can organise them in a systematic way is not always a sufficient condition to encourage the generation of creative insights. Kelly (1955) had argued that it was first necessary to go through the process of destructuring existing thought patterns before one could hope to gain any insights into a problem situation.

Some of the programs developed in the 1980s attempted to introduce mechanisms that would help people to destructure and restructure their thinking. *Brainstormer*, for example, was such a program and using the morphological approach divided a problem along major dimensions or themes. It presented a structured approach to creative problem solving and facilitated three-dimensional morphological analysis. *MORPHY* combined the morphological approach with randomly generated words to act as suggestions for descriptors or attributes to be listed under the problem dimensions identified by the user. The use of random words in the latter led to the consideration of attributes which might not normally be considered and thence to the revelation of unusual insights into a problem. *MORPHY* grew out of work conducted by its creator with an earlier program *BRAIN*. The latter made extensive use of random word generation and the production of semi-meaningful statements as stimuli to thought.

Creators of computer assisted creative problem solving aids adopted different approaches. One such approach was reflected in the *Idea Generator*. The program encouraged the user to employ a fairly wide range of analogical reasoning methods. Methods included asking the user to relate similar situations to the problem, thinking up metaphors for the situation, and developing other perspectives. The program also included sections which helped people focus on goals and on the reverse of goals. In addition there was a section which helped the user evaluate ideas. More recent developments of the *Idea Generator* are still being marketed at the time of writing.

Several of these early programs attempted to take people through a number of stages of the creative problem solving process (e.g. *BRAIN* and the *Idea Generator*), while others made specific use of the computer's ability to randomise events (*MORPHY*) or help in recording and restructuring ideas (e.g. *Brainstorm*). Some of the programs facilitated more than one of these features.

STRUCTURED APPROACH TO CREATIVE PROBLEM SOLVING IN COMPUTER PROGRAMS

It will be recalled from earlier in the book, that Van Gundy ([1981]1988) suggested six stages to the creative problem solving process:

1 Objective finding.
2 Fact finding.
3 Problem finding.
4 Idea finding.
5 Solution finding.
6 Acceptance finding.

This provides a potential theoretical framework against which to construct an integrated idea processing support system.

To be of assistance the computer assisted techniques should have the following features:

1 Facilitate movement through any or all of the stages of creative problem solving (i.e. problem definition, idea generation, idea evaluation, etc.).
2 Provide mechanisms which stimulate thought.
3 Provide a structuring framework within which to define problems, generate or evaluate ideas.
4 Facilitate or improve the use of conventional creative problem solving aids.

TYPES OF PROGRAMS

There is now a range of computer software which can be used to assist creative problem solving. This stretches from purpose built software to more general purpose software which can be used to stimulate creative thinking. In addition, some software is useful for the individual working alone while other software is of benefit to groups of individuals working on a problem or project together.

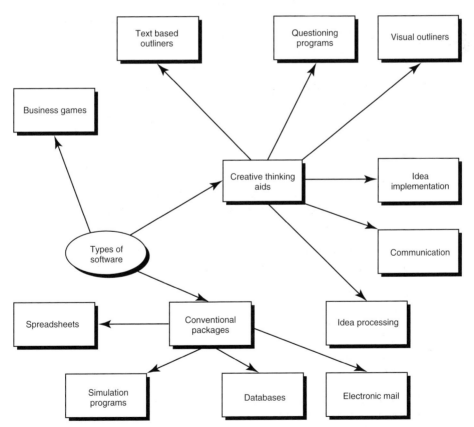

Figure 12.2 **An overview of the ways in which computers can help in the creative thinking process**

There are various ways of classifying creativity programs. These may be summarised under the following headings.

Text based outliners

Modern word-processing packages usually have an outliner mode built in. They are designed to help structure one's thoughts when preparing reports, articles or other literary works. *Brainstorm* was a forerunner of such features, the main idea of which is that one types ideas or thoughts into sections of an electronic page. One can then easily rearrange the sections in whatever order one chooses. It is also possible to collapse the sections to show just the first line. This enables a quick overview of what has been typed in to be obtained. Rearranging sections with just the first line showing facilitates the construction of a logically ordered document.

Visual outliners

Several programs attempt to automate the process of drawing graphical outlines, mind maps, and concept maps. These programs are useful for presentations and publication. There have been a number of good mind mapping programs produced commercially. A good example is *Inspiration*, and others include *Info Map Lite*, *Mindman* and *Idea Tree*.

Inspiration

Inspiration is a software program that facilitates mind mapping, a thinking process developed in the 1970s that takes superb advantage of the way the brain works. Instead of listing your ideas from *top to bottom*, mind mapping and *Inspiration* work from the *centre outwards*. This can, of course, be done with paper and pencil by starting with a central idea and adding thoughts, connecting them like spokes from a wheel's axle. The map which develops allows one to link and expand ideas so that the mind map which is produced grows like a web. *Inspiration* has advantages over paper and pencil methods. The structure encourages the user to build on ideas by recording everything added and keeps the mind map legible.

The mind map develops as a series of interconnected boxes. Starting with one box, one types in associations and *Inspiration* creates more boxes that branch out from the first. If you run out of ideas from one branch or something else occurs to you, you can click on another box and start a new branch. When the data entry is complete you can save, export or print mind maps.

Inspiration helps the user to generate insights, produce concepts in diagrammatic form and create outlines. In the diagram view you can make free-form visuals, diagrams and presentation graphics, while the integrated outline view allows the expansion of ideas into outlines and written documents.

Questioning programs

Several programs take input from the user, and then present sets of questions, keywords, or exercises to provoke new ideas. *IdeaFisher* and *MindLink*, for example, both make use of this approach.

IdeaFisher

Marsh Fisher, *IdeaFisher*'s developer, worked for more than ten years developing *IdeaFisher*, many of them spent sorting thousands of words into hundreds of boxes to create the associative categories on which the program is based. The result is a huge database of concepts associated in all sorts of ways. *IdeaFisher* helps one to create mental associations starting from the input of a word or concept. *IdeaFisher* includes a feature called the *Qbank* which provides several lists of questions to point users in the right direction if they do not know how to proceed in a project. It is also possible to construct your own lists of questions and these can be stored in the program for use on a future occasion. *IdeaFisher* is built around a database called the *IdeaBank*, which contains more than 60,000 words organised by major categories (such as Actions, Animals, Colours, the Senses, Emotions and Places) and topical categories (groups of related concepts such as achievement/success/failure or adolescence/stereotypes of teenagers). All of the entries in the *IdeaBank* are cross-referenced by concept and association. One can use free association, moving from one word or phrase to the next. *IdeaFisher* automatically records findings on the *Idea Notepad*, and the contents of this can be exported as a text file. The program permits the generation of new ideas based on combinations of words. One types in two words, and *IdeaFisher* creates a list of people, animals, verbs, adjectives, and phrases that are all associated with that word combination in some way or other.

   IdeaFisher generates massive lists based on single entries, but perhaps the application's most powerful feature is its compare option which filters associations shared between two categories. This is particularly useful when seeking a common ground between groups or ideas.

MindLink

MindLink Problem Solver integrates idea generation and problem solving by combining a collection of creative thinking tools and techniques into a flexible, learn-while-using problem solving program which includes a relational database for storage and retrieval of ideas. This allows users to create a database of ideas that can be retrieved for use on future problems (using Keywords and Text Searches). The computer package is divided into six modules. Any module can be accessed by clicking on its icon located in the opening window. Modules are ordered in a logical fashion, moving from the easiest to harder to use but more powerful modules. These are named respectively: Gym, Idea Generation, Guided Problem Solving, Problem Solving, Evaluate and Refine, and the relational database (*Thought*

Warehouse). The program provides a structured approach to creative thinking. A problem or challenge is typed in, and the program presents questions and exercises that help the user examine it from different angles. Responses to *MindLink*'s questions can be saved as a text file for use in other applications.

Idea processing

There are many different idea processors.

The *Axon Idea Processor* offers a visual workbench with a range of tools to record, process and manipulate ideas. It is a sketch-pad for visualising and organising ideas and its user interface is especially designed to support the thinking processes. It is unlike a word processor, which is designed for text formatting, and handles the upstream idea processing whereas a word processor handles the downstream formatting.

The *Idea Generator Plus* boosts creative thinking and planning skills by dividing the problem solving process into three logical parts:

1 *Problem Statement* helps users define their problems and related objectives and give their brainstorming session a tight focus.
2 *Idea Generation* allows users to choose from seven thought-provoking techniques to create many new ideas and solutions. For example, one technique is to consider other perspectives. Another is to think of metaphors for the situation. And a third technique is to reverse your goals (to discover what to avoid!).
3 *Evaluation* enables users to find their best ideas by ranking ideas against objectives and considering long and short term costs and benefits. Reports list the new ideas, numerically ranked, for further consideration and analysis.

Creative decision support systems

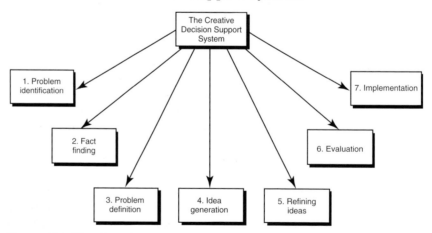

Figure 12.3 **The *Creative Decision Support System***

Decision support systems (DSS) (Figure 12.3) have been around for some years. Idea processing support systems (IPSS), however, are a relatively new concept discussed extensively by Young (1989). IPSS deal with the synthesis of ideas into problem contexts and exploratory problem definition.

A COMPUTER BASED IDEA PROCESSING SUPPORT SYSTEM

While there are many packages designed to assist creative problem solving, some of which have been referred to as *idea processing support systems*, there has not been any attempt until now to design a comprehensive integrated *idea processing support system*. Here, I will describe such a system in some detail.

The *Creative Decision Support System* (CDSS) is currently in its prototype version and undergoing testing. It is structured around a variation on the ideas of the creative problem solving process as outlined by Van Gundy ([1981] 1988). In this case, however, a seven-stage process has been adopted:

1 Problem identification
2 Fact finding
3 Problem definition
4 Idea generation
5 Refining ideas
6 Evaluation
7 Implementation

The package runs under *Microsoft Windows* and possesses all the usual save, load, cut, paste and print facilities. In addition, under the *utilities* menu there is a drag and drop facility which allows you to view any text file or run any program that you may have on the system. The latter facility means that even if certain procedures are not available within the package itself the user can readily access his or her favourite software. This permits access to one or other of the various mind mapping programs available, *PERT* scheduling programs such as *Time Line*, a word processor, a full blown spreadsheet, drawing packages, charting packages, and so on. Some of these facilities are incorporated into the software as it stands, but this access to outside packages readily improves the usefulness of the package.

Creative Decision Support System is a step-by-step approach to creative problem solving which one can follow through from beginning to end or access at any one of several different points *en route*. The user can start at the *problem identification* stage and work through all the subsequent stages, or can simply pick one of the stages, say *idea generation*, and work through that stage. All the stages are readily accessible through a multi-tiered menuing system.

Some of the mechanisms incorporated into the package are quite sophisticated, while others simply involve getting the user to work through a simple bank of questions. Figure 12.4 is produced by clicking the *problem identification* submenu and selecting the *considerations* option. The bank of

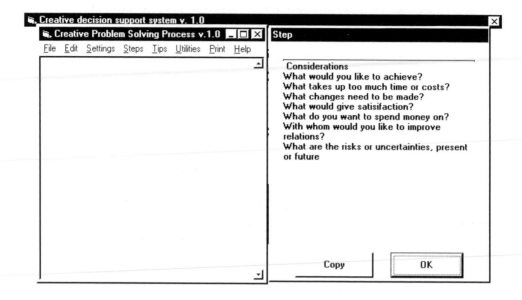

Figure 12.4 **Problem identification: considerations**

questions can be copied to the main text editor on the left and the questions answered or developed as required. Everything written or copied to the text editor can of course be reformatted, saved, reloaded and copied to other word-processing packaging. One can also paste material from other applications into it.

The *creative decision support system* contains several more sophisticated procedures which can help stimulate thoughts. These include databases, pictorial representations or visual images, and auditory stimuli. The databases relate to use of analogies to help stimulate ideation, phrases which stimulate perspectives on problems – e.g. reverse them, turn them upside down, etc. – and stages in potential problem analysis. All databases can be updated and so the user can add his or her own thoughts as and when they occur. Pictorial representations are used in the same way that conventional *trigger cards* are used in non-computerised creative problem solving methods. In essence one generates a picture or sets of pictures and asks people to link characteristics or associations which the pictures bring to mind with the problem in question. The use of pictorial representations helps to get round some of the barriers to creative thinking occasioned by a reliance solely on language as the means of stimulation and ideation.

Figure 12.5 illustrates the use of pictorial representation in one of the techniques used in the *creative decision support system*. In this case the user is using visual images as stimuli to thought. The user has to list all associations which are produced by the images and then, by selecting one or more groups of three associations (one from each image), hopefully obtain

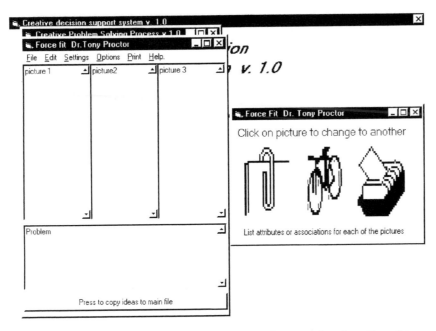

Figure 12.5 **Force fit uses pictorial representations to stimulate thought**

some insights into the problem. The associations and insights are listed in the text editing boxes on the left hand side of the screen from where they can be copied to the main text-editing screen illustrated in Figure 12.4. The user can make use of various forms of images as stimuli, including photographs. These can be created in a number of different formats for use with the package.

The *creative decision support system* also presents auditory stimuli to the user in another procedure. In this case the user is asked to produce lists of associations and again is expected to try and draw some kind of insights into the problem with which he or she is working.

Figures 12.6 to 12.8 show the database stimuli which are included in the program.

In the first of these instances, the *analogies database* (Figure 12.6), the idea is to take an analogous problem to the one that is being considered and to identify the various stages or procedures that are involved in solving it. The problem should be one with which the user has considerable familiarity. Of course, the analogous problem should have some similarities with the one under consideration, otherwise no subsequent transfer of useful ideas will be possible. Analogies should be based on everyday events which are readily understood. The purpose of having such a database is that one can relate step by step the stages in solving the analogous problem to the real problem with which one is having difficulty. This then may lead to some insightful solutions. For example, suppose one is deciding how to deal with the mass of items in one's in-tray. By considering the analogy of filling the boot of a car for going on holiday this would seem to suggest that the

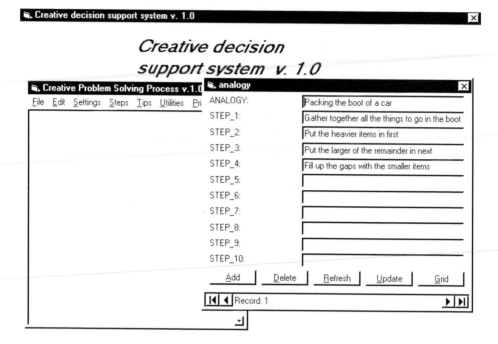

Figure 12.6 **The analogies database**

best course of action is to deal with the larger and heavier items first – i.e. those that are most important.

In the case of the *changes database* (Figure 12.7), one is being encouraged to look for solutions by changing one's perspective on the problem. For example, suppose one has the technical problem of material sticking to the sides of a rotating drum during a mixing process such that the actual mixing is impaired. The suggestion *drench it* taken from the changes database might lead one to spraying the mixture with water during the rotation process thereby preventing material from sticking to the sides of the drum. Of course the idea would only work provided that the water can be removed subsequently by centrifuging and that the water does not adversely affect the nature of the mixture.

In the case of both of the above, one is able to add data to the database which may be useful on a subsequent occasion for solving new or related problems.

Figure 12.8 shows the potential problem analysis database. Here one is trying identify possible things that go wrong when trying to implement an idea. One is also assessing the probability that things will go wrong and suggesting contingency plans for dealing with the subsequent problems. The probabilities shown in the database and the resultant index (RP × PS) reflect the risk that problems may still arise despite the contingency action suggested.

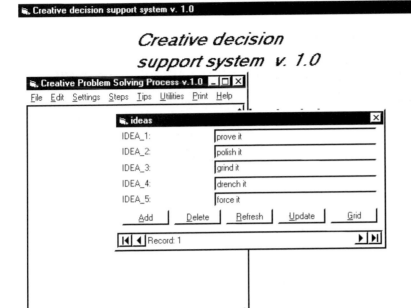

Figure 12.7 The changes database

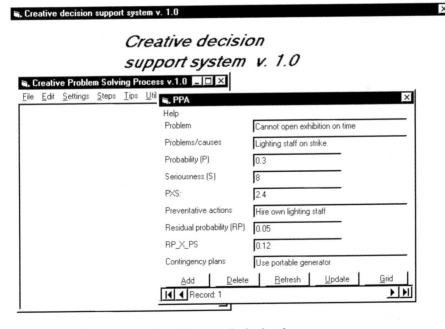

Figure 12.8 The potential problem analysis database

The ability to store such information in a database is useful for future reference when dealing with new problems.

HOW THE *CREATIVE DECISION SUPPORT SYSTEM* CAN HELP DECISION MAKERS

Organisations constantly encounter new problems and circumstances which demand innovative action to be taken. Unfortunately, innovative action has many pitfalls associated with it. Prather and Gundry (1996) identify what they call the five major pitfalls people and organisations tend to fall into when trying to become more innovative. These are:

1 Identifying the wrong problem.
2 Judging ideas too quickly.
3 Stopping with the first good idea.
4 Failing to get key people on board when trying to implement ideas.
5 Failing to challenge assumptions.

A tool such as the *creative decision support system* provides a systematic procedure by which the executive can work through the various stages of the creative problem solving process and hopefully avoid the five pitfalls mentioned above, along with others that may also exist. It provides a platform for producing new paradigms to deal with the increasingly complex nature of business.

Idea implementation

Once one has a good idea, it needs to be implemented. Depending on the size and scope of the project, a project management package could be used (e.g. *Time Line*), a task management package, or perhaps just a to-do list manager.

Communications (and the Internet)

World-wide communications, including the Internet, are good ways to bring people together for sharing ideas. Various Internet access providers (e.g. *Compuserve*), offer facilities for bringing people together in a virtual meeting room and aid the generation of ideas and discussion. Meeting room technology transforms the way people meet, improving the performance of people and the organisation. It can be used for brainstorming, problem solving, team building, strategic planning and interactive learning.

GROUP CREATIVE PROBLEM SOLVING AIDS

Networked personal computers permit the use of software which can assemble and amalgamate the ideas of different individuals working together on a problem. For example, a team of problem solvers can use such an application to evaluate and rank ideas which have either been generated in a group brainstorming session or which are the result of individual efforts collated on the network. This sort of software is time-saving and permits equality of opportunity to input ideas to all members of a group. It also makes it easier to gain a consensus of opinion.

Experience indicates that the merging of different perspectives and views is a productive way of obtaining new insights into intractable problems. *GroupSystems*™, developed at the University of Arizona in co-operation with IBM and other manufacturers, is built around idea generation, idea organisation, idea evaluation and issue exploration. The idea generation phase incorporates an electronic brainstorming tool which is used to record anonymous comments from group members. Traditional brainstorming, Delphi and nominal group methods are used to promote independent idea generation.

Other products aiming to achieve the same kind of goal include *TeamFocus*™, also developed at the University of Arizona, and *VisionQuest*™, developed by Collaborative Technologies Corporation of Austin, Texas. *TeamFocus*™ facilitates 'electronic meetings' on a 'decision network'. Team members can work from any location provided they have suitable computer hardware.

Aspects is a simultaneous conference program. It enables users of net-worked machines or modem linked machines to view graphic or text documents in a real time environment. Users can of course be in different rooms in different buildings and can make changes to documents at any time. In this way a consensus of opinion about the subject under scrutiny can be achieved. An added feature is that users can communicate with each other without interrupting the ongoing work. The software facilitates creative problem solving techniques.

OptionFinder™ is another package which can be used by a group. It is readily available in the UK and is designed to provoke thought and explore the different opinions held by the people who may use it. The system consists of a public screen and a single personal computer loaded with the software. The system is portable and is used to facilitate voting on issues identified by a facilitator. Voting is anonymous, but comment is not. Voting analysis is displayed in a graphical format, either on an x–y grid or as a bar chart on the public screen. This analysis of opinion enhances evaluation and feedback. It clarifies whether there is consensus of opinion or whether there is disagreement. Confirmation of conflicting beliefs can induce thought provoking exchanges and new ideas.

CONVENTIONAL SOFTWARE

Spreadsheets

Spreadsheets facilitate creative problem solving. Simple or complex mathematical models can be constructed with the aid of a spreadsheet and subjected to sensitivity analysis. This is both a powerful and a simple way of encouraging creative thinking. It encourages people to try out ideas in a risk free environment and provides a ready made tool for doing so. Jackson (1985) provided ample illustrations of the use of spreadsheets for this purpose. Her illustrations cover many aspects of business including: database management; statistical analysis; survey data; analysis of relationships; sales forecasting; financial planning; cost estimation; budgeting; decision modelling; sensitivity analysis and simulation. An example of a sensitivity analysis of the net savings to be derived from implementing a project is shown in Figure 12.9. Three scenarios are assumed, showing the added costs of the new method as 75 per cent, 70 per cent and 65 per cent of the savings effected on the old method. A projection for four years is shown.

Scenario 1		year 1	year 2	year 3	year 4	Total
Savings on old method		£75,000	£100,000	£125,000	£200,000	£500,000
Added cost of new method	75%	£56,250	£75,000	£93,750	£150,000	£375,000
Net savings		£18,750	£25,000	£31,250	£50,000	£125,000

Scenario 2		year 1	year 2	year 3	year 4	Total
Savings on old method		£75,000	£100,000	£125,000	£200,000	£500,000
Added cost of new method	70%	£52,500	£70,000	£87,500	£140,000	£350,000
Net savings		£22,500	£30,000	£37,500	£60,000	£150,000

Scenario 3		year 1	year 2	year 3	year 4	Total
Savings on old method		£75,000	£100,000	£125,000	£200,000	£500,000
Added cost of new method	65%	£48,750	£65,000	£81,250	£130,000	£325,000
Net savings		£26,250	£35,000	£43,750	£70,000	£175,000

Figure 12.9 **Sensitivity analysis with a spreadsheet**

Simulation packages

Simulation can be of enormous benefit to an organisation. For instance, the Exxon Corporation developed a model of gasoline supply at a refinery which was used to control the inventories of several blends of gasoline and maximise storage tank utilisation. Savings resulting from not building an additional storage tank amounted to $1.4 million (Golovin, 1979). In another instance a corporate simulation model was developed for Canterbury Timber Products Ltd to improve planning for domestic and export operations. The resultant ability to explore more alternatives with the model resulted in savings in direct and opportunity costs of at least $10,000 per annum (de Kluyver and McNally, 1980).

Simulation packages such as *MicroSaint* and *Dynametrics* can be used to enable complex processes in organisations to be modelled. Based upon sampling real data, simulations of activities can be carried out on a micro-computer. It might be difficult, expensive or even dangerous to experiment in the real world with such activities, but on the computer these problems are removed. As in the case of the spreadsheet, people are encouraged to try out their ideas in a risk-free environment. (See Figure 11.5 on p. 242 for an illustration of the use of *Dynametrics* in the context of implementing ideas.)

Databases

A firm's internal records can be scanned to help solve customers' problems. In addition, external databases can be searched for information which has an influence on pending organisational decisions. It is also possible to use databases to search for new product ideas as suggested by Bar (1988).

Electronic mail systems

The use of an electronic mail system for creative problem solving purposes illustrates how a general purpose computer installation can aid the creative thinking process. It facilitates the informal exchange of ideas. Moreover, from using electronic mail systems in this way a new kind of software called 'Groupware' has evolved. Groupware is the name given to computer soft-ware that enables remote users to swap ideas and other information. Several software houses offer groupware packages and among those available is *Lotus Notes*™.

Business simulators

Business games were designed as aids to management development and training. They provide a vehicle by which principles and practice can be learned and experienced. Yet the business game also contains something which is vitally important in the management situation but which is seldom found in practice: it allows the individuals to take risks and make mistakes; to play out hunches and follow up wild ideas. By their very nature, business games encourage creative thinking and ideas by helping people to overcome some of the well known barriers to creativity such as the pressure to conform and the fear of looking foolish.

Business simulators offer the opportunity for individuals to test out ideas and take risks. They can be made to provide positive feedback when satisfactory decisions or suggestions are made by the user or when creative and sensible suggestions are made. Conversely, negative reinforcers can be employed when rash or uncreative actions or suggestions are made.

Computer assisted creative problem solving is not eccentric. It has been around now for the best part of twenty years. As one the early developers of the area I have a keen interest. The chapter suggests some useful packages.

QUESTIONS

1 What do you consider to be the essentials of a creative problem solving program? Do you think it should provide a structured approach to the whole CPS process or should it just concentrate on one aspect of it?

2 Design a creative problem solving program which you think could help people to deal with different kinds of open-ended problems.

3 How do you visualise computer assisted creative problem solving developing in the future?

CASES

A new approach

Alpha Beta Ltd are looking ten years into the future. They want to start development work now on a series of computer programs that will help people with the creative problem solving process. Among the ideas that are being considered are interactive games which have a definite bias towards solving business and management problems, rather than just being used for intellectual stimulation and interest.

Of course, it would be a relatively simple matter to take the kind of approach adopted in adventure-type games and produce software which could be used for the purpose they have in mind. However, since the firm is looking ten years into the future it has to consider what developments in hardware and software might occur over the interim period. This is perhaps the most difficult part of the project, since developments in software and hardware capabilities will certainly have a substantial impact on the work they undertake.

The firm envisages adopting a multi-stage development approach whereby intermediate products are produced from time to time over the next ten years which make use of existing technology at the time the software is released. Also, whatever is developed at the end of the ten years should be capable of subsequent development in the future.

Questions

1 Do you think that the firm is correct in suggesting that it should develop software along the lines of the adventure games approaches? Why or why not?

2 Assuming it does adopt the approach how might the ideas be translated into interactive experiences suitable for creative problem solving in the business world? Are there any limitations on how it might be used?

3 Create a scenario for desktop computer hardware and software development over the next ten years. What kind of computer assisted creative problem solving methods do technological developments suggest might best be supported?

appendix *one*

CASE EXAMPLE OF THE CREATIVE PROBLEM SOLVING PROCESS

GREAT NORTHERN BUS COMPANY

The Great Northern Bus Company is based in Newcastle upon Tyne and runs regular services to other parts of the UK. The company defines its competitors as all carriers of passengers to all parts of the United Kingdom. The company is forward looking and recently appointed you as a consultant to advise on how it might get to grips with the current problems which it faces. These are summarised by the marketing director as follows:

'Recently we have experienced a drop in sales and loss of market share in our long distance business and we need to find ways to improve our position. We desperately need some good ideas and a specific plan of action to help us get to grips with this problem. Can you advise, or better still see, what solutions to our problem you can come up with?'

You, of course, want to help and decide that the best way is to make use of the creative problem solving process in which you are an expert. As a first step you decide to gather a small group of personnel with interest and expertise in the subject together to start the process rolling.

You start with *objective finding* and ask the group to defer judgement and list some major concerns in the company. The following list is generated:

 1 Recruitment of more qualified personnel.
 2 Improved customer service among long distance passengers.
 3 Increasing market share.
 4 Better prediction of customer responses to marketing.
 5 Developing a marketing slogan.
 6 Improving manager–subordinate relations.
 7 Reducing promotional costs.
 8 Improving target market identification.
 9 Determining customer preferences.
10 Improving focus group procedures.

Next you identify 'hits'. This is a subjective process and varies from company to company and from person to person. In this case suppose the company identifies items 1, 2, 4 and 9. Items 2, 4 and 9 clearly represent hotspots concerning customers. If the group members agree, they might identify an objective involving customers.

To identify this area, they apply the criteria of ownership, priority and critical nature. They decide they have ownership over all the hits, since customers are a prime marketing responsibility. Of the hits they decide that item 2 (improving customer service among long distance passengers) has higher priority than the other hits, since it is more likely to affect financial profit. (Remember, this was the concern of the marketing director.) It is also critical because an improvement in the financial position is critical and there is a definite need to increase market share. Improved customer service may result in more customers (or repeat business) and therefore more profit.

After reviewing the hits and applying the criteria, they decide on the problem statement: 'IWWMW improve customer service for the long distance passengers?' They are now ready to move on to the next stage – *fact finding*.

Fact finding

The purpose of this stage is to generate relevant data to improve understanding of the problem. This in turn allows you to consider different problem perspectives. To search for data systematically the group uses the 5 W's method. They generate a list of Who? What? Where? When? and Why? questions and answer them as follows:

Who are the potential customers?
The long distance travellers
People on business
People on vacation/holiday
People combining business and pleasure
Frequent travellers
People visiting families
Males and females

Young and old people
Rich and poor people
People travelling with other bus companies

Who provides customer service?
Couriers
Ticket counter personnel
Catering personnel
Drivers
Maintenance staff
Travel agents

What is customer service?
Learning customer preferences
Attending to customer needs
Solving customer problems
Anticipating problems before they occur
Interacting with customers with a positive attitude

Where is customer service most evident?
During journeys
When delays occur
At ticketing counters
When any other problem affects customers
During peak travel periods

When do most people notice customer service?
When they are ignored
When someone goes out of his or her way to help
When they receive prompt attention
When an employee overlooks a minor policy to help someone in trouble

Why is good customer service important?
It helps to attract new customers
It helps to retain old customers
Sustained profits depend on it
It helps the company project a positive image
It creates satisfied customers who are more likely to travel with us again

The group members then converge and identify hits among the fact finding
data. To do this they underline the most important responses to the
questions and list the results. For example:

The long distance traveller
People travelling with other bus companies
Couriers
Drivers

Ticket counter personnel
Learning customer preferences
Anticipating problems before they occur
During journeys
When delays occur
When someone goes out of his or her way to help
When they receive prompt attention
It helps attract new customers
It helps retain old customers
It produces satisfied customers
It helps the company project a positive image

Next the group examines the hits to see if might group some together as hotspots. The group members develop the following list:

Employees
Couriers
Ticket counter personnel
When someone goes out of his or her way to help

Customers
The travelling public
People travelling with other bus companies
Learning customer preferences
It helps to attract new customers
It helps retain old customers
It produces satisfied customers

Travel related data
During journeys
When delays occur

Problem finding

The group now is ready to enter the *problem finding* stage to consider a variety of problem perspectives. Restating the problem might unlock a new viewpoint that could lead to many creative solutions. To create these viewpoints, the group examines the fact finding hotspots and uses the hotspots to generate possible problem redefinitions. The group members generate the following list of problems:

In which ways may we
1 encourage employees to go out of their way to help customers?
2 attract passengers who regularly travel with other bus companies?
3 attract new customers?
4 increase long distance traveller customer satisfaction?
5 reduce the number of departure delays?

Next they converge and identify hits using the criteria of ownership, likelihood of stimulating many ideas, and freedom from criteria. After analysing all the statements they select problems 1, 3 and 4. Of these they decide that problem 4 is most likely to resolve their objective of improving the company's financial position. The primary reason for this choice is one of ownership. Their marketing data suggests that the long distance market is the most unstable because no bus company has established itself in a dominant market position, as is the case with short distance travel. Thus, they may be able to capture a larger market share and improve their financial position.

Idea finding

The group is now ready to begin *idea finding* using the problem 'IWWMW increase long distance traveller satisfaction?' The members start with a purge to list more conventional ideas:

- install more comfortable seats
- offer good entertainment
- provide more leg-room
- train personnel to be more courteous
- lower ticket prices

Next they select a formal idea generation technique such as the two words method to implement the approach. To implement this approach, they follow these steps:

1 List alternative word meanings for two keywords in the problem statement.
2 Examine combinations of two words, one word from each list.
3 Use combinations to suggest ideas.

For instance, they might focus on the words *increase* and *satisfaction* and set up the technique as follows:

Increase	*Satisfaction*
Improve	Pleasure
Enlarge	Ease
Enhance	Enjoyment
Renew	Peace of mind
Upgrade	Contentment

Different combinations of these words suggest such ideas as:

Gourmet food (upgrade–pleasure)
Seconds on food and drink (renew–satisfaction)
Free travel insurance (upgrade–peace of mind)

Better seats (enhance–enjoyment)
Shortening ticket-buying queues (improve–ease)

After generating these and other ideas, the group might try another technique such as brainwriting. Brainwriting is a brainstorming variation in which a group generates ideas silently and in writing. The steps for this method are:

1 Each group member is given a stack of index cards.
2 Each member writes down one idea per card and passes it to the person on the right.
3 The person receiving a card examines the idea on it for possible stimulation of a new idea.
4 Members write down (on another card) any new ideas suggested and pass the card to the person on the right.
5 After about ten minutes of this activity, the idea cards are collected and evaluated.

Some possible ideas from this technique are:

• Videocassette players built into seat backs.
• Free snacks.
• On board business card raffles.

In this example, the group has generated a total of twenty ideas for improving passenger satisfaction. Group members now need to converge, identify any hotspots, and select idea-finding hits. For hotspots, they identify:

• Travel comfort (e.g. more comfortable seats, more leg-room)
• Food enhancements (e.g. gourmet food, free snacks).

To select hits from among these hotspots, they decide upon three criteria: cost, ease of implementation, and likelihood of increasing passenger satisfaction. After examining all the ideas and applying the criteria, they reduce the list of twenty ideas to two:

1 More comfortable seats.
2 Video-cassettes built into seat backs.

The group is now ready to move to the next CPS stage and select a final problem solution.

Solution finding

Solution finding contains two sets of divergent activities. First, the group generates evaluative criteria:

1 Cost.
2 Time to implement.
3 Degree to which current equipment will require modification.
4 Effect on routine travel operations.
5 Acceptance by bus crew.
6 Passenger long term interest level.
7 Ability to interest a broad cross-section of passengers.

The second divergent solution-finding activity is to improve the ideas from idea finding. In this case the group members decide the ideas don't need improvement and move on to convergent solution finding.

Of the seven criteria they generated, the group members decide to delete criteria 2 and 5. They then construct a weighted decision matrix (Table A1.1). This allows different weighting for each criterion; thus cost may be seen as more important than acceptance of an idea by a bus crew.

Table A1.1 **Weighted decision matrix**

Criteria	Criteria importance	More comfortable seats		VCRs in seat backs	
		Idea score	Subtotal	Idea score	Subtotal
1 Low cost	5	2	10	3	15
2 Equipment modification	5	1	5	2	10
3 Routine travel operations	4	2	8	3	12
4 Passenger interest level	4	3	12	5	20
5 Interest to cross-section	3	3	9	5	15
Totals			44		72

The group rates each criterion on importance, using a five-point scale (1 = not very important; 5 = very important). Next, each solution is rated on the degree to which it satisfies each criterion. The lower the number, the less the criterion is satisfied. For instance, more comfortable seats were rated a 2 on the criterion of low cost. this means the group believes they will be relatively expensive. (Cost is always a confusing item since low cost will receive a high rating). Finally, they multiply the criterion ratings by the ratings for each solution ('idea score') and sum the products (subtotal). For instance, they multiplied the criteria importance rating of 5 for low cost by the rating of 2 for more comfortable seats and recorded a response of 10 as the subtotal. Then they summed the products in each column. As shown below, they rated VCRs the higher of the two options. In this case, however, the group decides to select VCRs.

Acceptance finding

It is not enough to select the best solution. Steps must also be taken to ensure the solution can be implemented successfully. This requires consideration of implementation obstacles and ways to overcome them.

A systematic way to ensure effective implementation is to conduct a potential problem analysis (PPA). Although different versions exist, the PPA used here was developed originally by Kepner and Tregoe (1976) and later modified by Van Gundy ([1981] 1988). The steps for conducting a PPA are as follows:

1 Generate a list of potential problems that might hinder solution implementation.
2 Select the most important problems and list the possible causes of each.
3 Rate the probability of occurrence of each (1 = not very probable; 5 = very probable) and the seriousness of each (1 = not very serious; 5 = very serious).
4 Multiply each probability rating (P) times each seriousness rating (S) to obtain a PS score.
5 Generate preventive actions for each problem cause.
6 Rate the residual probability (RP) that each problem cause still will occur after a preventive action has been taken.
7 Multiply the PS score by the RP score.
8 Develop contingency (back-up) plans for causes with the highest PS × RP scores.

An example of a PPA using the VCR is shown in Table A1.2. There are two problems with three causes each. The group estimates that all the preventive actions will reduce the probability of occurrence of each cause. For instance, equipment failure owing to lack of maintenance is reduced from a probability value of 3 to a 1 after the preventive action of checking the VCRs after every trip. Group members then multiply the PS ratings by the RP ratings to determine which causes should have back-up or contingency plans. In this case, the most important area seems to be equipment failure owing to misuse. If built-in 'help' functions do not prevent misuse, they suggest a computer diagnostic program that automatically signals potential misuse. If the group wanted, it could also have developed contingency plans for the other, more highly rated causes.

The last acceptance finding activity involves developing an action plan to guide solution implementation. A useful way to structure this plan is to use the Five W's questions of Who? What? Where? When? and Why? For instance, they might ask such questions as:

Who will be responsible for implementation?
What will they implement?
Where will they need to go to implement it?
When should it be implemented?

Table A1.2 **Example of a potential problem analysis (PPA)**

Potential problem/ causes	P	S	Preventive actions	PS	RP	PS × RP	Contingency plan
1 Equipment failure							
(a) Heavy use	4	5	Use industrial equipment	20	2	40	
(b) Misuse	5	5	Built in help	25	2	50	Computer diagnosis
(c) Lack of maintenance	3	5	Check after every journey	10	1	10	
2 Passengers do not know how to use equipment							
(a) Unfamiliarity	2	3	Instructional video/ film	6	1	6	
(b) Poor instructions	5	3	Write own instructions	15	1	15	
(c) Not user friendly	5	4	Test with passenger sample	20	2	40	

The Why? question can be used by asking 'Why?' of all the other questions – that is, asking why a particular person (or persons) should be responsible for an implementation activity (Who?); why a particular thing should be implemented (What?); why it should be implemented in a particular location (Where?); and why one time rather than another would be better to implement it (When?). This stage ends with a sequential listing of specific action plan steps. For instance, the group might want to survey customers, then contact VCR manufacturers and take bids, consult with engineers on installation problems, rewrite instructions if necessary, and so forth.

After implementation, the only remaining CPS activity is to follow up the effectiveness of the solution. In this instance, the group would want to know if it has solved the original problem of increasing passenger satisfaction. If so, the next task would be to relate improved satisfaction with increased revenues from ticket sales.

appendix two

ADDITIONAL CASES

On the following pages there are a number of small case study problems on which you can try out your creative problem solving skills. Use whatever aspect of the CPS process seems most applicable to the case in hand. Some cases are easier than others and one – that on the verge escapement (pp. 289–90) – may require you to undertake some searching of the technical literature not covered in this book.

DA International

DA manufactures electrical goods in Malaysia and supplies them to agents and distributors in a number of different South-East Asian markets. Recently it has decided it would like to open a manufacturing plant in Europe so that it can access nearby markets. It is trying to decide between a site in the UK and one in France. It is presently trying to enumerate the facts it would require to help it deliberate and choose between alternatives.

Question

What facts do you think the company should try to obtain and how should it set about obtaining them?

Recruiting management trainees

Management has a policy that all new graduates joining a company should start at the bottom of the organisation and gradually work their way up to more important jobs. This policy has been adopted because of the complex nature of the business and the perceived need that all executives should fully understand the workings of the business in detail. The firm anticipates that its management trainees would hold a first level managerial post within five years of joining the company.

Many new graduates who have joined the company have left after a very short space of time because other companies do not impose such a stringent requirement on their new recruits.

Question

What action do you think management can take to rectify this situation?

London furniture company

The firm is a furniture company situated in an area of London where the majority of the population is made up of adults aged between 21–40. The company manufactures and markets furniture to the local population. Some years ago the firm designed a new type of furniture which proved very successful, but recently its sales have taken an unprecedented tumble.

The initial statement of the problem is:

- The firm wants to increase its furniture sales volume and is looking for ways of doing this.

Using the boundary examination technique the firm restructures the problem perception as follows:

- The firm highlights the words *furniture* and *looking*. In the case of the *furniture* it is felt that there are hidden assumptions about shape, size and style. In the case of the word *looking* it is felt that a more proactive stance is in order and that one needs to create ways rather than just look for them.
  This leads to a new problem redefinition:

- How can the firm improve the style of the furniture in order to stimulate people to buy it.

The next step is to generate some insights or possible solutions to the problem. The Gordon–Little variation of brainstorming is chosen for this purpose. In this case only the leader of the creativity session knows the real problem and introduces the problem to the group in the first place in abstract form. The problem is gradually introduced through a number of stages of revelation – moving from the abstract to the concrete and original problem. In the final stage the group re-examines all previously generated ideas and tries to turn them into tangible ideas relating to the original problem.

The following episodes ensued:

1 Think of ways to improve something:

make it larger
polish it
add more features
use new technology

make it smaller
change its shape
make it interchangeable

2 Think of ways to improve something in order to stimulate people:

put wheels on it
make it lighter in weight
add some sugar
attach a winning lottery ticket to it
give it a face lift

make it easy to pick up
make it curvy
add some colours
use new material

3 Original problem: How can the firm improve the style of the furniture in order to stimulate people to buy it:

make it of stainless steel (from 'polish it')
use computers to design it (from 'use new technology')
design a chair which can also be used as a small table (from 'make it interchangeable')
paint it with an unusual type of varnish (from 'add some colours')
create a table lamp from wire (from 'use new materials')

While the firm felt it had generated some useful insights it decided that it would use the morphological analysis approach as well to see if this would produce further new ideas (Table A2.1).

Table A2.1 **Morphological analysis matrix**

Shapes	Kinds	Material	Function	Style
oval	chairs	wood	sleeping	period
square	beds	metal	eating	deco
round	tables	plastic	resting	modern
rectangle	desks	stone	sitting	Italian
pentagon	clocks	glass	reading	western
hexagon	stools	leather	thinking	campaign
cylinder	TVs	foam	entertaining	regency

The next step combined two or more sub-elements of the matrix to find useful ideas. The following were suggested:

- A circular, glass television with four screens capable of revolving for entertainment.
- A modern style plastic chair with storage space under the seat and behind the back.
- A hexagonal stone TV cabinet.
- An oval metal imitation regency style kitchen table.

The next stage involved evaluating the ideas in terms of their time and money requirements. Ideas were categorised into three groups: simple, hard and difficult. Simple ideas are those which can be put into action with the minimum of expenditure of both time and money. Hard ideas require more expenditure of time and money, while difficult ideas require substantial expenditure of time and money. Using this method ideas were classified as shown in Table A2.2.

Table A2.2 **Evaluating the ideas**

Simple	Hard	Difficult
Paint it with an unusual type of varnish	Oval metal regency kitchen table	Use computers to design furniture
Design a chair that can be used as a small table as well	Modern plastic chair with storage space	Hexagonal stone TV cabinet
Create a table lamp out of wire	Circular glass TV with screen along edges	
Make it of stainless steel		

This led to further possible practical solutions:

- Design furniture out of cheap material (wire, glass, etc.).
- Design strange shapes and styles (hexagonal, triangular, etc.).
- Invest in computer technology

Question

Evaluate the methods adopted by the firm in this instance.

Pink skirts

A manufacturer has had to stop production of skirts because there is no place to store the skirts. The problem is caused primarily by the fact that there is a large stock of unsold pink skirts which have been in the warehouse for a considerable amount of time taking up costly space. The firm has considered finding extra premises for storage but this does not really solve the problem. The pink skirts, 350,000 of them, cost around £5 each to produce. This means that not only is the firm having critical storage problems but it has around £1.75 m tied up in stocks!

The problem is so acute that immediate remedying of the situation is essential.

Question

What action should the firm take?

Universal creativity

It is 3575 and the Androids have taken over control of all commercial enterprise on the earth and in most parts of the universe which has been explored to date by mankind and other intelligent life-forms. Androids run all the businesses and all intelligent life-forms enjoy an existence of enforced idleness and pleasure. Disease has become a thing of the past and most earthling beings now live to at least 110 years of age. Moreover, poverty as it was known in the nineteenth, twentieth and twenty-first centuries on earth has disappeared. Affluence abounds everywhere and all human beings have a standard of living at least equivalent to the very richest people in the twenty-first century on earth.

The Androids are looking for ways to provide new entertainment for human beings and other intelligent forms on distant galaxies. Time travel is now possible, though it has only been experienced by relatively few intelligent beings who live on the planet A6183 in Galaxy 918. In addition, instant means of transportation over distances of thousands of light years has been made possible during the last decade as a result of new technologies.

Question

Can you think of any ideas which might be helpful for the Androids in their search for new ways to entertain intelligent life-forms throughout the galaxies?

Taylorism revisited

'The young people seem to like it but old hands resist it and any newcomers over 40 don't seem to stay long', John said dryly.

'Yes and I think we need to have a spread of all ages in the organisation. People have experiences from all walks of life that have relevance to banking. It isn't just young inexperienced people we need, it is older ones too', Jayne answered.

'I blame this "pay-related" work business. Banking is a profession; it isn't just about selling services. We need to offer people advice about their needs not sell them things that they do not want.' John spoke from thirty years' experience of banking.

'True, but you know banking is more competitive nowadays. The invasion of the building societies into our industry has made it much more competitive. If we don't keep abreast of competition, we'll all lose our jobs', Jayne smiled.

'Well, I've only a few years to go. But I don't agree with what is happening. In my younger days one joined the bank for a secure job. A hire and fire mentality seems to be the norm these days', John replied.

'Well, that's not really true, is it?', Jayne asked, somewhat irritated by John's negativity. 'The only difference that I can see is that those who work harder for the organisation get better rewards. And, in my opinion, that is how it should be.'

Question

How might banks seek to achieve their multiple objectives of profession-alism and competitiveness?

St Jude's

St Jude's college stands on a hill overlooking the M6 not far from Wigan. It is, or rather was at one time, an establishment for the training of priests. In more recent years its extremely spacious accommodation has been host to a number of local events to do with ecclesiastical matters, but its role as a training establishment has long since been defunct.

The driveway to St Jude's, nearly a quarter of a mile in length, is bordered by dense rhododendron bushes which hide extensive gardens to their rear. Beyond the building itself there are many acres of woodlands and even more extensive gardens. The building is imposing. Its ivy clad walls, huge front door and gothic towers making the visitor tremble with appre-hension when first it is seen. Inside the building there is a maze of corridors, rooms of all sizes, no less than five different floors and a basement, a chapel and extensive well equipped toilet and bathroom facilities. In addition there is a very large kitchen equipped with modern cooking equipment.

Of course, St Jude's is a problem for the archdiocese. Expenditure on maintaining the buildings and gardens far exceeds the meagre revenues which it generates. The Archbishop is opposed to the selling of the building but wants to find some way of keeping it and using it for ecclesiastical purposes, while at the same time trying to at least balance income and expenditure.

Question

What suggestions can you come up with in this case?

Super-liners

The 'queens' were the largest and heaviest ships ever built. Their working lives were curtailed by the advent of jet-powered air passenger services across the Atlantic. It was not the end of large passenger ships, however, for a new type of holiday became fashionable – the cruise holiday. Smaller, though very substantial ships were built to ply cruise routes around the Mediterranean, the Caribbean and other attractive holiday areas of the world. Modern day cruise liners are like floating hotels, offering many different forms of entertainment, accommodation and ranges of prices to suit the needs of customers.

Recently, a new breed of cruise liner has appeared on the scene. These are super-liners, larger than the old 'queens' and designed to be much more spacious. They even boast golf-courses! These are mini floating cities, not just floating hotels. Even-larger super-liners are planned and there seems to be no limit to how large these vessels can be.

Question

How might the new super-liners be suitably equipped to make best use of their size to provide entertainment and other facilities for customers?

Place marketing

Liverpool developed as a seaport during the nineteenth century. It was famed as a departure point for transatlantic traffic. One of the main attractions today is the Albert Dock, which has been redeveloped as a tourist attraction. It features a museum, art gallery, shops and restaurant facilities. Liverpool is a city with first class Victorian architecture. The waterfront, which incorporates the Pier Head and the Liver buildings, is a landmark as well-known as the New York skyline or Sydney Harbour Bridge. The liver birds are the city's logo, and Liverpool Football Club and the Beatles have enjoyed international fame exceeded by none.

However, when it comes to commercial development into the twenty-first century the story is somewhat different. While Manchester, less than 40 miles away, boasts an international airport second only to Heathrow in terms of importance in the UK, Liverpool's airport is much smaller and has regular flights mainly to the Isle of Man, Eire and Ulster. While Manchester was able to get permission to build a second runway, in the face of much opposition from local residents, Liverpool can hardly make best use of the facilities it has already. Yet Liverpool airport does have considerable potential for development as a centre for serving the North West of England.

In the 1970s there was sustained government intervention in the area of urban regeneration and place marketing. Development area status was granted to some areas of the country and special Enterprise Zones were established where there was high unemployment and failing industries.

Such areas were able to offer financial inducements and other incentives in order to persuade firms to relocate there. Today place marketing is an integral aspect of urban regeneration policies which strive to rebuild and redevelop local, regional and national economies. Over the last ten years a number of towns, regions, and cities have undertaken expensive marketing campaigns in order to promote themselves, and amongst these are Manchester and Liverpool.

Questions

What sort of things do you think the marketing of places should aim to promote? How might the marketing of a city like Manchester be different from that of Liverpool?

What they don't teach you at business schools

Business schools teach leadership, planning, control, decision making and problem solving. But is it this that enables aspiring executives to climb the organisational ladder? It will be remembered that Blake and Mouton in the book the *Managerial Grid* (1964) noted that the people most likely to get promoted were those who paid most attention to the work and least attention to their colleagues – although the book suggested that attention to both was the best way to manage. Perhaps there is a darker side, then, to success in the workplace – an aspect which is not recorded anywhere in writing and only spoken of in whispers, out of earshot of colleagues.

Of course, murder and assault is not common in the workplace – at least not in the physical sense of the words. However, metaphorically speaking, the reality is that this is often what does happen. People deliberately tell lies, or fail to tell all, simply to give themselves an advantage. Moreover, if one spots that a colleague is trying to make a threatening move against one then it is only fair play that one should anticipate the oncoming blow and mount a counter offensive. Maligning one's direct competitors for promotion in the workplace and plagiarising the ideas of others are seen as part of the game. After all, work is only a kind of game and no one really needs to get hurt – do they? And perhaps the most important skill of one-upmanship is deceit – convincing others that you really do know what you are talking about when you don't understand the subject matter at all.

Then there are 'cliques' and 'hole in the corner' meetings. Managing cliques is a world of its own. Off to the pub every lunch-time or after work to talk shop – or rather plot and counter-plot against other groups and individuals in the organisation. And, of course, kidding the other members of the clique that you really do have their personal interests at heart.

Most of the foregoing relates to being adept at political manoeuvring: the art of manipulating balance, power, rights, responsibilities, relationships and resources for the benefit of oneself, with no regard for its effect on others, is the name of the game.

Question

It is not advocated here that one should apply the above in an organisation; rather, it is argued that – being aware that such things do take place in organisations – one needs to know how to deal with these organisational misdemeanours when they occur. Can you suggest how you would deal with the above 'problems' in a manner that avoids meeting like with like?

Neural networks

Neural networks are not a new idea. We can trace some of the fundamental ideas behind neural networks in the work of the distinguished psychologist William James more than a century ago. The field of neural networks, and the development of neural network tools for personal computers, has developed rapidly since 1987. The list of applications has expanded from biological and psychological uses to include applications as diverse as biomedical waveform classification, music composition and prediction of the commodity futures market.

A neural network is constructed by connecting many simple computing elements that, as the name suggests, resemble the neurons found in the human brain. Each neuron has a single output whose value depends on the value of each input multiplied by a weight factor:

Input 1 → weighting ↘

Input 2 → weighting → NEURON (summates) → output

Input 3 → weighting ↗

This weighting can have a value of form anything from −1 to +1. If its value is zero, then that particular input will make no contribution to the neuron's eventual output. If, for example, the weighting is 0.01 then the contribution will be only marginal. The neuron produces an analogue output that varies continuously between a minimum and maximum value.

Such neurons can be connected in a multitude of ways. However, the pattern seeming most productive now is the 'three-layer feed-forward network'. It is called 'feed-forward' because each connection is towards the output of the network. A feed-backward network is where the output of a neuron can be directly or indirectly connected to one of its own inputs.

A network is not capable of predicting anything until it has been trained. Again there are several ways that training can be done, but the most promising appears to be supervised learning by back-propagation. Supervised learning means that the network is taught by presenting it with both the input data and the output this data is supposed to produce. Each record has to be presented to the network in turn and the desired output compared with the actual output.

Back-propagation is a particular algorithm that is used to adjust the weights on every neuron back down the network to minimise the error.

Once the weights have been adjusted, the next record is presented and the process is repeated. This is repeated for all cases again until the error for every record drops below a certain target threshold. The algorithm incorporates what are termed 'learning rate' and 'momentum' factors. How fast a network learns will depend on the 'learning rate' and the 'momentum'. The 'learning rate' determines to what degree the weights can be varied each time and the 'momentum' adds a smoothing factor to stop the network oscillating around a solution. Optimum values have to be determined by experiment.

Besides being able to learn number patterns, neural network programs are also able to learn binary data patterns.

Question

Suggest application for neural network programs in management and business.

Oil crisis revisited

Some of us will recall the oil crisis of the early 1970s. One day the availability of oil seemed endless and cars buzzed tirelessly along the newly built motorways. The next day we were told that oil was a precious commodity that had to be conserved. Output in the principal producing countries in the Middle East was restricted to conserve supplies, a 50 m.p.h. speed restriction was imposed on the motorways and the price of oil rocketed on international markets. Businesses and private citizens felt the pinch on their pickets and inflation took on proportions that had not been seen for many years. Since that time the coming on-line of North Sea oil and the discovery of potential oil deposits in other areas has taken the sting out of the 'need to conserve' argument. Nevertheless, motor vehicle manufacturers have taken note of the need to conserve and introduced more efficient engines and are actively researching for ways of improving fuel consumption requirements even further. There is also, of course, a drive towards finding viable alternative fuel sources – such as that provided by solar power and electrical battery power.

However, it seems inevitable that during the course of the next few centuries oil resources will eventually dry up. The resources are finite relative to consumption. It takes much longer for Nature to create oil resources than it does for the human race to consume them.

Question

Imagine the time when oil eventually runs out. What will be the implications of a world without oil? What substitutes need to be found that will provide for the myriads of uses of oil – quite apart from fuel and lubrication for the petrol engine?

Homes for the Elderly

The traditional providers of homes for the elderly have been local authorities. They have managed such homes successfully for many years. The funding of the running of such homes has been from the accumulated wealth and retirement incomes of those making use of the facilities afforded by the homes. Any shortfalls in terms of costs have been met from the local authority budget, which itself is a mixture of money collected from rates or council tax and a grant made available from central government.

During the 1980s and 1990s local authorities were squeezed with respect to their spending power. Central government not only effectively reduced the size of grants made available to local authorities but also prevented them from raising revenues from local ratepayers in the form of increased council tax. This led to local authorities seeking to make cuts in expenditure wherever possible and to look for more efficient and economic ways of dealing with the services it had to provide.

As we know, specialisation is thought to lead to increased efficiency through the effects of the well known 'experience curve'. The more experience you have of something the more proficient it is thought you become at doing that something and the more cost-effective is the expenditure of your effort – or so the theory goes. Many local authorities therefore decided to look for private providers of these services and to share the cost of running the homes with providers who had management experience and skills which exceeded their own. In this way it was believed that better use could be made of the proportion of the budget that they had available for these services.

Among those local authorities which opted to seek help from the private sector to run its retirement homes was Belford council. It enlisted the help of a specialised company called 'Homes for the Elderly' to manage a number of its homes. The council retained ownership of the premises and agreed that a set amount of money would be made available to the company on an annual grant basis to subsidise the running of the homes.

The arrangement ran reasonably well for a number of years. However, central government cuts and rate capping eventually forced the council to reconsider all its expenditure. At a meeting of the council it was decided to cut the grant made to Homes for the Elderly completely. The chief executive of Homes for The Elderly was stunned by the news. The local authority had in the past paid its employees in these homes above the average going rates in terms of salaries and wages. This was a policy which he had maintained after taking on the contract. The grant made by the local authority was sufficient to enable him to do so. The withdrawal of the grant, he felt, forced him to review the situation and he immediately announced that all wages and salaries of staff employed at the homes would be very substantially reduced. Various figures were floated about, but of course the chief executive had to take account of the impending legislation regarding the minimum wage.

The response from employees was not really surprising. Talk of strike action ensued and this in turn led to the chief executive threatening to send out dismissal notices to those workers who opted for strike action. Indeed the whole situation looked quite awkward and incapable of solution.

Questions

Suggest how the issue might be resolved. What actions might have been taken by both the council and the company to avert the crisis in the first instance?

The hinterlands

'Majorca, Alicante, Malaga, Biarritz, the Canaries, Goa, Madrid, Paris, Barcelona, and so on: that is where holidaymakers seem to want to go to. They enjoy the bright lights or the beaches; they bask in the sun, swim in the pool and eat English food. All of these things can be done back home at a fraction of the price.' Rebecca sighed. 'And when they come home they often complain that where they have been is not that much different to Brighton or London or Blackpool.'

'Culture, is what holidaying is all about', Marianne said knowingly. 'Experiencing different cultures. Take Turkey, for example. If you go to Turkey you can visit Kusadasi and just up the road are the ruins at Ephesus. Now that is a sight worth seeing. It's all about past civilisations and it makes you appreciate the history of the world.'

'Same in Egypt', Martha added. 'There's the Pyramids, the Valley of the Kings and all those tombs.'

'I don't think that culture is just history', Rebecca rejoined. 'Culture is about people of today as well. Take Turkey, for example, how can you really get to know what Turkish people are like? What are their homes like? What sort of interests and values do they have?'

'I knew someone who went to France for a holiday. She took an apartment in a small town thirty miles south of Paris. She stayed there for a month and learned a lot about the culture', Martha interjected.

'But that's France. I mean everyone speaks French – we learn it at school. But who speaks Turkish!', Marianne contributed.

'Hmmm. I see what you mean', Martha mused.

Question

Assuming that there was a sizeable market segment of holidaymakers who would be interested in going on holiday to find out more about local cultures what could tour operators do to exploit such a marketing opportunity?

The bully

'I cannot put up with him any longer. I think I will leave – or go sick.' Bill addressed the door, as if it were his best friend. 'Ever since he arrived he has been persecuting me. It is not as if I did anything wrong. He just doesn't like my approach to the job and wants me to go. He is rude, arrogant, pig-headed and at times plain stupid. I cannot stand the way he looks at me as if I am an idiot.'

The door remained firmly shut.

'Then there is his face – he looks like a criminal. Give him a machine-gun and he would make a fitting gangster.'

Bill looked through the window. It was raining and darkness was about to descend. His desk was covered with memos from the target of his aggression, demanding improved performance, correcting his letters which had never even left the building, and announcing a new schedule of meetings to take place at 7.00 p.m. after work on Tuesdays and Thursdays for the next six weeks.

Bill's new boss had arrived two weeks ago. He had summoned the whole of his staff – some 90 employees – and told them that he was going to issue new contracts with new terms and working conditions. There had not even been a murmur. All staff were white collar workers and none belonged to a union.

'I expect to make you all accountable', the new boss had said. 'Anyone who is failing in his work will receive my personal attention.'

In only his second week in the job the boss had hauled Bill's friend Alan over the coals for something over which he had no control. 'If that happens again, you're fired', he had said.

Bill sat hunched up over a coffee. Alan had left on the spot after the boss had given him a public dressing down for forgetting to sign a letter to a client. Now Bill had lost his best friend, though there were others with whom he had a good rapport.

Bill looked through the window again. The boss's white BMW was parked on the double yellow lines. The telephone rang. 'Come to my office immediately was the message.' Bill went. The boss sat smug behind his desk. 'I don't like the way you dress', he said. 'You look more like a hawker than an executive. Get a new suit and do something about your hair. It's too long.' Bill left the office. A cold wind blew through the open window. He felt as if he could take no more.

Question

How can Bill and his colleagues get to grips with the new boss?

The only one

At tea breaks Sally preferred to sit alone. She was the only female computer programmer in the building. It wasn't that she didn't like her male colleagues, it was just that they always spoke in a patronising way to her, talked about football all the time except when the conversation was interspersed with sexist jokes or sexist remarks. She could complain, she knew, but what good would it do? She wanted to keep her job.

Sally had taken to bringing the morning newspaper into the office so that she had something to read during the breaks. One day she left the newspaper open on the desk at the situations vacant pages while she went to the toilet. On her return she was teased by her colleagues about looking for another job. She thought nothing more of the matter, putting it down to the clownish behaviour of her male colleagues. However, it soon became a topic of conversation amongst her colleagues, which she could not help but overhear. Sally, they said, was looking for a new job because she was the only woman in the office. It soon became monotonous. Every day the same remarks would be made and Sally would simply smile, but it began to get on her nerves. So much so that she began to lose sleep, wakening in the night from dreams in which she was anxiously searching for jobs while listening to the taunts of her colleagues.

Question

What action should Sally take to deal with this problem?

Creative accountants

'No matter how hard I try,' began Jules, 'I just cannot see any application for creative thinking or creative problem solving in accounting matters. All the problems with which we deal require logical or vertical thinking and not lateral or creative thinking.'

'But there must be some problems that require creative thinking!', Angelica exclaimed. 'It can't all be logical thinking.'

'Well look at it from a manager's point of view then', Jules replied. 'What kind of financial problems does the manager need solving? As far as I can see it is all figure work where numbers rather than words are the name of the game. Who needs creativity where numbers are concerned?'

'I see what you mean', Angelica said, doubtfully.

Question

Can you think of problems in accounting that require creative thinking?

Problems with the tunnel

The tunnel was built over sixty years ago and in its time was one of the small 'Wonders of the World'. It is over a mile in length and connects the city centre with large residential areas on the other side of the estuary. It carries two lanes of traffic in either direction and has been essentially unmodified since it was first opened. A standard toll of £1 is paid by all car-drivers to use the tunnel and higher rates are charged for commercial vehicles.

Some ten years ago or so a second tunnel was opened about two miles further along the estuary to relieve the congestion that was occurring in the old tunnel. The effect of this was to reduce the amount of traffic passing through the old tunnel by a considerable amount. Now, however, traffic has begun to build up again in the old tunnel at peak hours. This is particularly the case in a morning between 7.30 a.m. and 10.00 a.m. when commuters are heading into work. A temporary solution to this problem has been to restrict traffic leaving the city centre at these times to using only one of the four lanes and to allow traffic coming into the city to use three of the lanes. The problem, however, is becoming worse and outward bound traffic flows around 5.00 p.m. in an evening are now becoming a problem. It is anticipated that in the next ten years the problem created by heavy usage of both the road links under the river will have become critical once more. While building a third tunnel is not altogether out of the question its siting and cost do not look very attractive propositions. The city has hovered on the verge of bankruptcy for years and has extreme difficulty in balancing its books.

Crossing the river by road is not the only option available. An electric railway winds its way under the river bed, linking the city centre to stations at most of the residential centres on the other side. At the time the old tunnel was first built there were also frequent ferry services over the river to three destinations on the other side. At each of the three landing stages there were excellent bus services to all the residential districts which were not actually sited on the bank of the river itself. Over the years the ferry services were curtailed and bus-links severed. People switched to using the tunnels as the commuters came to own cars and use them to go to work in the city centre. The ferry service has almost closed down altogether on more than one occasion over the last twenty years.

Questions

How do you think the congestion problem should be approached? What actions do you think should be taken in the next ten years? What problems do you see arising with respect to the implementation of your ideas? Are there any ways of getting around these problems?

The verge escapement

The earliest form of escapement mechanism used in watches was the verge. Its use in clocks dates back as early as the beginning of the 1300s. The verge escapement comprises a crown escape wheel, a verge which has two flags called pallets, and a balance. The verge is now entirely discarded, although verge watches still exist and continue to go. Wear on the train was excessive and good time-keeping was almost impossible. Exceptional verges could keep the time to a couple of minutes a day but most of the better ones were no more accurate than ten minutes a day. More often than not, however, verges were no more accurate than thirty minutes a day. This, of course was of little use in an age when the railways were to replace the horse-drawn coach as the means of long distance travel.

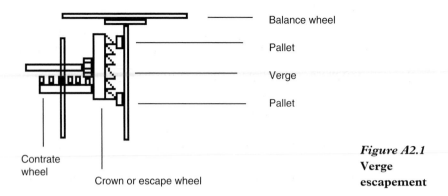

Balance wheel

Pallet

Verge

Pallet

Contrate wheel

Crown or escape wheel

Figure A2.1
Verge escapement

Watchmakers in the eighteenth and nineteenth centuries strove to improve the verge movement or to replace it with a better movement. Marine navigation needs eventually led to the development of the chronometer escapement – but this was generally too expensive to include in everyday watches. Three other types of escapement were eventually invented which proved economical to produce: the cylinder, the duplex and the lever. After many modifications the lever escapement has settled down to one theoretical shape and become the standard movement of mechanical and automatic watches today.

Some notes on the technical specifications of the verge movement are as follows. The balance in this escapement has no free arc and its vibration is limited to about 110 degrees each way. The crown wheel has generally either 11 or 13 teeth, and in the plan of the watch its arbor lies horizontally. The balance staff, or verge, is made as small as proper strength will allow, and planted close to the wheel so that the tips of the teeth just clear it. The pallets which form part of the verge are placed at an angle of 95 or 100 degrees with each other – with a preference, generally, for the latter. The width of the pallets apart, from centre to centre, is equal to the diameter of the wheel. The escape wheel will recoil until the impetus of the balance is exhausted. The teeth of the wheel are undercut to free the face of the pallet during recoil. An increased vibration of the balance and less recoil can be obtained with a larger angle, but to get sufficient impulse the verge must be planted closer to the wheel. To ensure good performance the body or arbor of the verge should be upright, the drops of the pallets should be equal and the balance wheel teeth true.

Question

Can you suggest what improvements might have been made to the verge either to improve the accuracy of the verge or as a move towards the modern lever movement?

The conference

'It's to be a conference on creativity and innovation', Dennis announced.

'What sort of conference is that?', Maggie asked, seeming to express both interest and surprise.

'Well, anything to do with creativity and innovation really, I guess.'

'Well that can include a multitude of very diverse subjects. Is it for managers, artists, writers, politicians?'

'It's for managers or, rather, business executives.'

'That narrows down the scope a bit, I suppose. And where and when is it to be held?'

'Dunno, I haven't worked that out yet. Somebody, said Paris in the spring would be good.'

'It is something else you need to think about, Dennis. Why are you making it a conference? Why not an exhibition, seminar, or symposium?'

'I just thought a conference was . . .'

'The only thing you could think of, I guess. Well that's something else you may need to think about again.'

'Hmm!', Dennis grunted. 'I suppose you are right, as usual.'

Questions

What would the purpose of the conference? What ideas have you got to help answer the kind of questions that Maggie has raised for Dennis to consider.

appendix three

NOTES ON CASES AND PROBLEMS

CHAPTER 1

Doppler system

In the Doppler system of aircraft navigation two beams of radio waves are aimed at the ground from transmitters under the fuselage, the forward beam striking the ground slightly ahead of the aircraft and the back beam slightly astern; both alternate twice each second from port to starboard. The forward beam signals reflected back to the aircraft are increased in frequency in proportion to its speed over the ground, the back beam signals decrease. The difference in frequency is measured automatically to give the navigator an accurate indication of the speed of the aircraft and of the drift angle so that the course can be corrected accordingly. This in turn has led to the development of automatic flying and landing devices. The first pilot-less aircraft successfully completed an Atlantic crossing as long ago as 1947.

Tank refurbishers

Instead of cutting off both ends of a tank only one end needs to be removed. Cleaning and painting can be performed adequately in this way. It also saves the cost of re-welding both ends of the tank.

Keeping prices competitive

Organisations can often disguise price rises, permanent or temporary, by making it appear that no price rise is in fact occurring. This can be achieved in any one of the following ways:

1 The discount structure can be altered so that the total profit to the company is increased but the list price to customers remains the same.
2 The minimum order size is increased so that small orders are eliminated and overall costs thereby reduced.
3 Delivery and special services are charged for.
4 Invoices are raised for repairs on purchased equipment.
5 Charge for engineering, installation and supervision.
6 Customers are made to pay for overtime required to get out rush orders.
7 Interest is collected on overdue accounts.
8 Lower margin models in the product line are eliminated and more profitable ones sold in their place.
9 Escalator clauses are built into bids for contracts.
10 The physical characteristics of the product are changed – e.g., it is made smaller.

Price and innovation

Unless Sally feels confident that her firm can take on the role of market leader, it would probably be better to hold prices steady – but there may be more creative solutions!

CHAPTER 2

Perceptual block

There are in fact 18 occurrences, but most people do not get it right first time despite having at least two chances to read through and count the occurrence of the letter.

Why are 1996 coins worth more than 1984 coins?

Because there are more of them – 12 more to be precise.

The clock problem solved

Each broken piece has
numbers which sum to 20

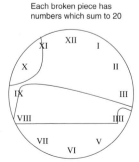

Figure A3.1 **Broken clock solution**

Hint: normal sum of clock numbers 1–12 = 78 not divisible into whole numbers when divided by 4. Need to artificially find an extra 2. The answer usually involves reversal of the IX (or IV if this is used instead of IIII).

CHAPTER 4

Seven letters problem

SUPERMARKET

Parcel delivery problem

Reducing the number of sorters, introducing a clear system of coding to identify relevant delivery vans, and training sorters on how to implement such a system.

CHAPTER 6

Reducing wear and tear

In order to reduce the amount of resurfacing work on motorways the white lines should be repositioned every few years. Resurfacing costs, it was estimated, could be reduced substantially as a result since repair work would need to be done at considerably longer intervals.

CHAPTER 7

Points about 'Challenging assumptions: what can we take for granted?'

Total expense would go up after outsourcing components because fixed costs had not been reduced, but one still had to pay suppliers for components. The assumptions must also include either that the fixed cost can be reduced (e.g. plant, machinery, etc. sold off, etc.) or that fixed costs are relatively small in relationship to the savings that can be achieved by outsourcing. Outsourcing only some of the components means that the remaining components still produced by the company must now shoulder an increased overhead of fixed costs, thereby making the possibility of outsourcing these components a more attractive proposition.

Over-utilisation of assets, such as assembly plant, leads to the creation of extra inventory and not extra sales. Inventory absorbs overheads and is shown as an asset in the balance sheet and can therefore give a misleading picture of the company's financial position.

The CEO resigned because he must have known the true state the company was in. Subsequently many thousands of workers were laid off and the company nearly went out of business. The build up of inventory given a significant increase in demand for the firm's products might have resulted in a favourable situation for the company as its inventory would have transformed into sales and generated cash-flow and profit. Any other scenario was a recipe for disaster.

Solution to the nine dots problem

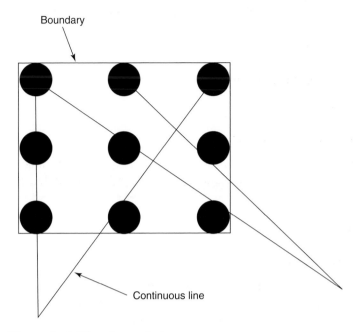

Figure A3.2 **Nine dots solution**

appendix four

PUBLICATIONS

PERIODICALS

Brain/Mind Bulletin, Interface Press, Box 42247, 4717 North Figueroa Street, Los Angeles, CA, tel: 213 223-2500.

Creativity and Innovation Management, Blackwell Publishers, 108 Cowley Road, Oxford, OX4 13F, UK.

Creativity Research Journal, Mark A. Runco, Editor, published quarterly, Creativity Research Journal EC 105, California State University, Fullerton, CA 92634.

Creativity Today, Creative Management Group, 226 East High Street, Charlottesville, VA 22901-5177, tel: 804 296-6138; fax: 804 979-4879.

Human Intelligence International Newsletter, School for Human and Educational Services, Oakland University, Rochester, MI 48063.

Journal of Creative Behavior, Creative Education Foundation, 1050 Union Road, Buffalo, NY 14224.

BOOKS

The Essence of Management Creativity, Tony Proctor, Hemel Hempstead: Prentice-Hall, 1995.

Creating Product Strategies, Beth Rogers, London: International Thomson Business Press, 1996.

The Creative Marketer, Simon Majaro, Oxford: Butterworth Heinemann, 1991.

Creative Thinking, Michael Le Boeuf, London: Piatkus, 1994.

A Whack on the Side of the Head, Roger Von Oech, London: Thorsons, 1990.

Idea Power, Arthur B. Van Gundy, New York: AMACOM, 1992.

Managing Ideas for Profits, Simon Majaro, Maidenhead: McGraw-Hill, 1992.

Problem Solving Through Creative Analysis, Tudor Rickards, Aldershot: Gower, reprinted 1982.

Problem Solving in Business and Management, Michael J. Hicks, London: Chapman & Hall, 1991.

The Ideal Problem Solver, John D. Bransford and Barry S. Stein, New York: Freeman, 1993 (2nd edn).

Techniques of Structured Problem Solving, Arthur B. Van Gundy, New York: Van Nostrand Reinhold, reprinted 2nd edition 1993.

Cognitive Psychology: A Student's Handbook, Michael W. Eysenck and Mark T. Keane, Hillsdale, NJ: Lawrence Erlbaum Associates, 1990.

Creative Management, Jane Henry, London: Sage, 1991.

Managing for Innovation, Neville I. Smith and Murray Ainsworth, London: Mercury, 1989.

Fundamentals of Creative Thinking, John S. Dacey, Lexington, MA: Lexington Books, 1989.

Psychology: The Science of Mind and Behaviour, R. Gross, London: Arnold, 1988.

Introduction to Social Psychology, M. Hewstone, W. Stroebe, J. Codol and G.M. Stephen, Oxford: Blackwell, 1994.

Systems, Management and Change, Ruth Carter, John Martin, Bill Mayblin and Michael Munday, Paul Chapman Publishing (in association with the Open University), reprint 1988.

Creativity for Managers, Alan Barker, London: The Industrial Society 1995.

Business Creativity: A Guide for Managers, Paul Birch and Brian Clegg, London: Kogan Page, 1995.

Creative Action in Organisations, Cameron Ford and Dennis Gioia, London: Sage 1995.

There is much information on 'Compuserve Creativity Forum' on the Internet. If you can access it please do so and join the forum.

Bibliography

Ackoff, R. L. and Vegara, E. (1988), 'Creativity in problem solving and planning', in R. L. Kuhn (ed.), *Handbook for Creative and Innovative Managers*, New York: McGraw-Hill.

Adams, J. L. (1974), *Conceptual Blockbusting*, New York: W. H. Freeman.

Amabile, T. M., Conti, R., Coon, H., Lazenby, J. and Herron, M. (1996), 'Assessing the work environment for creativity', *Academy of Management Journal*, 39, 5.

Arnold, J. E. (1962), 'Education for innovation', in S. J. Parnes and H. F. Harding (eds), *A Sourcebook for Creative Thinking*, New York: Scribners.

Bar, J. (1988), 'Computer-aided creativity: a systematic technique for new product idea generation', *Creativity and Innovation Year-book*, 1: 20–9, Manchester: Manchester Business School.

Barron, F. (1988), 'Putting creativity to work', in R. J. Sternberg (ed.), *The Nature of Creativity*, New York: Cambridge University Press.

Beggs, W. B. (1989), 'Humour in Advertising', *Link*, Nov.–Dec.: 2–15.

Bennis, W. and Nanus, B. (1985), *Leaders: The Strategies for Taking Charge*, New York: Harper and Row.

Bessant, J. and Buckingham, J. (1989), 'Organisational learning for effective implementation of computer-aided production management', *Creativity and Innovation Year-book*, 2, Manchester: Manchester Business School.

Blake, R. and Mouton, J. (1964), *The Managerial Grid*, Houston, TX: Gulf Publishing Company.

Bloch, A. (1990), *Murphy's Law Complete*, London: Mandarin.

Bransford, J. D. and Stein, B. S. (1993), *The Ideal Problem Solver* (2nd edition), New York: Freeman.

Brooks, J. D. (n. d.), *Review of Operational Mechanisms for Innovative Management Course*, Pittsburgh, PA: Industrial Studies Program, US Steel Corporation.

Bujake, J. E. (1969), 'Programmed innovation in new product development', *Research Management*, 12: 279–87.

Burnett, J. (1993), *Promotion Management*, Boston: Houghton Mifflin, chapter 7.

Buzan, T. (1991), *Use Both Sides of Your Brain*, New York, Dutton (Penguin Books).

Buzan, T. (1994), *The Mind Map Book*, New York, Dutton (Penguin Books).

Carson, J. and Rickards, T. (1979), *Industrial New Product Development*, Farnborough: Gower Press.

Coch, L. and French, J. R. P. (1948), 'Overcoming resistance to change', *Human Relations*: 512–32.

Colley, R. H. (1961), *Defining Advertising Goals for Measuring Advertising Effectiveness*, New York: Association for National Advertising.

Cyert, R. N. and March, J. G. (1963), *A Behavioral Theory of the Firm*, Englewood Cliffs, NJ: Prentice-Hall.

Dacey, J. S. (1989), *Fundamentals of Creative Thinking*, Lexington, MA: Lexington Books.

De Bono, E. ([1970] 1971), *Lateral Thinking for Management*, New York: McGraw-Hill (republished in Pelican).

De Kluyver, C. A. and McNally, G. M. (1980), 'Corporate planning using simulation', *Interface*, June: 1–8.

Duncker, K. (1945) 'On problem solving', trans. L. S. Lees, *Psychological Monographs*, 58, 5 (Whole No. 270).

Eden, C. Jones, S. and Sims, D. (1983), *Messing About In Problems*, Oxford: Pergamon Press.

Ekvall, G. (1988), 'Change centred leaders: empirical evidence of a third dimension of leadership', *Creativity and Innovation Year-book*, 1: 36–46.

Forsth, L. and Nordvik, B. (1995), 'Building a vision – a practical guide', *Creativity and Innovation Management*, 4, 4: 251–7.

Gelb, M. (1988), *Present Yourself!*, Torrance, CA: Jalmar Press.

Geschka, H. (1979), 'Methods and organization of idea generation', Paper presented at the Creativity Development Week II, Center for Creative Leadership, Greensboro, North Carolina, September.

Geschka, H., Schaude, G. R. and Schlicksupp, H. (1973), 'Modern techniques for solving problems', *Chemical Engineering*, August: 91–7.

Gilliam, T. K. (1993), 'Managing the power of creativity', *Bank Marketing*, 25, 12 (Dec.): 14–19.

Golovin, L. (1979), 'Product blending: a simulation case study in double time', *Interfaces*, 9, 5.

Gordon, W. J. (1961), *Synectics*, New York: Harper and Row.

Gordon, W. J. (1969), *Synectics – The Development of Creative Capacity*, New York: Harper and Row.

Grossman, S. R. (1984), 'Releasing problem solving energies', *Training and Development Journal*, 38, 94–8.

Guilford, J. P. (1967), *The Nature of Human Intelligence*, New York: McGraw-Hill.

Guilford, J. P. (1975), 'Creativity: a quarter century of progress', in I. A. Taylor and J.W. Getzels (eds), *Perspectives in Creativity*, Chicago: Aldine Publishing Company.

Haefele, J. W. (1962), *Creativity and Innovation*, New York: Reinhold.

Halpern, D. (1989), *Thought and Knowledge: An Introduction to Critical Thinking*, Hillsdale, NJ: Lawrence Erlbaum.

Hamilton, H. R. (1974), 'Screening business development opportunities', *Business Horizons*, August: 13–34.

Hart, S., Borush, M., Enk, G. and Hornick, W. (1985), 'Managing complexity through consensus mapping: technology for the managing of group decisions', *Academy of Management Review*, 10, 3: 587–600.

Hayes, J. R. (1989), *The Complete Problem Solver* (2nd edition), Hillsdale, NJ: Lawrence Erlbaum Associates.

Henle, M. (1962), 'The birth and death of ideas', in H. E. Gruber, G. Terrell and M. Wertheimer (eds), 'Contemporary Approaches to Creative Thinking', A Symposium at the University of Colorado.

Henry, J. (1991), *The Creative Manager*, London: Sage.

Herrmann, N. (1990), *The Creative Brain*, Lake Lure, NC: Brain Books.

Hicks, M. J. (1991), *Problem Solving in Business and Management*, London: Chapman & Hall.

Higgins, J. M. (1994), *The Management Challenge* (2nd edition), New York: Macmillan.

Humphrey, G. (1948), *Directed Thinking*, New York: Dodd Mead.

Isenberg, D. J. (1984a), 'Field research on managerial thinking: seven findings, seven puzzles', Working paper 9–785–040, Division of Research, Harvard Business School, August.

Isenberg D. J. (1984b), 'How senior managers think', *Harvard Business Review*, 62, (Nov.–Dec.): 80–90.

Jackson, M. (1985), *Creative Modelling with Lotus 123™*, Chichester: Wiley.

Janis, I. L. and Feshback, S. (1953), 'Effects of fear arousing communications', *Journal of Abnormal and Social Psychology*, 48, 1: 78–92.

Jensen, J. V. (1978), 'A heuristic for the evaluation of the nature and extent of a problem', *Journal of Creative Behavior*, 12: 268–80.

Jones, L. J. (1987), 'The development and testing of a psychological instrument to measure barriers to effective problem solving', Unpublished MB.Sc. Dissertation, Manchester Business School.

Kelly, G. A. (1955), *The Psychology of Personal Constructs*, New York: Norton.

Kepner, C. H. and Tregoe, B. B. (1976), *The Rational Manager*, Princeton, NJ: Kepner–Tregoe.

Koestler, A. (1964), *The Act of Creation*, London: Hutchinson.

Kotter, J. (1997), 'Rethinking leadership', in R. Gibson (ed.), *Rethinking the Future*, London: Nicholas Brealey.

Langer, S. K. (1942), *Philosophy in a New Key*, Cambridge, MA: Harvard University Press.

Larsen, E. (1961), *A History of Invention*, London: Phoenix House.

Lavidge, R. J. and Steiner, G. A. (1961), 'A model for predictive measurements of advertising effectiveness', *Journal of Marketing*, October: 58–62.

Lawrence, P. R. and Greiner, L. R. (1970), 'How to deal with resistance to change', in G. W. Dalton, P. R. Lawrence and L. R. Greiner (eds), *Organizational Change and Development*, Homewood, IL: Irwin.

Le Boeuf, M. (1994), *Creative Thinking*, London: Piatkus.

Levitt, T. (1988), 'In this issue', *Harvard Business Review*, Jan.–Feb.: 3.

Locke, J. (1690), 'An essay concerning human understanding', in J. V. Canfield and F. H. Donnell (eds), *Readings in the Theory of Knowledge*, Appleton Century Crofts.

Luchins, A. A. (1942), 'Mechanisation problem solving: the effect of Einstellung', *Psychological Monographs*, 54.

McClelland, J. L. (1981), 'Retrieving general and specific information from stored knowledge of specifics', *Proceedings of the Third Annual Meeting of the Cognitive Science Society*, pp. 170–2.

McClelland, J. L. and Rumelhart, D.E. (1986), 'A distributed model of human learning and memory', in D. E. Rumelhart, J. L. McClelland and the PDP

Research Group (eds), *Parallel Distributed Processing*, Volume 2: *Psychological and Biological Models*, Cambridge MA: Harvard University Press.

Machiavelli, N. (1993), 'Concerning the way to govern cities or principalities which lived under their own laws before they were annexed', *The Prince* (in translation), Ware, Herts.: Wordsworth Reference.

Majero, S. (1991), *The Creative Marketeer*, London: Butterworth Heinemann.

Majaro, S. (1992), *Managing Ideas for Profit*, Maidenhead: McGraw-Hill.

March, J. G. (1988), *Decisions and Organisations*, Oxford: Blackwell.

Maslow, A. H. (1954), *Motivation and Personality*, New York: Harper and Row.

Minsky, M. (1974), 'A framework for representing knowledge', Cambridge, MA: MIT Artificial Intelligence Laboratory, Artificial Intelligence Memo No. 306.

Mintzberg, H. (1976), 'Planning on the left side and managing on the right', *Harvard Business Review*, July–August.

Moore, L. B. (1962), 'Creative action – the evaluation, development, and use of ideas', in S. J. Parnes and H. F. Harding (eds), *A Sourcebook for Creative Thinking*, New York: Scribner's.

Morgan, G. (1989), *Riding the Waves of Change – Developing Managerial Competencies for a Turbulent World*, San Francisco: Jossey-Bass Publishers.

Newell, A. and Simon, H. A. (1972), *Human Problem Solving*, Englewood Cliffs, NJ: Prentice-Hall.

Newell, A. Shaw, J. C. and Simon, H. A. (1962), 'The processes of creative thinking', in H. E. Gruber *et al.* (eds), *Contemporary Approaches to Creative Thinking*, New York: Atherton Press.

Oech, R. Von (1990), *A Whack on the Side of the Head*, London: Thorsons.

Olson, R. W. (1980), *The Art of Creative Thinking*, New York: Barnes and Noble.

Oldman, G. R. and Cummings, A. (1996), 'Employee creativity: personal and contextual factors at work', *Academy of Management Journal*, 39 (June).

Osborn, A. (1953), *Applied Imagination*, New York: Scribner's.

Parker, M. (1990), *Creating Shared Vision*, Oslo, Norway: Norwegian Centre for Leadership Development.

Parnes, S. J. (1963), 'The deferment of judgement principle: a clarification of the literature', *Psycho. Reports*, 12: 521–2.

Parnes, S. J. (1981), *The Magic of Your Mind*, Buffalo, NY: The Creative Education Foundation, in association with Bearly Ltd.

Parnes, S. J., Noller, R. and Biondi, A. (1977), *Guide to Creative Action*, New York: Scribner's.

Poincare, H. (1952), *Science and Methods*, trans. F. Maitland, New York: Dover Publications.

Polya, G. (1957) *How To Solve It*, Garden City, NY: Doubleday Anchor.

Pounds, W. F. (1969), 'The process of problem finding', *Industrial Management Review*, Fall: 1–19.

Prather, C. W. and Gundry, L. (1996), *Blueprints for Innovation*, New York: American Management Association.

Prince, G. (1970), *The Practice of Creativity*, New York: Harper and Row.

Quillian, M. R. (1968), 'Semantic memory', in M. Minsky (ed.), *Semantic Information Processing*, Cambridge, MA: MIT Press.

Rickards, T. (1985), *Stimulating Innovation: A Systems Approach*, London: Frances Pinter.

Rickards, T. (1988), 'Creativity and innovation: a transatlantic perspective', *Creativity and Innovation Year-book*, Manchester: Manchester Business School.

Rickards, T. (1990), *Creativity and Problem Solving At Work*, Farnborough: Gower.

Rogers, B. (1993), 'Giving creativity a shot in the arm', *Involvement and Participation*, Summer: 6–10.

Rogers, B. (1996), *Creating Product Strategies*, London: International Thompson.

Rogers, C. (1954), 'Towards a theory of creativity', *A Review of General Semantics*, 11: 249–60 (reprinted in P. E. Vernon (ed.), *Creativity*, Penguin, 1975).

Rogers, E. (1962), *Diffusion of Innovations*, New York: Free Press of Glencoe.

Rokeach, M. (1979), *Understanding Human Values: Individual and Societal*, New York: Free Press.

Rumelhart, D. E. and Norman, D. A. (1983), 'Representation in memory', *CHIP Technical Report No. 116*, San Diego: Center for Human Information Processing, University of California.

Saaty, T. L. (1980), *The Analytic Hierarchy Process*, New York: McGraw-Hill.

Saxberg, B. O. (1993), 'Vision management: translating strategy into action', *Personnel Psychology*, 46, 1: 180–3.

Schank, R. and Abelson, R. (1977), *Scripts, Plans, Goals and Understanding: An Enquiry Into Human Knowledge Structure*, Hillsdale, N.J.: Lawrence Erlbaum.

Shaw, M. L. (1982), 'PLANET: some experience in creating an integrated system for repertory grid applications on a microcomputer', *International Journal of Man–Machine Studies*, 17: 345–60.

Simon, H.A. (1969), *The Science of the Artificial*, Cambridge, MA: MIT Press.

Simon, H. A. (1985), 'What we know about the creative process', in R. L. Kuhn (ed.), *Frontiers in Creative and Innovative Management*, New York: Ballinger.

Stein, M. (1974), *Stimulating Creativity*, New York: Academic Press.

Tauber, E. M. (1972), 'HIT: heuristic ideation technique – a systematic procedure for new product search', *Journal of Marketing*, 36: 58–61.

Thompson, J. D. (1967), *Organizations in Action*, New York: McGraw-Hill.

Torrance, E. P. (1965), *Rewarding Creative Behavior: Experiments in Classroom Creativity*, Englewood Cliffs, NJ: Prentice-Hall.

Van Gundy, A. B. (1993), *Techniques of Structured Problem Solving*, New York: Van Nostrand Reinhold Co.

Van Gundy, A. B. (1987), 'Organizational creativity and innovation', in S. G. Isaksen (ed.), *Frontiers of Creative Research: Beyond the Basics*, Buffalo, NY: Bearly Ltd.

Wakin, E. (1985), 'Creative Thinking', Presentation at the 31st Annual Creative Problem Solving Institute, Buffalo, NY, June.

Wallas, G. (1926), *The Art of Thought*, London: Jonathan Cape.

Weihrich, H. (1982), 'The TOWS matrix: a tool for situational analysis', *Long Range Planning*, 15, 2: 54–66.

Weinman, C. (1991), 'It's not art but marketing research can be creative', *Marketing News*, 25, 8 (April 15): 9–24.

Weisberg, R. W. (1986), *Creativity, Genius and other Myths*, New York: W. H. Freeman.

Weizenbaum, J. (1984), *Computer Power and Human Reason*, Harmondsworth: Penguin.

Wertheimer, M. ([1945]1959), *Productive Thinking*, New York: Harper and Row.

Wertheimer, M. (1962), 'Contemporary approaches to creative thinking', A Symposium at the University of Colorado.

Whiting, C. S. (1958), *Creative Thinking*, New York: Van Nostrand Reinhold.

Wilson, P. (1997), 'Simplex creative problem solving', *Creativity and Innovation Management*, 6, 3 (September): 160–6.

Young, L. W. (1989), *Decision Support and Idea Processing Systems*, Dubuque, IA: W. C. Brown.

Zwicky, F. (1948), *Discovery, Invention, Research through the Morphological Approach*, New York: Macmillan.

COMPUTER AIDED CREATIVE PROBLEM SOLVING PROGRAMS

Aspects, Group Technologies Inc., 800 North Taylor St., Suite 204, Arlington, Virginia, VA 22203.

Axon Idea Processor, Axon Research, 5, Langkok Merak, Singapore 248860

BRAIN, Sound Thinking.

BRAIN, ORACLE, MORPHY produced by the author.

Brainstormer, Software Systems, USA.

COPE (University of Bath and University of Strathclyde – now marketed as *Decision Explorer*) is available from Banxia Software Ltd, 141 St James Road, Glasgow, Scotland.

Dynametrics, James L. Allison, Neptune Systems, 703 Neptune Lane, Houston, TX 77062 (USA) – email: 71565.303@compuserve.com – versions are available for Microsoft Windows 95 and Windows 3.1.

Expert Choice Pro is produced and marketed by Expert Choice Inc., 5001 Baum Boulevard, Suite 650, Pittsburgh, PA 15213; phone: (412) 682-3844; fax: (412) 682-7008.

IdeaFisher, IdeaFisher Systems Inc., 2222, Martin St, 110 Irvine, CA 92715.

Idea Generator, Experience in Software, 200 Hearst Avenue, Berkeley, California, CA 94709 (in 1985).

Idea Tree, L. E. Cohen, Mountain House Publishing, Waitsfield, VT 05673-9621.

Info Map Lite, CoCo Systems Ltd, 2 Mortens Wood, Amersham, Bucks, HP7 9EQ.

Inspiration, Inspiration Software Inc., 2920 SW Dolph Court, Suite 3, Portland, Oregon, 97219.

MicroSaint, Rapid Data Ltd, Crescent House, Crescent Rd, Worthing, West Sussex BN11 5RW.

MindLink, MindLink Software Corporation, 247 Kings Highway, North Pomfret, VT 05053-9987.

Mindman, Michael Jetter, Moosanger, 2, D82319, Starnberg, Germany, (e-mail 100423.57@compuserve.com)

Option Finder, Option Technologies Ltd, Winchfield, Hants.

THUNDER THOUGHT, T. A. Easton, R. K. West Consulting, PO Box 8059, Mission Hills, CA 91346.

Time Line for Windows™, Symantec Corporation, 10201 Torre Avenue, Cupertino, CA 95014.

Author index

Subject index